German Business
after the
Economic Miracle

FRANK VOGL

A HALSTED PRESS BOOK

JOHN WILEY & SONS
New York – Toronto

First published in the United Kingdom 1973 by
THE MACMILLAN PRESS LTD

*Published in the U.S.A. and Canada
by Halsted Press, a Division of
John Wiley & Sons, Inc., New York*

Library of Congress Cataloging in Publication Data

Vogl, Frank, 1945–
  German business after the economic miracle.

"A Halsted Press book."
    1.   Germany (Federal Republic, 1949–   )—
Industries.   2.   Germany (Federal Republic, 1949–   )
—Commerce.   3.   Industrial organization—Germany
(Federal Republic, 1949–   ).   I.   Title.
HC286.6.V64   338'.0943   73–15016
ISBN 0–470–90970–6

Printed in Great Britain

Contents

1 A General Introduction

The structure of West German industry is now undergoing a major transformation as a wide range of assorted forces make it imperative for managers to adopt new attitudes and new methods of operation. The era of the 'Economic Miracle' has ended with the country increasingly falling into line with rates of inflation and economic growth that have long been existent in the great majority of developed Western countries. New business strategies are having to be devised to cope with important and new domestic social, political and economic developments, with the increasing integration of the European Economic Community and with major changes in international monetary and trading relationships.

West Germany is today the strongest industrial nation in Western Europe and can boast of a large number of strong companies with able managements. Yet, many of the current problems that face industry there came to the fore so swiftly that they caught managers by surprise and the sharp profit declines in a vast number of companies in 1970 and 1971 largely reflected this. The modest recovery in company earnings in 1972 reflects to some extent the efforts that top managers have made to modernise their companies and get into better shape to tackle the difficulties that with increasing clarity seem certain to lie ahead.

West Germany differs from most developed Western countries in that its labour force is far too small for the needs of its expanding industry. The acute tightness in the labour market is now one of the country's major problems and it is a factor that is likely to produce major changes in the structure of the economy. German industry has been importing labour for many years, but as the total of foreign workers increases so the strain on the country's social services intensifies. The labour shortage will be a major factor in the coming years in forcing German companies to invest more abroad, especially in areas where labour is in plentiful supply. Furthermore, the labour shortage will speed up the already clear trend towards an expansion of labour intensive service industries and a contraction here of manufacturing.

West Germany currently has a population of about 61·5 million, which is growing at an annual rate of about 250,000 persons. The country's total labour force is slightly above 27 million people, with about 12·5 million people employed in manufacturing industries. The work force is supported by approximately 2·5 million temporary workers* from foreign countries. The density of population is not great compared to some European industrial countries, with about 247 inhabitants per square kilometre. However, population density is considerable in the main industrial areas and the total figures for the country as a whole must be considered after noting that of a total land area of 249,000 square kilometres, some 136,000 is devoted to agriculture and a further 72,000 is given over to forestry.

The level of population density varies in fact most considerably from one region to the next. According to Federal Statistics Office figures the density of population per square kilometre in the Düsseldorf area, for example, was about 4,200 persons at the end of 1971 and similarly high figures can be found for the other major industrial areas of the country. The major industrial area is clearly the *Land* of Nordrhein-Westfalen with a total population of 17·1 million, followed by Bayern with 10·6 million, then Baden-Württemberg with 9·1 million and then Niedersachsen with 7·2 million and Hessen with 5·5 million. The other main industrial area is the city state of Hamburg with a total population of 1·8 million. West Berlin is of marginal importance as a manufacturing centre and has a population of slightly over 2 million.

Measured in industrial turnover terms West Germany is the third largest industrial nation in the world, behind the United States and Japan. West Germany's annual industrial turnover is now in excess of DM 600,000 million and is second only to

---

* There were 2·35 million temporary foreign immigrant workers in West Germany in October 1972, according to official Federal Labour Office statistics. There is believed to be a considerable number of immigrant workers on an illegal basis in West Germany, who are not registered in any way.

Japan as the largest exporter of manufactured goods in the world. West Germany is by far the largest exporter of manufactured goods in the European Economic Community, but she is greatly dependent on her European Economic Community partners for her foreign sales, with her eight partner countries taking approximately 46 per cent of her total exports.*

The major manufacturing companies are large by any standards of comparison, but most are heavily dependent on export sales and few have substantial foreign investments. The revaluations of the Deutsche Mark in 1969, 1971 and 1973 substantially weakened the international competitiveness of industry in this country. The international currency crisis in February 1973 underlined the fact that the Deutsche Mark will never again be allowed to reach such an under-valued level as was reached in early 1969. With a currency competitive position no longer existent it is going to be most difficult for the industry of this country to continue maintaining the sort of exceptionally high export levels seen in recent years.

Measured in turnover terms Volkswagenwerk AG is the largest German company and largest automobile manufacturer outside the United States. Siemens AG is the largest private sector employer in the Federal Republic and second only to Philips NV of the Netherlands as the largest electrical equipment producer in Europe. Bayer AG, Hoechst AG and Badische Anilin- und Soda-Fabrik AG, rank among the leading chemical companies in the world and all closely follow Imperial Chemical Industries Ltd of Britain in the list of largest European chemical concerns. The August Thyssen-Hütte AG steel group is larger than any Continental rival and is second only to the British Steel Corporation as Europe's largest steel maker, and other European giants are to be found in Germany in most other industrial sectors, such as shipbuilding, textiles, coal mining, brewing, mechanical engineering and tobacco.

West Germany produces more cars, more lorries, more beer, more steel, more machine tools, more electrical equipment and more of most sorts of industrial products than any other country in the European Economic Community. In terms of gross national product this country is now considerably larger

* This figure is an estimate made by the Bonn Government's Economic Advisory Council in its annual report, published in December 1972.

than any of its neighbours,* but this has been a relatively recent development. However, at the moment there seems little likelihood that West Germany will lose its leading position.

This book aims to describe the present structure of this powerful industrial country, to outline the major problem areas from the labour market to the foreign exchange market, and to show how attitudes in politics, business and trade unions are changing and the likely effects that these changes will have. The main aim of this book is to show that there is little substance in the West Germany of the 1970s in the popular views that still maintain that an 'Economic Miracle' continues, but that instead, this country now faces a vast volume of industrial problems and its overall long-term industrial outlook is far from bright. There are bright spots on the horizon, but the difficulties are great and one often wonders if these difficulties are fully realised abroad when one notes the heavy volume of foreign industrial and portfolio investment spending in this country. This book is as much about the state of German industry today, as about the general likely future development of industry in this country. To get this into context it is worthwhile to start by looking at the general development of the economy and business in this country in the recent past.

THE POST-WAR RECOVERY

West Germany's battered and war-weary economy only began to take on some semblance of an orderly shape after the Currency Reform of 1948. This measure produced the impetus for the start of economic recovery: it produced the basis for a stable economic environment, bringing an end to the severe post-war inflation. The war, itself, produced new scientific and technological processes, which could be used as the basis for constructing modern industries. The economic recovery was greatly aided by foreign contributions in terms of both finance and administration. The Marshall Plan aid, approved by the United States Congress in March 1948, was a key factor in starting the industrial reconstruction ball rolling. The devaluation of the Deutsche Mark in 1949 followed on from the

* See table in Appendix 3.

Currency Reform and paved the way for greater stability in the economy.

In addition, West Germany had the good fortune of having able political leaders in these early years, who were capable of tackling the enormous problems of rebuilding a country that lay in ruins. Dr Ludwig Erhard was given a free hand to manage the economy and his policies were largely based on *laissez-faire* concepts, which suited those men charged with the responsibility of developing new companies and rebuilding the old concerns of this once powerful industrial nation.

In the early years of reconstruction the largest German industrial enterprises were mainly led by managers with substantial business experience gained through running large companies in the war and pre-war periods. Middle management was largely filled by men with previous experience of big business or with administrative talents acquired in the army. The leaders of German industry today are largely those men, who after the war held middle management positions in the large companies. The existence after the war of numerous outstandingly able managers was a factor of vital importance in producing the success that German industry had by the early 1950s already come to enjoy.

The Korean War was a further boost to economic revival and in the years 1950, 1951 and 1952 this country could already boast of an annual average real economic growth rate of around 8·7 per cent. At the time these were the highest growth rates in Europe. Only a marginally slower rate of economic expansion was achieved in the following five years. And in this early period small companies started to get off the ground, growing swiftly and selling their products abroad, where in many cases the economic development and hence the demand for sophisticated products, was greater than that in existence in Germany at the time.

Probably the most important single factor that produced such swift economic recovery was the attitude towards work and economic success that prevailed among the citizens of the young Federal Republic. This is a factor that cannot be quantified and is often largely neglected. The German people quite clearly were determined to build again a powerful Germany. Only by this means did they believe that price stability and security of employment could be achieved and that these were essentials if prosperity was to be obtained. The inflations and severe periods of unemployment in the Weimar Republic of the 1920s and in the immediate post-war era, produced a generation utterly convinced that job security and price stability were the most important priorities. This was a generation quite prepared for hard work and for the acceptance of firm leadership in politics and business. It was a generation, perhaps, so used to living in a country ruled by an iron dictator that it was ready to accept with few disputes the conditions of employment offered by the managers of industry. In the early years the trade unions found themselves with little more than ideals: they lacked strong support from the working classes and they lacked substantial political influence in the generally conservative Government of Konrad Adenauer.

Erhard and Adenauer gave the people the sort of stable government that was generally desired at the time and the strong mandate that these men enjoyed for many years, enabled the possibility of a high degree of political policy continuity. This continuity gave business leaders a clear idea of government attitudes, it enabled them to make detailed medium-term plans and made it more possible for the economy to gain in strength in a relatively short time at a fast pace.

A further significant factor was the 'Cold War'. The Germans in the West saw themselves in the front line against the Communist countries of eastern Europe and, at the height of 'Cold War' fears, the need to build swiftly a strong Federal Republic took on an added element of urgency. Under such circumstances the Social Democrats in this country stood little chance of gaining power.

It has often been suggested in recent years that the goal of economic reconstruction played too great a role in the minds of the people and in politics in the early life of the Federal Republic, with the result that many social services, such as health, education, care for the old, were largely neglected. Much evidence can be put together to support this view and it is clear that many social reforms are desperately needed and that new schools, roads and hospitals are a desperate and urgent necessity. However, West Germany could never have pulled off such a tremendous rate of economic expansion and development in the first fifteen years of its existence had the policies of the Adenauer governments been more socially orientated.

The momentum needed to sustain a strong pace of economic advance was supported by a high increase in the labour force total, through large immigration. By 1954 some four million people had settled in this country from eastern Europe, mainly from the German Democratic Republic. The flow of immigrants from the Communist countries continued at a substantial pace until the construction of the wall between East and West Berlin in 1961. A more temporary type of immigration has been seen in the last decade with workers from the less developed areas of Europe obtaining jobs for an average of two to four years in this country. The rate of inflow of these temporary foreign workers (they are known somewhat jeeringly as *Gastarbeiter*, meaning guest workers in Germany) has been considerable and continues today.

West Germany's proportion of manufactured exports was only half Britain's total in 1950. By 1957 German exports were at the same total volume level as British exports and West Germany's total level of exports was significantly greater than the British volume by the early 1960s. By the early 1960s this country had become a major industrial nation and some noticeable changes in certain public attitudes were becoming evident. These changes were mainly due to the spreading of affluence, labour shortages which added to general job security, the taking for granted of low rates of inflation and high rates of real economic growth, the increasing feeling that the now old Adenauer had been in power long enough and the improved international political situation, which decreased the level of 'Cold War' fears.

The memories of massive unemployment and high inflation were fading fast and poverty in the country no longer existed. The position of the Social Democratic Party was strengthened by these changing attitudes and it became only a question of time before this party obtained a measure of political power. The recession of the mid-1960s put the Social Democrats in the Bonn Government as junior coalition partners. In 1969 the Social Democrats did not win as many votes at the polls as the Christian Democrats and Christian Socialists together, but they managed to establish a coalition Government where they held the upper hand with the small Free Democratic Party. In 1972 the Social Democrats won a major election victory, winning more votes than any other party. The Social Democrats were still forced to form a coalition with the Free Democrats, but their power had never been greater and they were certain of at least four full years of running the Federal Republic.

But perhaps I am racing ahead a little too fast, for in large measure the 1960s was a decade of both economic and political transition. While the 1950s was a period of complete Christian Democrat and Christian Socialist power in Bonn and continual dynamic economic expansion, the 1960s was a period during which the economy began to stumble and the degree of power enjoyed by the Christian Democrats and Christian Socialists began to decline. These developments in the last decade were to a great degree the result of the changing public attitudes towards economic development and politics mentioned above.

The decline in the economic growth rate in the early 1960s forced the Government to intervene more directly in the economy. The first few years of the last decade were difficult and a major crisis did not seem far distant for many business leaders. The ending of immigration from the East produced labour shortages, of which the strengthened trade unions took full advantage. Overhead costs in industry surged ahead and international cyclical economic developments saw a decline in demand for German products. A further burden for German industry, which was greatly export-orientated, was the five per cent revaluation of the Deutsche Mark in terms of the United States dollar to a level of four marks equals one dollar in 1961.

The mid-1960s saw the first recession since the Currency Reform. I believe that this recession marks the turning-point in the economic development of the Federal Republic. The greatest company sales and profit records were to be established at the end of the 1960s yet the recession was the start of a shake-up in almost every aspect of German life: it was the cause of the fall of Erhard and the rise of the Social Democrats into the Government; it saw the sinking of poorly managed and weak companies and forced massive rescue operations to save industrial giants, such as Krupp, from bankruptcy; it momentarily placed the trade unions in a weak position as unemployment fears were widespread, but the taking advantage of this weakness resulted later in such bitterness by the unions that they eventually managed to get the highest wage rises in post-war history; it forced a far greater direct intervention by government in the managing of the economy and led to important changes as a result.

By 1969 the system of economic management had undergone substantial changes. At the heart of Dr Erhard's economic policies lay the conviction that governments should play an advisory and to a small extent supervisory role in the economy, leaving the development of the economy primarily to the free interplay of market forces. Industrial disputes were viewed as matters for employers and employees alone to settle, free of intervention by politicians. The forming of monopoly positions was not something that dismayed the authorities and the cartel laws of the late 1950s were by no means severe. A system of checks and balances was created to prevent to some extent too much direct government intervention. An Economics Ministry was established with powers over monetary policy that were curbed by the establishment of an independent Federal Bank. The Federal Bank Law of 1957 created an institution, which today enjoys a greater degree of autonomy than any other central bank in the European Economic Community. The Finance Ministry was created to be in charge of fiscal policy and public expenditure, but powers for economic planning and the raising of capital for the State on the markets were given to the Economics Ministry. The result was a system that forced negotiation between the central bank and the two Bonn ministries for a co-ordinated wide-ranging economic policy to be made effective and this in itself restricted the actions in the economic sphere that German governments could take.

The recession showed clearly that some German managers had been pumping all their profits for too long into new investments to produce expansion and had neglected sufficiently the building of adequate capital reserves. Some companies by the time of the recession had become flabby, employing too many people, neglecting rationalisation, simply because managers had become so used to ever higher sales and profits that they had become negligent and failed to recognise that a recession could come about. The mini-recession, for by international standards it was certainly not a recession of major proportions, produced substantial rationalisation in many companies. Unemployment was not a major problem, because those first hit were the temporary immigrant workers, who left the country in large numbers at this time. However, the fear of recession was greater than at any time in the previous fifteen years.

The crisis produced once again in German history the demand for strong government. Dr Erhard was forced out of power and more significantly the neo-Nazis, the NPD, began to emerge as a political force of importance. The shift to the right of the political arena at the first indication of an economic set-back was a clear example to many observers that changes in political and social attitudes in West Germany have not been as rapid as many people would like to believe. However, the total crushing of radical parties in the general elections of 1972, when inflation was the major election theme and the rate was the highest seen for a very long time, tends to suggest that some changes to the good are taking place in the democratic thinking of the German people.

However, the recession also made it quite clear that the authorities must have some sort of emergency powers to intervene firmly in the economy when the economic situation appeared to be getting out of control. The formal system of checks and balances with great reliance on the interplay of market forces was not adequate in times of economic crisis. The result was the 1967 'Stability and Growth Law', which clearly outlines the economic priorities of the government and gives the government a wide range of special powers of a dirigistic type for use in emergency situations. This piece of legislation is of vital importance and gives the Bonn governments exceptionally wide-ranging powers, which in effect, if used, can almost totally overthrow the free market economic system that Dr Erhard constructed and which still is the basic philosophy of all German central bankers, Finance and Economics ministers.

By the time the new law was passed through Parliament the recession had almost ended. That it came to an end so swiftly was in large measure due to the trade unions accepting very minor wage gains in contract negotiations, which enabled companies to get back on to higher profit margins, while also placing them in a position to continue as most forceful and effective competitors on world markets. The strong revival of the economy in the last years of the last decade speedily cast aside all hopes that radical political parties may have had of gaining power. Low wage agreements aided the revival, as did rationalisation that managers were belatedly forced to push through. At the same time, partly owing to the Vietnam war, a notable upswing in international economic activity was developing. Further, West Germany had managed to maintain a rate of inflation well below the international average, resulting in the effects of the 1961 revaluation, in terms of pegging the currency at a realistic rate in terms of other currencies, being completely eroded by the mid-1960s, and the Deutsche Mark was once again a greatly under-valued currency, which naturally helped to strengthen the international competitive position of German industry.

Throughout the last decade the rate of annual consumer price increases was rarely above 2·5 per cent, with the annual real economic growth rate rarely below 3·5 per cent. The gross national product, measured at 1962 prices,* rose from DM 328,400 million in 1960 to DM 419,500 million in 1965, then in 1966 as the recession started to bite it climbed to only DM 431,000 million and then fell back in the following year to DM 430,800 million. The recovery was swift, however, with the gross national product reaching DM 462,300 million in 1968 and DM 499,300 million in the following year.

German companies in 1968 again started to register healthy profits and substantial turnover development and in the following year record results were widespread. In that year of great prosperity, booming conditions and of still better prospects, the German people hesitantly cast aside the Christian Democrats and Christian Socialists. The swift haul away from recession into bustling economic activity and immense affluence was largely credited to the ability of Dr Karl Schiller, the one-time Hamburg professor of economics, who since 1966 had been the Economics Minister. The charm and proven skill of Schiller, combined with the distinct charisma of the one-time mayor of Berlin, Willy Brandt, proved the main assets for the Social Democrats, who came to power in the autumn of 1969.

* Figures based on Federal Government Statistics Office tables and calculations.

1969–72 – A NEW ERA STARTS

The election result in 1969 can fairly be seen as the start of a new era in German politics and in the country's economic development. A political party, that for years had longed for power, that had many ideals and little experience of the realities of government, finally came into office. The necessity to form a coalition with the Free Democrat Party forced the Social Democrats at the very start to abandon some of their more radical reform plans, especially as between them the Free Democrats and the Social Democrats had only a very slender Bundestag majority.

The Brandt administration made many promises that it could not keep, but it set out in a direction of basic reform in domestic social sectors and in international relations that won applause from the German public. In November 1972, the Government was forced to face the public in a general election, for the crossing of some members of the Bundestag into the Christian Democrat and Christian Socialist camp left the Brandt coalition without a majority. Brandt's election victory in 1972 underlined the fact that a new era had started in 1969. Despite the appeals of the Christian Socialists and Christian Democrats that they alone could restore economic stability, the German people gave Brandt a substantial vote of confidence. It is probably too early to draw too many conclusions about the last election, yet it seems certain the re-election of the Brandt administration, despite increasingly high rates of inflation, reflected to some extent the fact that memories of the past periods of massive inflation and high unemployment had faded. A large number of major economic developments took place in the period of the first Brandt administration, which have changed the picture of the German economy considerably and which have promoted a major transformation in the shape and structure of the economy and of German industrial life. This following section deals with the major economic developments between 1969, when Herr Brandt became Chancellor, and the elections of 1972, and forms the essential basis for grasping the full depth of the changes taking place here that are looked at in more detail in the following chapters of this book.

The Social Democrats came to power at a time when the

trade unions felt bitterly annoyed about the way in which they had entered into low wage rise agreements with employers in 1967 and 1968. The trade unions felt that the wool had expertly been pulled over their eyes and they were out for revenge. The trade unions had been told of the prospect of severe depression and heavy unemployment unless they agreed to almost minimal wage rises. In fact, the years 1968 and 1969 saw the strongest profit increases and profit levels in post-war German industry. This strong earnings boom was achieved on the backs of the workers, argued the unions. A significant worsening of industrial relations was about to take place. A major crisis could have been avoided had employers been slightly more generous in the immediate post-recession period, but their failure to take such a line resulted in their having to pay a high price in late 1969 and early 1970.

The Social Democrats owed much of their electoral success to trade union support and were not therefore in a position to demand that the unions modify their wage demands. The employers, basking in their record profits, had few arguments to convince the unions that they were not in a position to pay high increases in wages. The trade unions not only demanded high rises for 1970, but their demands also involved increases to compensate for the low wage gains made in the previous years. Average hourly wages rose by more than 15 per cent in 1970, which according to the Federal Bank, was the highest rate of increase since the time of the Korean War. When shorter working hours are taken into consideration and higher insurance and social security costs, the rise in wage costs in industry in 1970 was in many cases well over 20 per cent. The average rise in Nordrhein-Westfalen according to the Cologne Chamber of Commerce was over 21·5 per cent, while the German chemical industry, for example, maintained that the rise was in excess of 24 per cent.

The high wage rates, which were among the highest in Europe, not only produced a substantial inflationary push, but also significantly weakened the competitive position of industry. The problems of industry were increased by mounting pressure for a change in the value of the German currency. By the end of 1969 West Germany had a most sizeable balance of payments surplus and it was universally recognised by bankers and economists that even after the French and British devaluations the Deutsche Mark was greatly under-valued. Fearing the consequences on foreign sales of a revaluation the leaders of German industry were quite naturally opposed to such a measure. It was argued that a revaluation would wreck all hopes of Germany remaining a major exporting nation; it would cripple German industry and lead to a flood of imports.

By the end of 1969 West Germany had a total trade surplus of DM 15,584 million.* The Social Democrats favoured a re-valuation and after they were elected they pegged the currency at DM 3·6600 to one U.S. dollar. This compared with the parity set in 1961 of DM 4·0000 to one U.S. dollar. Despite the protests of the business community that the new rate was far too high and would produce immense hardship, it was in fact a rate that still left the Deutsche Mark somewhat under-valued. It took another two years and a major international monetary crisis to finally see the German currency pegged at a rate that most bankers and economists in the country considered to be realistic. However, the persistent belief abroad that the Deutsche Mark was under-valued, coupled with Germany's continuing high trade surpluses, produced further changes in the value of the Deutsche Mark in terms of the U.S. dollar in 1973.

The German balance of payments figures suggest that the effect on German exports of the 1969 revaluation was not nearly as great as industrialists had suggested. The degree of this country's involvement in international trade and the character and structure of this foreign business is worth some examination, especially as it shows just how dependent German business is upon exporting. In the European Economic Community and the European Free Trade Area only Italy, with a trade surplus of DM 231 million in 1969, exported more goods to West Germany than it imported from West Germany. The situation changed due to the revaluations and in 1972 West Germany had a deficit in trade with all her five European Community partners except for France. After a total trade surplus with these partners in 1970 of DM 1,823 million, Germany had a total trade deficit of DM 3,169 million in 1972.

* Figures quoted here are based on statistics compiled by the Federal Bank. A full discussion of Germany's international trading position is given in Chapter 4.

However, the period of stagnation early in 1972, followed by a gentle economic upturn, resulted in relatively low domestic demand for foreign products and for domestic goods, especially capital goods. The swifter pace of economic development in many foreign areas, however, produced a large demand for German goods from abroad and with low domestic demand German companies were in a position to deliver large volumes of products abroad swiftly. These cyclical factors of a general economic nature played a most important role in the West German trade pattern in 1972 and overshadowed the negative effects on German exports produced by the D-Mark's revaluation.

The upswing in foreign demand for German goods in the first half of 1973 was so great, due to the generally strong pace of economic activity in most industrialised countries, that the record 1972 trade surplus of DM 20,251 million looked like being exceeded. However, by this time the full impact of the series of recent revaluations of the German currency had not been registered in the trade figures and many business leaders felt certain that, in due course, the strong rises in the prices of German goods would lead to significant declines in demand and that, in the medium term, West Germany would have to content itself with considerably smaller trade surpluses. It is probably useful at this point in the context of German trading relationships to outline where this country's companies sell their goods abroad on the basis of the 1972 trade figures. The countries of Western Europe are by far the most important trade partners for this country. The total volume of German exports to the five other members of the once small Common Market of six countries equalled DM 59,434 million in 1972, while total German exports to all countries amounted to DM 149,004 million.

Apart from the members of the Common Market in 1972 this country's chief European trade partners were Britain, which imported DM 7,046 million of German goods, Switzerland, which imported DM 8,761 million, Austria, with imports from Germany of DM 7,472 million and Sweden with imports from this country of DM 5,027 million. Outside Western Europe the most important trade partner by far for this country is the United States. Total exports in 1972 to the United States from

West Germany amounted to DM 13,818 million. It may well be, however, that the combined effects of recent D-Mark revaluations may in time make the United States a substantially less important export market for companies here. Japan is another non-European industrial country of particular importance in the German trade map. In 1970, trade between Japan and this country was almost in equilibrium, by 1971 the Japanese had a trade surplus with this country of DM 713 million, which rose to DM 1,208 million in 1972. Japanese exports to Germany totalled DM 3,176 million in 1972 and with gathering momentum a wide assortment of Japanese companies are now seeking to build on this base and make West Germany a foreign export market of major significance.

On the imports side the figures show that West Germany is even more dependent on her European neighbours than on the export side. In 1972 this country's total import volume was DM 128,753 million, with DM 62,023 million accounted for by Italy, Holland, France, Belgium and Luxemburg alone. British exports to Germany were DM 4,583 million, while those from Switzerland were DM 3,719 million, from Austria DM 2,654 million and from Sweden DM 3,195 million. U.S. exports to West Germany were DM 10,766 million.

Apart from the main industrial countries the Germans are actively seeking to strengthen their trade with Eastern Europe in particular. In 1970 West German trade with all Comecon countries excepting East Germany involved exports of DM 5,400 million and imports of DM 4,394 million. In 1972 West German exports to these countries had increased by more than 40 per cent, while imports had increased by close to 25 per cent and the West German trade surplus had risen to DM 2,336 million from DM 1,006 million in 1970. East Germany is for political reasons not seen by the Bonn authorities as a foreign area, but the total volume of trade between the two German countries is close to DM 5,000 million now, with a considerable surplus for the West Germans.

Trade with developing countries, as defined by the Development Assistance Committee, is considerable and roughly balanced. In 1972 West Germany exported DM 24,877 million worth of goods to these countries and imported from them a total volume of DM 24,196 million worth. In coming years it may well be that greater efforts are made by Germans to build strong market shares in developing countries for these clearly may well prove to be major areas of growth. However, as in the case of Eastern Europe, limits are set through payment difficulties should the West Germans manage to achieve large trade surpluses.

It seems to some extent remarkable that the West Germans have managed to sustain such a high level of exports in recent years and to some extent this is due to their determination to hold on to large foreign market shares, even if this means taking losses on exports from time to time. After the 1969 revaluation it was widely argued within German industry that higher inflation rates abroad would swiftly permit the re-establishment of satisfactory profit margins on exports. This led to a policy of holding prices down, rather than immediately making price increases to offset the revaluation losses and resulted in companies managing to maintain very high export sales in 1970, albeit with a lower earnings return. It was not possible to repeat this tactic after the 1971 revaluation. Firstly, it was not so necessary with regard to main European markets, for the rate of the revaluation in terms of other European currencies was far smaller than in 1969. Secondly, Germany in 1972 was well in line with international inflation averages and faced the prospect of still higher inflation, and the one country that got the largest benefit from the revaluation, the United States, managed to hold inflation in 1972 well below German levels. The result was a significant decline in German sales to the United States for much of 1972, resulting directly from the currency re-alignment. To keep a high sales volume in the United States would have demanded some German companies taking vast losses on sales to the United States, and German companies were by no means strong enough to take such sacrifices. Volkswagen, with annual unit sales to the United States of some 500,000 cars, was the largest sufferer and had to consider trying to sell to the United States from foreign-based plants, rather than from its main German factories.

In early 1970 it was not surprising that many manufacturers should have taken a bleak view of the future. The international competitive position of German industry had been weakened by the revaluation and major difficulties existed in trying to digest the high wage increase rates. Further, the higher wages were producing a consumer spending boom giving opportunities to businessmen to raise their prices, and Germany started to fear a serious inflation problem. These fears resulted in the Federal Bank tightening credit and thereby adding to industrial investment costs and making life still tougher for many company managers.

The Federal Bank's policies in 1970 were probably more responsible for increasing the inflation tempo than for curbing it. The Federal Bank increased its discount rate in one go by 1·5 per cent to 7·5 per cent, while the lombard rate – the rate of borrowing against collateral – was increased from 9 per cent to 9·5 per cent. These decisions in early March 1970 resulted in Germany having an interest rate level substantially above the international average and particularly above U.S. levels. The Federal Bank President, Dr Karl Klasen, said at the time that these decisions should prove adequate for dampening the overheating economy and bringing prices on to a more stable path.

This high interest rate policy was a mistake simply because it produced a massive inflow of foreign funds on account of the high yields available and thus stimulated the expansion rate of the money supply and only added to the country's inflation problems. The Federal Bank, however, believed at the time that it was essential that some action should be taken on the inflation front and with the Government doing nothing it believed its only choice was to impose tougher credit restrictions. The Government was mindful of its election promises of no tax increases, it was also ambitious to go ahead with reform plans and was therefore not prepared to make cuts in public spending. Dr Schiller pleaded for tax increases early in 1970 and his defeat in the cabinet on this suggestion was the start of increasing internal cabinet hostility between Schiller and several other prominent ministers. After his defeat Schiller took a holiday, officially a rest for health reasons, and speculation mounted on whether or not he was going to resign. In the event he remained in the Government, with his love of politics and being at the centre of the political stage clearly greater than the hurt to his pride that a cabinet defeat involved.

At the start of 1970 few experts predicted a serious economic crisis. By the spring the Federal Bank acted to curb the inflation;

its official foreign exchange reserves at the time totalled DM 28,518 million and due primarily to the heavy cash inflows from abroad, that followed the interest rate rises the reserves reached DM 49,018 million by the end of the year. The economy was becoming increasingly over-heated and by July it was clear that the Federal Bank's policies were not having the desired effect. Finally, Dr Schiller got his way in the cabinet and a series of measures were decided upon by the Government. The most important decisions included the suspension for six months of tax-deductable depreciation allowances and the imposition of a 10 per cent surcharge on income tax, that would be frozen at the Federal Bank and repaid within a maximum of three years. This latter measure counteracted the foreign cash inflows to some extent by draining DM 5,900 million out of the economy, with about DM 2,000 million of this coming from companies, who were already suffering through the increased cost of investments resulting from the suspension of tax-deductable depreciation allowances.

The July measures had a modest effect in cooling down the economy. The willingness to invest on the part of industry declined significantly as companies fought to digest the high wage costs, the lower profit margins on foreign sales, the higher interest rates and the blows produced by the July mini-budget. Companies were forced to reduce their profit forecasts sharply, and there were widespread fears that the forced cuts in investment spending could in the medium term produce a slow-down in the economic rate of growth and a further weakening of German industry's international competitive position. In the autumn of 1971 the trade unions started to prepare their new wage contract demands and, determined to gain high rises once again, they were not greatly put off by the fact that high rises would inevitably lead to further declines in company profits and produce a further stimulus for the inflation.

The trade unions won rises modestly below the previous year's levels. The actual increases gained were about 11 per cent to 12 per cent on average. Many companies announced sharp profit declines for 1970 and warned of still greater falls in 1971. In 1970 and 1971 together, average wage costs in industry rose by well over 30 per cent and the revaluation losses to industry had been most substantial. However, at the start of 1971 there was reason to question the pessimism of industrialists, for higher rates of inflation abroad than in Germany were increasing the scope for German companies to raise prices abroad and there were signs that the July measures were starting to bite, resulting in a slow-down in the inflation rate. By international standards the rise in the West German cost of living index in 1970 was modest at 3·8 per cent, but by previous German standards this was seen as being intolerably high.

Hopes of a brighter corporate profit outlook and reduced inflation were dashed by the international money crisis that was clearly developing early in 1971. The high yields offered on deposits in Germany, coupled with the country's continuing high current account balance of payments surplus and the comparatively low rate of inflation, made the Deutsche Mark one of the most sought-after currencies in the world. The increasing belief among bankers, finance experts and economists that an international currency realignment was essential, involving primarily a devaluation of the dollar, especially in terms of the Japanese Yen and the German currency, started to produce massive short-term international capital movements early in 1971.

The volume of currency speculation gathered momentum and Federal Bank cuts in the discount rate tended to make little difference to the volume of currency inflows spilling into Germany. The rate of German money supply expansion quickened, leading to ever higher inflation. The country was enjoying a consumer spending boom of vast dimensions. The belief that the Deutsche Mark might well be forced to another revaluation stimulated foreign demand for German goods, as companies abroad believed that placing orders in fixed Deutsche Mark terms could produce high savings should a revaluation take place. German industry early in 1971 was working at more than full capacity with the demand for labour huge and over-time work plentiful. By early May 1971, the foreign exchange and gold reserve holdings of the Federal Bank amounted to DM 68,636 million – an increase of close to DM 20,000 million since the start of the year and a rise of over DM 40,000 million since the start of 1970.

The Bonn Government faced a fairly simple choice: it could either follow suggestions made by some of its European Economic Community partners and take advantage of the 'Stability and Growth Law' to impose rigorous foreign exchange controls; or it could revalue the currency immediately; or it could follow the advice of the country's leading economic research institutes* and set the Deutsche Mark free to float to a realistic value. The former course of action was favoured by business leaders, who feared that a revaluation or float would wreck export sales and lead to massive increases in imports. Further, a de jure revaluation or a float, which would have been a de facto revaluation, would produce immediate losses to companies that had yet to complete delivery or orders contracted earlier at fixed Deutsche Mark currency rates.

Dr Schiller, the Economics Minister, believed that exchange controls always proved to be an obstacle to free trade, that they rarely worked well and that they were philosophically in complete opposition to the free market economic system that he and Dr Erhard so favoured. Dr Schiller seriously feared that the tight imposition of exchange controls across Europe could lead to the establishment of Europe as a highly protectionist bloc and produce far greater strains in political relations between the United States and Europe than were anyway resulting from the international currency upheaval. On 5 May 1971 West German authorities closed the exchange markets and after a series of marathon sessions in Brussels in the Council of Finance Ministers, West Germany, followed by the Netherlands, announced on 9 May, that the Deutsche Mark and the Guilder respectively were to be set afloat.

All currencies were eventually forced into an effective float on 15 August 1971, when President Nixon announced his package of economic measures: these involved an immediate prices and wages freeze in the United States, the suspension of full dollar convertibility and the imposition of a 10 per cent surcharge on all imports to the United States. The latter measure and the de facto revaluation of the German currency produced by the

---

* In a joint report, published on 3 May 1971, the economic research institutes of West Berlin, Hamburg, Kiel, Munich and Essen called for the free floating of the Deutsche Mark. The West Berlin institute added that the float should be followed at an appropriate time by a revaluation. When floating the currency the German authorities insisted that in time the DM 3·66 parity rate would be restored.

May float, hit German exports severely. The impact of the float was clearly visible by the autumn of 1971. Order book levels in German industry declined sharply and many companies had no alternative other than to introduce a large measure of short-time working in their factories. The situation was particularly serious for the iron, steel and mechanical engineering industries. The year 1971 saw a heavy decline in international demand for steel and coupled with the domestic German problems it was not surprising that the largest worker lay-offs in the late months of 1971 in Germany were in the iron and steel industry. The American measures hit Volkswagen, with its huge U.S. sales, particularly hard and other German car makers were suffering as foreign manufacturers took full advantage of the currency situation to boost sales in Germany.

In the late autumn of 1971 the trade unions were forced to take a more moderate stand in wage contract negotiations than they had in the two previous years. Usually the I.G. Metall trade union, the largest in the country, representing more than four million employees in the iron, steel, electrical, car and engineering industries, is the first major union to put in pay claims for the following year. The I.G. Metall contracts are vitally important, because the settlements reached tend to set the guidelines for all other trade union negotiations that follow. The inflation in Germany had gathered momentum strongly in the first months of the year, the Government had failed to take fiscal measures to dampen demand and the effect of the massive currency inflows on the economy had been substantial. The inflows were effectively neutralised by the float, but the float had come fairly late in the year to affect the inflation trend in 1971 substantially. The I.G. Metall was determined to win pay rises greater than the increase in the cost of living.

Employers felt that they were in a desperate position. Profits had fallen substantially and demand for all manner of goods was declining sharply. Employers were determined to have a show-down with the unions, they also realised that a short strike would, in the industries involved in the I.G. Metall negotiations, not be all that inconvenient, as plant closures for a short period seemed inevitable due to the sharp fall in demand. Strikes took place in December, which by German standards were the most severe ever seen. A final wage settlement was reached, that acted as a guide to other unions in 1972 and which brought average wage increases for 1972 down to a tolerable level of slightly above 9 per cent.

At the end of 1971, West German industry was in many respects in major difficulties. Profit margins on foreign sales had become paper thin, due to the combination of the 1969 revaluation and the May 1971 float. The Deutsche Mark was finally pegged on 18 December 1971* at a rate of DM 3·2250 to one United States dollar. Industry found that its wage costs were the highest in any major European industrial nation. Furthermore, a major recession was feared as order-book levels declined swiftly with foreign rivals taking full advantage of the currency realignment and the higher prices of German products, forced up by the wage cost explosion. Imported cars, for example, had accounted for slightly less than 22 per cent of all German car registrations in 1970, and one year later the market share of imports had climbed to over 26 per cent.

It was widely recognised in German industry that new strategies had to be devised and that major rationalisation had to take place. In many companies top managers were forced to resign, carrying, sometimes unfairly, the blame for the slump in profits in 1970 and 1971. In addition to the general problems outlined above, some industries faced special difficulties. The chemical companies, for example, confronted serious problems due to a substantial international over-capacity of artificial fibres output. The electrical industry, to take another example, was severely hit by the U.S. measures, which forced Japanese manufacturers to look for sales opportunities in Europe now that their sales chances in the United States had declined, and a considerable volume of Japanese electrical products were dumped on the European markets.

There also appeared to be few bright spots on the horizon for German industrialists. There were certainly hopes that the general situation would improve, but it was widely recognised that the times when German industry could steam ahead with low wage costs and an under-valued currency were finally over for good. Among the questions that had to be asked was the problem of where best to locate new plants and concentrate

* This rate was negotiated in line with an international currency re-alignment concluded at the Smithsonian Institute, Washington.

new investment spending. In addition, German managers had to try and work out ways of saving relations with the trade unions from getting worse and they had to reach a better relationship with the Government. The list of general and particular problems that faced the leaders of German business was great at the outset of 1972 and the chief worry concerned the uncertainties: would the Government with its shrinking majority manage to hold on to power? what would be the effect of the latest revaluation on sales and profit margins? how best could investment projects be financed after two years of vast profit declines? what policies would the Government and the Federal Bank adopt to curb the increasing inflation? would the Americans shortly lift their import surcharge and would the European Economic Community's Commission manage to reach a trade agreement with the Japanese?

The list of questions was immense and all were vital in determining not just the short-term, but also the medium- and long-term outlook for German industry. The high degree of pessimism that was to be found in German industry late in 1971 largely resulted from the firm conviction that the Government was totally incapable of averting a serious recession and that many of its attempts could well further weaken industry. There were large fears of tighter cartel laws, stiffer controls on borrowing abroad and higher corporation taxes.

The Government itself was in a muddle on the economic policy front, which by no means helped the situation. Major internal cabinet rows between the Finance Minister, Herr Alex Möller, and Dr Schiller, had resulted in the former resigning in the spring of 1971. The Chancellor, Herr Brandt, appeared to take little interest in economic policy; his chief concern was with foreign affairs and he trusted Dr Schiller completely. So much so that on Herr Möller's resignation the Finance and Economics ministries were pulled together to form a vast and unwieldly department of State under the sole command of Dr Schiller. The Hamburg professor of economics had become the most powerful man next to Brandt in the cabinet and this itself produced hostility to Schiller among other ministers, who believed that Schiller enjoyed too much power.

In addition, the Government's majority had become paper thin and it was by no means certain that it could last out its official term of office, which was due to end in autumn 1973. Dr Schiller was in many respects to the right of his party and by no means a full supporter of many of the social reform plans of his colleagues. Further, Dr Schiller seemed reluctant to push ahead with major tax reforms that the Social Democrats saw as their most important contribution to producing a fairer distribution of income.

In the first few months of 1972 the situation appeared to be getting gloomier as fresh foreign currency inflows started and it became clear that the international currency re-alignment had not at a stroke solved the international monetary crisis. The Federal Bank continued to increase its holdings of foreign currencies as international speculators remained convinced that a further adjustment in currency values would take place. The money supply expansion rate continued to increase, producing a still more serious inflation situation. The cost of living index in 1971 had risen by 5·2 per cent and real gross national product development had been only 3 per cent. These taken together were the worst figures of their kind in over twenty years in this country and the outlook clearly indicated higher inflation and lower real economic growth.

Consumer spending remained high and to achieve some of its reforms the Government had embarked on a course of high spending. The increase in public spending demanded large borrowing, for the tax income was expected to fall in view of the serious corporate profit situation. Very minor tax increases on petrol and tobacco were introduced. The heavy public borrowing became the main cause of the increasing inflation rate, according to Karl Schiller and the Federal Bank, but this was only realised late in 1972. Further, it placed a great strain on the capital market and lessened the opportunities of the private sector to float bond issues. Many companies were forced to go outside Germany to borrow and this only added to the internal money supply expansion rate.

To some extent in those early months of 1972 the experts had misjudged the situation. The final currency re-alignment had narrowed the revaluation premium between the Deutsche Mark and some major currencies from the level that had existed when Germany's currency alone was floating. The Government had increased public expenditure in the belief that this would give the economy a boost and avert a recession. But the recession fears themselves had been exaggerated. Slowly order books with major industries began to fatten as demand from abroad rose. The pace of improvement varied greatly from one industry to another. Some companies, such as Volkswagen, with products that were out-dated, did not enjoy an upswing in sales and the iron and steel industry continued to suffer as its prices remained uncompetitive, due partly, among other factors, to sharp increases in domestic coal and coke prices.

The best improvements were being registered by manufacturers of consumer goods as the high wage level had produced little interruption in the high level of public demand for all manner of products. The construction industry benefited strongly from the high volume of public sector contracts and the strong private demand for housing. The electrical industry was aided by the Munich Olympic Games, which produced a particularly high demand for such products as colour television sets. World demand for artificial fibres was rapidly increasing and helping the German chemical industry to recover. An upswing in economic activity in most European industrial countries and the United States, from the early spring of 1972, helped promote a more satisfactory demand level for all manner of German products. Many German companies remained hesitant, however, delaying new orders for capital goods. Renewed confidence in German industry only really started to set in in the summer, and swiftly thereafter the mechanical engineering and other investment goods industries started to register higher order book levels. But the rate of inflation gathered pace.

In many respects the first third of 1972 was a period of stagnation mixed with high inflation in West Germany. The upswing in demand for industrial products was slow and only started to gather momentum towards the end of the first half of the year. The rate of real economic growth in the first six months was negligible, but it was a time when many companies pushed through drastic consolidation and rationalisation programmes, producing some easing in the labour market tension, although no large unemployment. The improving trend of the economy was hidden for much of the first half of the year and the easing of labour market tension convinced some experts that the feared recession would really take place. The Government was also aware of the need to increase its popularity as a general election could not be long avoided.

To stimulate the economy and fully neglecting the inflationary situation, the Government decided to start repaying the tax surcharge imposed in July 1970. The repayments were fully made in June and July of 1972 with the authorities hopeful that the DM 5,900 million repayments would go into savings or in expenses abroad resulting from summer holidays. Earlier in the year the Government had tried to curb foreign borrowing abroad by German companies by introducing a cash deposit system. This system, known as the 'bardepot', forced companies borrowing more than DM 2 million a year abroad to deposit a portion of their borrowings, free of interest, at the Federal Bank. The amount to be deposited with the Federal Bank could be up to 50 per cent of the amount borrowed, thus effectively doubling the cost of the borrowing. The scheme at first had little effect as the German companies found too many ways around the complex cash deposit system's rules. The system also had little support from Karl Schiller, who introduced it under strong pressure from the Federal Bank, but who doubted if it would work and who opposed it on the basis that it was a clear break with free market economic system ideas.

To counter the effect on the domestic economy of the increasingly large inflows of foreign funds, the Federal Bank took a series of measures in the summer to tighten commercial bank minimum reserve requirements, but it held back from increasing its key interest rates for fear that rises would lead to still greater short-term capital movements into the Federal Republic. By June however the situation had once again become almost unmanageable without radical measures being taken. The inflation rate was steaming ahead and cash inflows became substantial as speculation on a devaluation of the British and Italian currencies mounted. There were also fears that such devaluations could force another major international currency crisis, involving a further devaluation of the United States dollar and the result was the heavy selling of dollars for Deutsche Marks. Early in June the Economics Minister had announced plans to cut total Federal Government spending by DM 2,500 million and this was to be followed by cuts of DM 1,500 million in the budgets of the regional governments. But these measures alone were insufficient to deal with the inflation crisis.

The Federal Bank President, Dr Karl Klasen, suggested to the Bonn cabinet in late June that as a first step to restore price stability the Government should take advantage of the 'Stability and Growth Law' to impose tight exchange controls. He suggested that all foreign purchases of German domestic bonds should be made subject to special Federal Bank approval and that the cash deposit scheme on foreign borrowing by German companies should be tightened. The first measure was thought the best means of curbing foreign currency inflows, for the Federal Bank had realised that in the first half of 1972 foreign purchases of German securities, mainly fixed interest bearing bonds, had totalled close to DM 10,000 million. Dr Klasen's suggestions were made after detailed consultation with other European Economic Community central bankers and with the knowledge that the immediate currency crisis was likely to end, as Britain had decided upon a currency float and the EEC had agreed to special arrangements for the Italian currency.*

The majority of the cabinet fully supported Dr Klasen's suggestions. Dr Schiller, however, was a hostile opponent. He believed that the free market economic system was about to be wrecked, that an increasing number of exchange controls would in time be introduced. Further, he feared that other countries would follow the German example and the result would be widespread protectionism, imposing strong limits on German exports. Dr Schiller also believed that some kind of plot had been hatched between Dr Klasen and members of the cabinet. The cabinet opposed Schiller, they accepted Klasen's suggestions and, shortly after, Schiller resigned from the

---

* At this time the Common Market was operating a narrower currency band system, where each member country could intervene in the exchange markets to ensure that no currency became so weak or so strong as to fall out of the narrower band system. Such support was to be repaid by the country whose currency had been supported in a proportion to the reserves that the country held. From July to the end of 1972, Italy enjoyed special arrangements, whereby she could make repayments in dollars and did not have to fear the loss of her gold or special drawing rights reserves. The arrangements were in fact unnecessary as speculation tended to end after the pound's float—at least as far as 1972 was concerned.

Government, being replaced as Economics and Finance Minister by Herr Helmut Schmidt.

The Government's decisions were welcome by industry, due to fears that unless tough measures were taken the currency would sooner or later have to be floated again, with such a step being impossible to digest by an industry that had already taken two revaluations in little more than two years. The Cabinet measures involved the cutting of the foreign borrowing limit in the cash deposit scheme to DM 500,000 a year from DM 2 million and an increase in the amount that had to be deposited with the Federal Bank to 50 per cent from 40 per cent. At the same time the Federal Bank took a series of minimum reserve requirement measures to cut liquidity by over DM 8,000 million.

By the autumn, international interest rate levels were starting to rise and the Federal Bank, in a series of measures, increased its discount rate from 3 per cent to 4·5 per cent by the end of November. At the same time, the capital market had become so tight that during the autumn effective yields on new issues rose from 7 per cent to over 8·4 per cent. The economy in the autumn was starting to enjoy an upswing, largely due to strong foreign demand for all manner of products and gradually increasing domestic industrial demand for capital goods. The consumer spending boom continued and the inflation continued to surge ahead at an annual rate of well over 6 per cent. The Government was forced to call a general election, which it won on 19 November, despite a massive campaign by the Christian Democrats and Christian Socialists, warning of economic ruin if Herr Brandt was re-elected. At the end of 1972 companies could announce slightly improved profits, largely due to savings made on rationalisation. The economy appeared to be moving gradually into yet another boom, but there was little sign of a decline in the inflation rate.

By the summer of 1973 it was clear that many companies were reaching maximum capacity utilisation, due largely to heavy foreign demand, which in turn had stimulated domestic demand for all manner of products. The inflation rate, however, seemed set for an annual average in excess of 8 per cent. The Bonn Government and the Federal Bank took a large series of measures in the first six months of the year to combat

the inflation, including exceptionally tight credit restrictions
and significant tax increases. Many industrialists felt certain
that the sharp pace of foreign demand could not last for long,
especially in view of the swift increase in value of the Deutsche
Mark. The worries of industrialists were all the greater, for
the deflationary measures of the authorities added most considerably to investment costs and the costs of financing business.
At the end of the 1960s West Germany could boast of a record
of almost uninterrupted substantial economic growth over 20
years and constantly low rates of inflation. Her industry enjoyed
generally low wage cost levels and a substantial advantage over
foreign rivals due to an under-valued currency. Three years
later, at the start of 1973, West Germany found itself in a
position where her real economic growth rate had become lower
than that of many of the world's industrial nations and her
inflation rate was marginally above the international average.
West Germany still had barely any unemployment and
increasing tension in industrial relations and in the labour
market seemed to stare industry in the face. The managers of
German industry had been forced early in the 1970s to take a
close look at their situation and design new policies to meet a
decade that promised to be much more difficult than the 1960s
or 1950s.

The wealth of problems that German industry confronts
today is greater than is often realised. The following chapters
attempt to discuss the most important of these new problems
and, in so doing, these chapters attempt to outline the present
structure of German industry and the likely trends that will
develop in German industry. This chapter has sought only to
outline the background and the general economic situation.
To support this, Appendix 3 contains a series of tables sum-
marising important economic data.

The specific problems of companies and industries naturally
vary considerably and a book of this type can not hope to give
a detailed account of every company's and every industry's
problems and difficulties. This book can only deal with the
general situation and the most important wide-ranging problems. However, in order to place many of the remarks made
in this and the following chapters into the context of the chief
companies and industries the special problems of these com-

panies and industries are discussed in brief form in Appendix 1
and Appendix 2.

The following five chapters deal with the most important
areas of change and development, while the final chapter
attempts to draw the various strands together to present a
global picture, adding a few more relevant details that make
the general picture more complete and looking ahead to the
future economic development and the plans that the Brandt
Government has. With the Brandt administration now enjoying a substantial majority and certain of holding on to power
until at least late 1976, it is somewhat easier now to discuss its
plans than it was only a couple of years ago, when from day to
day one did not know how long the Government would last.
A new era in German economic history is starting and the
trends and developments must be appreciated by all who in one
form or another do business with this country. This is particularly
true of all the members of the European Economic Community
of nine nations, with whom West German industry does the
largest proportion of its foreign business.

It is also true, however, of the United States and Japan. The
trading relationship between West Germany and the United
States is likely to change greatly in coming years, as a result of
the latest international monetary developments, which place
U.S. industry in a much more competitive position in terms of
the Germans and the Japanese, and as a result of international
trade negotiations, where the Americans will almost certainly
continue to seek concessions from the Japanese and the European Community. As for Japan, the sharp change in the
relationship between the Yen and the Dollar will probably
result in Japanese companies being forced to turn their attention more fully on Europe, to compensate for losses in sales in
the United States. Here the Germans will come under great
pressure and the trade fight, in third markets in particular,
between the West Germans and the Japanese should have
fascinating consequences in years to come.

2 The Ownership and Control of West German Industry

A vast number of large German companies are closely controlled today by a relatively small number of financial institutions and organisations. These groups, through the holding on their own account of large blocks of shares or through representing by proxy the interests of many thousands of small share-holders, enjoy great influence over every aspect of the development of German industry.

The power of these groups is further aided through the existence of lax public controls in the fields of stock market supervision, monopoly controls and cartel regulations. The often close relationship between the various powerful groups has made it frequently possible for a concentration of industry to take place, through merger or take-over, without the sort of damaging stock market public battles that are commonly seen in some other countries.

The system of ownership and control of industry in West Germany is now, however, going through a period of almost revolutionary change. Stiffer cartel and monopoly regulations are being imposed by both the German and the European Economic Community authorities. These regulations are setting limits on the manner in which the holders of major blocks of shares use their influence. At the same time further curbs are being imposed by the trade unions, who are meeting with success in their efforts to increase their direct influence in the decision-taking process within industry and, supported by the Social Democratic Government, they are acquiring important powers through the development of new worker co-determination systems.

The general public is taking an increasing interest in the operations of public companies and the bourses, due to a large extent to rising prosperity and greater exposure of company and stock market affairs in the press and on television. This increasing interest has led to the formation of a large number of minority shareholder organisations who, as they grow and gain experience, become important checks on the influence of major shareholding groups, through skilful use of existing company laws. There is now growing pressure from small shareholders, trade unionists and an increasing number of politicians for greater public controls on the banks, public companies and stock exchanges. These pressures will almost certainly result in new laws substantially curbing the activities and degree of influence in the industrial field currently enjoyed by financial institutions.

These developments taken together will have a profound effect on the managements of German companies and the way in which top executives in large companies operate. These developments are a part of the basic changes that are now taking place within the economic system of this country. To understand fully the extent of the basic transformation in the structure of industry it is essential to understand how companies here are governed and it is important to know who owns the major companies and how the influence of owners is becoming restricted. It is probably accurate to suggest that in few western countries today is the erosion of powers held by large share-holders in their companies as swift and dramatic as it is in West Germany now.

In a narrower context, concerning foreign portfolio managers and foreign investors interested in German securities, the changes in the way in which large companies are controlled here is also of vital importance. Many of the developments are likely to have a negative effect on the overall development of German companies and it is somewhat surprising that just as the powers of large shareholders in their companies here declines, the volume of foreign investment in German securities appears to be increasing. Part of the reason may well be that foreign investors are not fully aware of the developments taking place now.

A few facts and figures serve to illustrate just how important this topic is for foreign investors today. The Federal Bank in its monthly report in December 1972 noted that non-resident purchases of German securities in 1972 amounted to about DM 10,000 million. In a letter to me on this subject in April

1971 the West German Banking Federation pointed out that foreign shareholders own close to 20 per cent of the share capital of all quoted German joint stock companies. This percentage is rising swiftly as foreign purchases of German shares increase, as has been the case in the last two years. So much so, in fact, that the Commerzbank AG in a report on the stock exchanges in 1972, stressed that share purchases in Germany from Britain, France and Switzerland were of paramount importance in influencing German stock market trends. British investment had been particularly heavy due to Britain's entry into the European Economic Community and the total German bourse turnover increased by about one-third in 1972, to a record DM 20,000 million, with fully 30 per cent accounted for by non-resident orders.*

This chapter deals primarily with the two-tier board system in major companies, the various legal forms of companies and the degree of influence that shareholders can and do wield in the companies they partly own. The way in which shareholder powers are being curbed is discussed in this chapter, with a number of important aspects, such as the growing power of the trade unions, discussed more fully in later chapters.

THE AKTIENGESELLSCHAFT

The most common legal form of large companies is the Aktiengesellschaft, whose structure is precisely detailed in the company laws of 1937 and 1965.† Responsibility for the affairs of an Aktiengesellschaft is divided among three main organs of control: the general meeting of shareholders, the supervisory board of directors, which is elected by the general meeting of shareholders and is known as the Aufsichtsrat, and the executive board of directors, which is appointed by the supervisory board and is known as the Vorstand. The laws have aimed at establishing a system of checks and balances between these three organs

* See the Commerzbank publication *Rum um die Börse*, published on 15 December 1972.

† Literally translated Aktiengesellschaft means 'share company'. The shares of this sort of company need not be publicly quoted. A shortened term for Aktiengesellschaft is AG, which is usually incorporated into the name of companies: e.g. Volkswagenwerk AG, AG Weser, Daimler-Benz AG, Siemens AG, Degussa AG.

to ensure that efficiency is maintained in the running of a company and that the company is directed in a manner that is in the best interests of the shareholders.

Each of the three organs has, under the existing laws, specific powers and responsibilities. These powers and responsibilities are carefully defined, yet the relationship that exists in practice can vary greatly from one company to another. For example, the balance of real power between the Aufsichtsrat and the Vorstand can vary greatly depending on whether the company is owned by a vast number of small shareholders or by just one or a handful of individuals or institutions. In the latter situation the Vorstand is often little more than a mere subordinate body to the Aufsichtsrat with the Aufsichtsrat taking the majority of the key management decisions. In a company where no large shareholders exist the Vorstand can often enjoy a great deal more power over a company's affairs than can the company's Aufsichtsrat.

It is more difficult to ascertain where real power lies in a German company than it is in major companies in other countries that do not have a two-tier board system. Outside Germany there is often confusion over the relative status of individuals in German companies. The confusion partly arises through the German love of important-sounding titles, with heads of departments in companies often having a director title, which to a foreigner may appear to suggest that the individual called a director is in fact a board member, which is often not the case. Further, the confusion exists because of the two-board system itself and there is no simple method for a person unacquainted with a German company to know if the company's Aufsichtsrat chairman is in fact more powerful than the company's Vorstand chairman. In most cases the chairman of the Vorstand is the most powerful man in a German company with the greatest burden of responsibility for his company's affairs.

The Vorstand is by law the servant of the general meeting of shareholders and of the Aufsichtsrat. To ensure that Vorstand members enjoy a degree of managerial independence they are designated by law as the official representatives of their company to third parties. The members of the Vorstand are responsible for all the internal operations of their companies, subject only to certain important limitations discussed later in this chapter. The members of the Vorstand are meant to be appointed solely on the basis of their managerial talents and do not have to have any shares in the company they work for.

It is most rare that a Vorstand member is a large shareholder in the company he manages and no single person is allowed to sit on both the executive and supervisory boards of the same company. However, it is common practice for Vorstand members of large companies to hold positions on the supervisory boards of subsidiary companies. For example, the Vorstand chairman of Volkswagenwerk AG is usually Aufsichtsrat chairman of VW's largest subsidiary Audi NSU Auto Union AG and, to take another example, the Vorstand chairman of Bayer AG always has a position in the Aufsichtsrat of Agfa-Gevaert AG, for this latter company's single largest shareholder is Bayer.

Companies with a basic capital of more than DM 3,000,000 must have Vorstands consisting of at least two persons under Aktiengesellschaft laws. Generally, large companies have Vorstands consisting of more than six persons, with the large banks often having more than a dozen persons in their Vorstands. The appointment of the Vorstand is solely the affair of the Aufsichtsrat and herein lies the single greatest power of the Aufsichtsrat. The Aufsichtsrat has the power to dismiss the Vorstand or members of the Vorstand under a set of special circumstances defined by law. The power of Vorstand members is partly curbed by their not having contracts that can run for more than five year periods. The time limit on contracts has been placed in the existing laws to ensure that the Aufsichtsrat has a perfectly free hand, at least once every five years, to determine whether to retain or dismiss a Vorstand member and this is meant to assure the continued efficiency of Vorstand members.

The Aufsichtsrat can dismiss a Vorstand member during a contract period if it can prove that the Vorstand member in question has acted in a way harmful to the company, been generally negligent or acted in direct contradiction to orders given by the general meeting of shareholders or the Aufsichtsrat. The Aufsichtsrat's powers to impose its will on the Vorstand are limited and carefully defined. However, in companies where an institution has a majority shareholding the representative of the institution in the Aufsichtsrat, who is almost always the Aufsichtsrat chairman, can virtually pick on any pretext to force a Vorstand member to resign. At Krupp, the company's shares are held by a special foundation set up in 1967, the Krupp Trust, whose chairman is Herr Berthold Beitz, who is also Krupp's supervisory board chairman. In 1971 Herr Beitz disagreed with the management methods of the company's Vorstand chairman, Herr Vogelsang, and after a series of arguments the latter saw no alternative other than to resign. Herr Vogelsang's successor, Herr Krackow, took office as Krupp Vorstand chairman at the start of October 1972 and yet by November of that year he had already had a major row with Herr Beitz and the result was that he was forced to leave Krupp in December 1972.

Vorstand members have a degree of protection against being summarily dismissed during their contracts by Aufsichtsrats. A dismissed Vorstand member can sue the Aufsichtsrat if he believes there are insufficient grounds under the law for his early dismissal. Such legal action, however, can only take place once the Vorstand member has left his company. To avoid legal action and damaging publicity for a company, Aufsichtsrats usually seek to avoid dismissing the Vorstand men they themselves have anyhow appointed, prior to the expiration of contracts. In cases where this has happened an agreement has often been made giving the dismissed Vorstand member a large financial compensation and arranging matters so that the public gains the impression that the Vorstand member resigned of his own free will.

In the late summer of 1971 the Vorstand chairman of Volkswagenwerk, Dr Kurt Lotz, was forced to resign. The final statement issued by the Aufsichtsrat stated that Herr Lotz had resigned from the company and was leaving VW on a basis of good relations. Herr Lotz was given a handsome payment from VW, which at least equalled the loss in the remuneration he would have had should he have stayed with the company to the end of his contract period. By this means the VW Aufsichtsrat ensured that a bitter legal battle with Herr Lotz was avoided. It was public knowledge that an assortment of reasons was leading to a clash between Herr Lotz and the Aufsichtsrat and after Herr Lotz's resignation little effort was made by VW to attempt to suggest that health reasons had prompted Herr Lotz's resignation. In many cases, where disputes have been kept secret, health reasons are cited for the resignation in mid-term of Vorstand members.

At companies which do not have large single shareholders, early dismissals of Vorstand members are rare indeed. The most important forced resignations of Vorstand members in large companies in 1971 and 1972 exclusively took place in companies where institutions have large shareholdings.* Apart from the threat of dismissal or the non-continuation of contracts, Vorstand members are restircted through the possibility of Aufsichtsrats holding special matters concerning a company's development for their sole jurisdiction. These must be matters basic to the structure of the company and usually tend to concern the taking of major long-term loans, alterations of the company's basic capital and diversification on a large scale into new business areas.

Under no circumstances can the Aufsichtsrat reserve for itself matters that could hinder the day-to-day management operations of the Vorstand. Usually decisions on even the most basic and important issues are taken by the Aufsichtsrat in conjunction with the Vorstand and mostly in a manner advised by the Vorstand. In many companies the Aufsichtsrat does little more than rubber stamp the decisions of major importance taken by the Vorstand. This is the case simply because the Vorstand is generally more involved and better informed about a company's affairs than is the Aufsichtsrat and the latter body recognises that all its information comes from the Vorstand. Should the Vorstand suggest that a certain decision be taken and should this be opposed by the Aufsichtsrat, then the Vorstand can seek to overrule the Aufsichtsrat by taking the

* Among the most dramatic dismissals in 1971 and 1972 were the dismissals of Lotz, Holste and Hahn from Volkswagen's Vorstand, the dismissal of Friedrich Krämer as Vorstand chief of Preussag AG and the dismissal of BMW AG's sales chief, Paul Hahnemann. All these companies are largely controlled by powerful institutions. The Federal Government and State of Lower Saxony between them hold 36 per cent of the VW shares and are VW's only large shareholders. BMW is more than 60 per cent owned by the Quandt group, the Westdeutsche Landesbank owns over 26 per cent of Preussag and is the sole major shareholder in the company.

controversial matter in question to a general meeting of shareholders. This rarely takes place, because the largest shareholders
are directly represented in the Aufsichtsrat and because the
Vorstand, in order to meet with success in its fight against the
Aufsichtsrat, can only get its way if supported by more than
75 per cent of the shares represented at a general meeting.

Vorstand members are generally assigned specific areas of
responsibility, covering such sectors as finance, production,
personnel, sales and purchasing. The final responsibility for all
decisions rests with the Vorstand as a whole, rather than with
any one member of it. There is legislation designed to ensure that
the Vorstand works as a team of equals with joint collective
responsibility. By law the Vorstand is obliged to meet frequently and each member of the Vorstand of a company is
forced to get himself well informed on all areas of his company's
activities. Decisions taken within the Vorstand can be reached
by a simple majority vote.

The position of the Vorstand chairman is a somewhat complex one. In theory he has no more power than any other
member of the Vorstand. In practice he is the most powerful
executive in the company, usually representing the company
on major occasions, usually presenting the views of the Vorstand
to shareholders, the Aufsichtsrat and the general public and
usually in a position to co-ordinate and to a certain extent
direct the work of the other Vorstand members. The chairman
of the Vorstand is usually the highest paid person in a company.
The level of remuneration that Vorstand members get is
usually based on a complex formula involving a set salary,
plus a scale of bonuses dependent on profits of the company,
plus additional fees resulting from Aufsichtsrat positions that
Vorstand members hold in subsidiary companies.

The remuneration of the Vorstand chairman tends to be
higher than that of his colleagues because he gets the first choice
of the best Aufsichtsrat positions going in the company's subsidiaries. For example, the Vorstand chairman of a large bank
may be on the Aufsichtsrat of ten major companies, due to the
large shareholdings the bank may have in these companies,
while a young and new member of the same bank's Vorstand
may find that he has only a couple of Aufsichtsrat positions in
only medium-sized companies. German companies are not

forced to publish the salaries of their top executives and at best figures that are often published in the German press are little more than informed guesses.

However, it would not be too inaccurate to suggest that the Vorstand members of some of the largest stores groups and major companies held largely in private hands are at the top of the salary scale, followed closely by the chief executives of such huge companies as Volkswagenwerk AG and Daimler-Benz AG. These top Vorstand salaries may well be around DM 600,000 a year, as a conservative estimate. The average annual income, including bonuses and Aufsichtsrat remuneration, of Vorstand members in the approximately 420 German public companies is probably around DM 200,000 a year. In the large banks, the salaries of top Vorstand members probably range between DM 250,000 to DM 550,000 and the total earnings of chief bank executives could well be double this amount in a good profit year and including Aufsichtsrat fees. Aufsichtsrat members usually get about DM 15,000 to DM 40,000 a year, depending on the size of the companies.

The Aufsichtsrat must have at least three members by law and its actual size is partly dependent on the size of a company's capital, with the maximum size being twenty-one members. In all cases the Aufsichtsrat must have a total that is divisible by three and usually* two-thirds of the total are elected by the general meeting of shareholders, with the remaining one-third elected by the company's employees. The maximum period that a person can serve on an Aufsichtsrat before having to be re-elected is four years. The Aufsichtsrat must by law meet at least every six months, but in most large companies it meets on a quarterly basis. In addition, the Aufsichtsrat chairman usually has an office in the company's headquarters and keeps in continual touch with Vorstand members.

The Aufsichtsrat must meet when one of its members wants a meeting or when the Vorstand asks for a meeting. All Auf-

---

* Under worker co-determination laws in 1951 and 1952 the employees representatives on the Aufsichtsrat in the coal, iron and steel industries are the same number as the shareholder representatives, with the Aufsichtsrat having a neutral chairman. Fuller details of the co-determination system are given in the next chapter. The system where there exists equal employee and employer representatives on the Aufsichtsrat is called the parity co-determination system.

sichtsrat decisions hold force when at least half the members are present or where there are no written objections to a set of proposals from any Aufsichtsrat member.

The chairman of the Aufsichtsrat has the responsibility of ensuring that meetings are held, that at least one shareholders' general meeting is held per year and he usually chairs general meetings of shareholders. The Aufsichtsrat chairman, by keeping in continual touch with Vorstand members, acts to some extent as the direct link between the employees of the company and the shareholders. He can enjoy immense power if he represents the majority shareholders of the company in a direct form, such as by being the chairman of the largest institutional shareholder in the company.

Apart from the chief responsibility of appointing Vorstand members and dealing with special matters basic to the structure and health of the company, the Aufsichtsrat has a number of other tasks. Most important among these is its responsibility to sign the annual accounts, its duty to examine and approve the profit distribution suggestions of the Vorstand and its duty to ensure that everything stated in the company's annual report is accurate. By law companies need only provide shareholders with half-yearly reports and the interim report is not subject to strict regulations, so that, for example, it is rare that companies give clear net profit figures in their half-year statements. The Aufsichtsrat, together with the Vorstand, must represent the company in the courts in legal matters and the Aufsichtsrat is responsible for guaranteeing credits that may be given to company employees.

Probably the most fascinating aspects of the Aktiengesellschaft laws are that they attempt to define clearly the various responsibilities of the various company organs and yet they leave large grey areas all the same, on matters where Vorstand responsibilities end and Aufsichtsrat responsibilities start. The result has been that the balance of power in two-tier boards in large companies depends to a large degree on the personalities of the individual Aufsichtsrat and Vorstand members, as well as on the extent to which company shares are widely distributed.

The question of personalities becomes clearer by looking at a couple of examples. The Deutsche Bank AG, the largest joint stock bank in West Germany has its shares very widely distributed with no institutions having a particularly large holding. Herr Hermann J Abs is probably the most powerful and influential man in the Deutsche Bank, despite the fact that he is only Aufsichtsrat chairman and not in the Vorstand and despite the fact that he does not enjoy the backing of any type of major Deutsche Bank shareholders. Herr Abs's strength lies almost entirely on his reputation and his personality. He was the chief architect of the Deutsche Bank's post-war development, having joined the Bank's Vorstand at the age of 36 in 1937 and having been in the Vorstand for a full thirty years. He works most days in an office in the Deutsche Bank's headquarters in Frankfurt and while he leaves most aspects of the Deutsche Bank's management to the Vorstand, it is almost inconceivable that any management suggestions or business ideas he may put to the Vorstand would be refused. Many Aufsichtsrat chairmen would not make suggestions that are directly involved with day-to-day company business, but holding back in this manner is not Herr Abs's style and his direct power in the Deutsche Bank is greater than that enjoyed by most Aufsichtsrat chairmen in their own companies.

Professor Karl Winnacker is another of the rare exceptions and falls into the same category as Herr Abs. Professor Winnacker was chiefly responsible for the rebuilding of Farbwerke Hoechst AG, a company with no large shareholders. He moved up from the Vorstand to the chairmanship of the Aufsichtsrat in June 1969, handing over the top Vorstand job to one of his protégés, Dr Rolf Sammet. Professor Winnacker retains a strong interest in Hoechst and probably exercises a great deal more influence on the company's affairs than most Aufsichtsrat chairmen can in their own companies.

A somewhat contrasting example is to be found in the powerful Bayerische Hypotheken- und Wechsel-Bank AG, which again has no large shareholders. The Vorstand chairman, Dr Anton Ernstberger, joined the Hypo in 1960 after a varied career as a lawyer, industrialist and banker. He personally owns a substantial holding in a Munich-based private bank and is a man of considerable wealth. Dr Ernstberger has always insisted on considerable freedom of action, he has made enough money to no longer be dependent on his high income from the Hypo and he has left little doubt that he will resign the instant he feels the Aufsichtsrat at the Hypo is blocking his plans for the rapidly expanding Bavarian bank. Some of Dr Ernstberger's deals and ventures may well have given the generally conservative Hypo Aufsichtsrat sleepless nights, but so far he has been left to do as he wishes and has left little doubt that he is the master of the bank he serves.

The single most important factor in determining where real power lies in a major company is the distribution of the company's shares. It is impossible here to outline a comprehensive list of 'Who Owns Whom?'* in German industry, but several examples will suffice here to illustrate the power that major shareholders can wield over their companies and the relationship between these shareholders (represented in companies directly by their own appointees on Aufsichtsrats) and Vorstand members. The holders of major blocks of shares in the largest companies tend to fall into three institutional categories: the privately owned family holding groups of such multi-millionaires as the Flicks, Quandts and Fincks; the financial institutions, mainly the large banks and insurance companies and, finally, assorted types of Federal State and Local State organisations.

THE HOLDERS OF LARGE BLOCKS OF SHARES

The holders of more than 25·1 per cent of a company's share capital have great influence, simply because many of the Aktiengesellschaft laws demand approval by more than 75 per cent of a company's shareholders for certain actions to be taken. These clauses are discussed in greater detail in the section dealing with general meetings later in this chapter but, with regard to general distribution of shares, it can be said that a holder of at least 25·1 per cent of a company's shares is in a position to veto any major company decisions. This power of veto is what many institutions seek and they often content themselves with holdings of shares of just 25·1 per cent in companies. The fact that institutions need not seek 50·1 per cent of a company's shares in order to have a power of veto, has

* One of the best guides to who owns German companies is the Commerzbank AG publication *wer gehört zu wem*. Another is the Westdeutsche Landesbank und Girozentrale publication *Besitz- und Beteiligungsverhältnisse Deutscher Unternehmen*.

made it possible for many institutions to spread their investments more widely than would have to be the case in a system
where blocking power could only be reached by holding a
majority of a company's shares. Total power of control over a
company only comes when an institution has more than 75·1
per cent of a company's shares* and, usually, institutions content themselves with 25·1 per cent holdings, rather than seeking total powers of control through much higher investment.

The large banks probably account between them for less than
10 per cent of the share capital of all German publicly quoted
companies and yet they are by far the most important and
powerful controllers of major companies through shareholdings.
The banks derive their power by combining shareholdings on
their own accounts and holdings of their clients, which have
been placed on deposit with the banks and where the clients
have given by proxy the voting powers of the shares they own
to their banks. The banks are the sole stockbrokers in West
Germany and can buy and sell shares on both their own account
and on behalf of their clients. The banks do not publish a full
and detailed list of all their holdings and there is no means of
discovering how great the shareholding power of the banks is
when the proxy vote system is taken into account. The banks
tend to publish annually a list of those companies in which, on
their own account, they hold more than 25·1 per cent of the
outstanding shares.

At the end of 1971 the Deutsche Bank AG, according to its
annual report, held more than 25·1 per cent of the shares of
more than 20 companies. The most important holdings of the
Deutsche Bank, which are in excess of 25 per cent of the issued
shares, are in Daimler-Benz AG, one of Europe's leading automobile makers, Karstadt AG, one of Germany's huge department store companies, Continental Gummi-Werke AG and
Phoenix Gummiwerke AG, West Germany's two largest tyre
manufacturers, Pittler AG, one of the country's leading machine
tool manufacturers and such important food manufacturers as
Süddeutsche Zucker AG and Gebrüder Stollwerk AG.†

* As discussed later in this chapter, minority shareholders have minor
powers of curbing total domination of a company by holders of more than
75·1 per cent of a company's shares.
† The Deutsche Bank sold its Stollwerk holding in late 1972.

In addition, the Deutsche Bank has a large number of sub-sidiaries, which in turn have their own holdings in public companies. Furthermore, the Deutsche Bank has interests in a number of investment companies with holdings of their own. For example, the Deutsche Bank owns 75 per cent of the shares of the Deutsche Gesellschaft für Anlageverwaltung mbH, which in turn holds 25 per cent of the shares of the large Horten department stores group. The remaining 25 per cent of the shares in this Deutsche Bank investment company are interest-ingly held by the Commerzbank AG, which is one of the Deutsche Bank's chief banking rivals.

The shareholdings in excess of 25 per cent of a company's share capital owned by the other major joint stock banks in the country, the Dresdner Bank and the Commerzbank, are just as impressive as the list of holdings owned by the Deutsche Bank. These three major banks have widespread portfolios, ranging from shipping and retailing to automobiles, metals and brewing. The Vorstand members of these three banks hold positions in the Aufsichtsrats of all the companies in which the banks have major direct holdings, plus a large list of other companies, where the banks can exert influence through the proxy vote system.

An interesting feature of the holdings of the country's three largest joint stock banks is that these institutions often have large holdings in the same companies. This can be interpreted in two ways: either the banks are not such great rivals as they would like to make out, or they want to watch closely what their rivals are doing by holding large blocks of shares in those companies where their rivals are also major shareholders. The former interpretation seems the most valid. To illustrate the ex-tent of the partnership one need only look at such institutions as the Deutsche Gesellschaft für Anlageverwaltung mbH mentioned above, or note that both the Dresdner Bank and the Commerzbank have large blocks of shares in the Kempinski hotel company and that all three of these major banks have most substantial holdings in most of the country's largest department store groups.

The large block shareholdings that the banks have and their position as stockbrokers place them in a position to play a major role in bringing about mergers or take-overs. The heavy interest of the Deutsche Bank in the country's leading tyre companies could, for example, produce a major concentration of the German tyre industry and co-operation between the Dresdner Bank, Commerzbank and Deutsche Bank, through a reshuffle of their shareholdings, could result in a most substantial reorganisation of the German retailing business, through a merger of such stores groups as Karstadt and Kaufhof.

For the time being the major stores groups plan to remain fully independent, yet in the recent past developments in the business operations of the stores groups suggest that the major banks have been playing a definite role in bringing some of the stores groups close together. It now seems most likely, for example, that a small group of companies will soon completely dominate the German travel business. The country's largest tour operating company is Touristik Union International, which counts among its largest shareholders the Hapag-Lloyd shipping company, which itself is more than 25 per cent owned by the Dresdner Bank and more than 25 per cent owned by the Deutsche Bank. In 1972 Touristik Union International concluded wide-ranging co-operation agreements with two of its largest rivals, Transeuropa and International Travel Services. Transeuropa is more than 25 per cent owned by the Karstadt stores group, which counts the Commerzbank and the Deutsche Bank among its largest shareholders. International Travel Services is a subsidiary of the Kaufhof stores group, which counts the Dresdner Bank and the Commerzbank among its largest shareholders.

A full merger between these three travel companies seems most likely and this will clearly be a result of behind-the-scenes action by the three largest banks in the country. The development of the travel business, in terms of integration, is likely to go further, however, because of additional work by the banks. Hapag-Lloyd has recently entered the air charter business and it would be no surprise if its chief customers were the three travel agencies and the common link between all these companies is clearly the three large banks.

The brewing industry is a sector where recent developments clearly show the influence that major shareholders can have and how co-operation between banks works. A major concentration of the German brewing industry is now in mid-stream, due solely to the activities of a few banks and a couple of vastly rich private families. West Germany has more than 1,800 breweries and in mid-1972 the Vorstand chairman of the Bayerische Hypotheken- und Wechsel-Bank, Dr Anton Ernstberger, was quite correct when he said that 'compared with breweries in England, France, Holland, Italy and the United States, our largest breweries are mere dwarfs'.

But Dr Ernstberger knew full well when he said this that the situation was changing at great speed for he has been the chief architect of the brewing industry concentration. The bank that Dr Ernstberger heads controls through various shareholdings about 18 per cent of the West German beer market. Other major shares in this market are held through diverse holdings by the Dresdner Bank, the Oetker group of companies, which is owned by the Oetker family, and, finally, the Reemtsma Cigarettenfabriken GmbH, which is largely owned by the Reemtsma family. Other companies with smaller but all the same important holdings in the brewing industry, include the Bayerische Vereinsbank and a number of insurance companies.

In the recent past the Bayerische Hypo has formed a close relationship in several business sectors with the Dresdner Bank, notably in international banking areas, and this relationship has been the basis for the largest merger in the history of the German brewing business. The Bayerische Hypo bought a sizeable block of shares in the Dortmunder Union Brauerei from the Reemtsma group in early 1972. The Bayerische Hypo had gradually been building up strong holdings in the Dortmunder Union and in the Schultheiss Brauerei and the Dresdner Bank also had substantial interests in both these leading breweries. The purchase of shares in Dortmunder Union by the Hypo and this bank's increasingly close relationship with the Dresdner Bank, made it possible in the autumn of 1972 for a full merger between the Dortmunder Union and the Schultheiss breweries to take place, producing a company with more than a 14 per cent market share in Germany.

The Oetker, Reemtsma and Hypo groups continue to increase their brewery interests and some swapping of holdings between these groups seems most likely. The result may well be that in the not too distant future a few more large brewing companies will be created through behind-the-scenes operations by a handful of powerful institutions. The general public is usually left in the dark about the stock market wheeling and dealing of the powerful financial institutions and has little chance to make profits on the stock markets from mergers and take-overs. The secret activities of the banks in this field, particularly the co-operation between banks and the seeming conflict of interest that must arise when a bank advises customers and acts on its own behalf in the share markets, has produced increasing public criticism in Germany. The result may well be that new legislation may be brought in to sharply restrict the share market activities of the banks and to improve the degree of disclosure made by companies. But the behind-the-scenes share dealings are by no means confined to the banks alone.

A small group of vastly rich families also enjoy immense influence over German industry. It is difficult to ascertain the size of these private family holdings, but it seems fairly certain that the Flick family is the wealthiest. It is perhaps amusing that newspaper articles and books concerned with the richest men in the world tend to often overlook the Germans. This is generally because the German billionaires are intensely secretive about their wealth and partly because one would simply not assume that massive fortunes could be built up, to rival those of the wealthy Americans, in the short time since the last war. Friedrich Flick died at the age of 89 in summer 1972, having built up in the 1950s and 1960s possibly the largest private industrial empire in Europe. Flick had already been the architect of one gigantic industrial empire between the world wars, but this was largely confiscated by the allies and Flick spent a short time in prison after the last war as a result of his industrial aid to the Nazis.

On leaving prison, Flick was forced to sell his steel and coal holdings and, with the relatively small sum of compensation he obtained, he started again in his sixties to build a complex and huge industrial empire. When Friedrich Flick died he left his heirs about 40 per cent of the shares in Daimler-Benz AG and large shareholdings in over 300 assorted companies. These holdings, with the exception of Daimler-Benz and a few others, were managed by the Verwaltungsgesellschaft für Industrielle

Unternehmungen Friedrich Flick GmbH. This company controls all the companies in which the Flick family has more than a 50 per cent shareholding and the total turnover of these companies in 1972 was in excess of DM 6,500 million, placing the consolidated Flick group among the twenty largest industrial groups in West Germany. If 40 per cent of the Daimler-Benz turnover was added to this, then the Flick group would feature prominently among the ten leading industrial groups in this country.

By comparison, the holdings of Dr Herbert Quandt and his family are modest. All the same, Herr Quandt's holdings include more than 60 per cent of the shares of Bayerische Motoren Werke AG (BMW), about 14 per cent of Daimler-Benz AG, more than 25 per cent of the large Varta AG battery company and sizeable interests in a long series of financial institutions and other manufacturing companies. Men like Flick, Quandt, Finck, Oetker, Henkel, Reemtsma, to mention just some of the most wealthy private holders of vast numbers of industrial shares, enjoy probably more power in the companies, whose shares they hold in large number, than do the banks in those companies where they are the large shareholders. The main reason for this assertion is that the banks are not by their structure in a position to take such quick decisions or such risky decisions regarding a company's future as individuals like Flick,* Quandt and Finck. Where the banks and the wealthy individuals meet on the same company supervisory boards, the private individuals tend to have somewhat greater power in that, so often, they themselves are major clients of the banks and the banks are loath to oppose suggestions made by the wealthy private tycoons for fear of loosing clients.

A model example is Daimler-Benz AG, the largest commercial vehicle manufacturer in Europe and one of West Germany's six largest companies. The Aufsichtsrat reflects to some extent the power of the massive institutions of this country, that have so far been mentioned in this chapter. The chief shareholders in the company are the Flicks with about 40 per cent, the Quandts with about 14 per cent and the Deutsche Bank with about 27 per cent. In 1971, according to the Daimler-Benz

* Friedrich Karl Flick is today the chief governor of the Flick family fortunes and Flick industrial empire.

annual report, Herr Friedrich Flick was honorary president of the Aufsichtsrat, with his son, Friedrich Karl Flick, deputy Aufsichtsrat chairman and with the long-time Flick family trusted aides, Otto Friedrich, Konrad Kaletsch and Günter Paefgen, all holding Aufsichtsrat seats. The chairman of the Aufsichtsrat was Franz Heinrich Ulrich, Vorstand chairman of the Deutsche Bank, with this bank's Aufsichtsrat chairman, Hermann J Abs, also holding a seat on the Daimler super-visory board. The second deputy chairman of the company's Aufsichtsrat was Dr Herbert Quandt and one of Quandt's chief aides, Herr Horst Pavel, also held an Aufsichtsrat seat. The remaining Aufsichtsrat seats, other than those held by represen-tatives of the employees, were taken by Hans Deuss, chairman of the Commerzbank Aufsichtsrat and by Jurgen Ponto, Vorstand chairman of the Dresdner Bank.

The shareholdings of the major private and financial groups in Daimler-Benz were accurately reflected in the distribution of the Aufsichtsrat seats. Few companies can boast of an Auf-sichtsrat so full of powerful bankers and tycoons. The Flick family on account of its 40 per cent holding in Daimler-Benz is the most powerful group in the Aufsichtsrat and the Flicks have never been fearful of using their power. In German busi-ness circles one often hears of certain Daimler-Benz Vorstand members being talked of as personal Flick appointees and it is often said that company decisions are often made by a phone call between a Daimler-Benz Vorstand member in Stuttgart and a Flick family member in Düsseldorf. The increase in Daimler-Benz's dividend in 1971, despite lower company profits, is often said to have been solely due to demands by Friedrich Flick for more cash from this huge company, to compensate for lower earnings in some of his other enterprises.

It is not inconceivable that a merger between BMW and Daimler-Benz may one day be settled by a private arrangement made between the Flicks and the Quandts, with the Vorstand members of the companies being informed about the deal after the event. The degree of influence enjoyed by Vorstand members often appears to be greater than it really is in companies which are dominated by powerful individual shareholders, such as BMW or Reemtsma or Oetker or Daimler-Benz. Many of the private individuals who own vast shareholdings in major companies tend to avoid making public statements about their interests and, by leaving all public declarations about the affairs of their companies to the Vorstand men they have appointed, they manage to appear to the public to have less real influence than is in fact the case.

The vast holdings of a variety of public authorities in industry are also generally not well known. These public authorities are no less keen to interfere with company Vorstands than are the banks and the powerful private holders of large blocks of shares. In some cases the intervention in the management of companies by public authorities through their shareholdings, seems counter to the spirit, if not the actual word, of the Aktiengesellschaft laws.

The Federal Government has major shareholdings in a considerable number of assorted types of companies. The State owns, for example, 40 per cent of Veba AG, which in turn owns a range of different types of companies, including Veba Chemie AG, the fourth largest chemical company in the country, 25 per cent of Chemische Werke Hüls AG, 36 per cent of Chemie Verwaltung AG, 14·1 per cent of Ruhrkohle AG, which produces over 80 per cent of Germany's coal and coke, 86 per cent of Preussische Elektrizitäts AG and substantial holdings in other companies. The State also owns, among other things, 16 per cent of Volkswagenwerk AG, 74·3 per cent of Deutsche Lufthansa which itself owns West Germany's largest charter airline, Condor. The fifth largest steel company in Germany, Salzgitter AG, is fully State owned and owns in turn a wide range of companies in the engineering and metal industries and is the majority shareholder in the country's largest shipbuilding company, Howaldtswerke-Deutsche-Werft AG.

The regional States own vast industrial holdings, some of which are controlled directly and others of which are controlled by the local Landesbank. The industrial holdings vary considerably, from the Bavarian State having blocks of shares in breweries to the State of Lower Saxony owning 20 per cent of Volkswagenwerk AG. The largest of the State banks, the Westdeutsche Landesbank und Girozentrale, acts with regard to shares in the same way as the joint stock banks and its portfolio not only includes holdings of more than 25 per cent of the shares of such large companies as Preussag AG, Berliner Kindl

Brauerei and Werkzeugmaschinen-Fabrik Gildemeister, but also sizeable shareholdings in a number of foreign companies.

The direct holdings of the local States are managed by the politicians who happen to be in the local government and often their decisions are politically motivated. One of the factors, for example, that made Dr Lotz unpopular with the VW Aufsichtsrat and which may have resulted in his dismissal as VW's Vorstand chairman, was that he was an active Christian Democrat, while in 1971 the governments of the Federal State and the State of Lower Saxony, whose representatives form a major section of the VW Aufsichtsrat, were Social Democrat.

The appointment of Vorstand members in companies that are largely owned by public authorities is often not based solely on management abilities, and politics plays a role. Many of the appointments in the recent past to top positions in companies largely owned by the Federal State, for example, have gone to men with either a good Social Democratic or Free Democratic record. Apart from the fully nationalised industries, such as the posts and the railways, most of the companies largely dominated by public authorities, through shareholdings, are run on strict capitalist lines, despite the preponderance of socialist governments in Germany now.

The trade unions have in some respects proved to be the best of capitalists to the surprise of many. The Bank für Gemeinwirtschaft is among the largest banks in the country; it is wholly owned by the trade unions, it makes a handsome profit and it invests readily in the shares of a wide range of companies. The BfG has huge holdings as have a number of other trade union owned companies in the insurance and financial field. The unions seek to ensure that they do not have a commanding position in many companies to prevent a situation where a conflict of interest arises, with trade unionists having to operate as powerful capitalists and as radical socialists at one and the same time.

The final group of significance as owners of large blocks of shares in West Germany are foreign investment institutions and foreign companies. The British Slater, Walker Ltd opened a bank in Frankfurt in late 1972 and has already made an impact by buying large blocks of shares in a number of German companies. Other British merchant banks may well follow suit now that Britain is a member of the Common Market. A considerable number of the largest companies in West Germany are primarily owned by foreign companies. Among the 50 biggest companies in this country today one finds Adam Opel AG, the wholly owned General Motors subsidiary, Ford, Esso, Deutsche Shell, Deutsche Unilver, British Petroleum, IBM Deutschland, British American Tobacco (which apart from being a major German cigarette maker is also the holder of 25 per cent of the Horten stores group), Deutsche Texaco, Mobil Oil, Deutsche Nestlé and Brown, Boveri & Cie Mannheim, which is 56 per cent owned by the Swiss Brown, Boveri company.

GENERAL MEETINGS OF SHAREHOLDERS

There is no simple way of deciding whether it is healthy or not for an economy to have a small number of individuals and institutions in positions to greatly influence developments in vast industries. The owner of a large block of shares should clearly have the right to influence the affairs of those companies where he is a major investor. Similarly the banks, if they are to prosper themselves and produce profits for their own shareholders and benefits for their clients, should have the right to influence the developments of those companies where they hold, directly or indirectly, a large portion of shares.

Yet it is equally clear that the interests of major shareholders do not always coincide with the interests of the general public as a whole. For shareholders the pursuit of profit is often a more important priority than ensuring that the companies they own do not pollute the environment or produce unemployment. The banks in West Germany claim that they do not enjoy anything like the vast power over industry that their critics often suggest. The amount of power that the banks can wield over industry is impossible to quantify, but it is clearly considerable.

The main theme of the critics of the present relationship between large shareholders, especially the banks and large companies, concerns the degree of secrecy attached to the affairs of the big shareholders and the large companies. Pressure is building up now in the Federal Republic to make the activities of large companies and large holding companies more open to public scrutiny. Fearing drastic reforms and aiming to satisfy critics with compromises, many institutions and large companies are voluntarily now increasing the amount of disclosure of their affairs. The stock exchanges are making efforts to improve the volume of information that the public can obtain about publicly quoted companies and seeking to reduce the presently great abundance of 'insider information'.

At the moment the general meeting of shareholders is probably the most important forum and the best means of discovering what companies are planning and doing. New laws imposing much stricter regulations on the banks, improving the stock exchange system and the system of disclosure are already being prepared, and in time the presently clouded situation of shareholder-company relationships with regard to major block shareholders will become more transparent. Without waiting for new legislation, small shareholders have in the recent past sought with a high degree of succcess, to greatly improve public knowledge of company affairs and of the wheeling and dealing that goes on behind the scenes, among the banks and other institutional holders of large blocks of shares.

Under the laws governing the Aktiengesellschaft the general meeting of shareholders is the most important controlling organ in a company. The powers of the general meeting are restricted to some extent by the special responsibilities given under the laws to the Aufsichtsrat and the Vorstand. Thus, for example, the general meeting cannot question the manner in which the company's annual balance sheet is compiled, so long as the balance sheet has been signed and approved by the Aufsichtsrat and inspected and approved by the auditors elected by the general meeting. The general meeting can, however, appoint special auditors to re-examine the company's books and should large discrepancies arise, the Aufsichtsrat can be dismissed by the general meeting. In practice this never happens.

The Aufsichtsrat can be dismissed by a number of methods, such as rejection by the general meeting of the suggested dividend payments. In all cases the suggestions made to the meeting by the Aufsichtsrat, which could result in the dismissal of the Aufsichtsrat if the suggestions were opposed, can only be overruled if the motion in question is defeated by a vote of more than 75 per cent of the shares represented at the general meeting. A special general meeting can be called to dismiss an individual company director if a call for such a meeting is supported by at least the holders of 10 per cent of the company's share capital. But even at such special meetings the resignation of an Aufsichtsrat or Vorstand member can only be forced through the backing in a vote of more than 75 per cent of the company's shares.

Most decisions placed before the general meeting of shareholders require simple majority votes, but the exceptions concern the dismissal of directors and increases in the company's basic capital. The refusal, by one large group holding over 30 per cent of the Atlantis AG's shares, to agree to a doubling in this company's basic capital, resulted in this company being forced into liquidation in late 1972 and it would not have mattered to the company's future if the holders of the remaining 70 per cent of the shares had supported the capital increase. The 75 per cent system was designed to ensure that minority shareholders had their interests safeguarded, but the laws did little to protect the interests of holders of less than 25 per cent of a company's shares.

A general meeting can be called by a simple majority vote in either the Vorstand or Aufsichtsrat of a company, and by law at least one general meeting of shareholders must be held each twelve months. The laws specify a number of items that have to be voted on at annual general meetings, including the election of part of the Aufsichtsrat, approval of the profit distribution proposals and election of the auditors. The chairman of the general meeting, who is usually the Aufsichtsrat chairman, has sufficient power under the laws to ensure that an orderly meeting is held, to limit the speaking time of shareholders and even to have disruptive shareholders ejected from the meeting.

The most important right that small shareholders have is the right to ask questions at general meetings on all matters concerned with the activities of the company. By law these questions must be answered by directors to the best of their ability. A director can be forced to pay heavy damages in a court of law if a shareholder can prove that an answer given by a director to a general meeting of shareholders was untrue or inadequate. The shareholders' right to fair replies poses considerable difficulties for directors, for the problem arises that at times a fair answer would involve the giving of information that could benefit rivals of the company and prove greatly harmful to the company's development. Directors sometimes but rarely plead the excuse that divulging information would do the company harm and, possibly mindful of possible court action, they attempt to give detailed and comprehensive replies to questions.

In restricting the speaking time of shareholders at general meetings the chairman can intervene only when he believes the speaker is discussing matters that have nothing whatever to do with the company. There is no way of restricting the number of questions a shareholder asks, even if a shareholder comes to a meeting with a list of many hundreds of questions. The central court of the local State where the company has its headquarters is responsible for dealing with all legal actions that may arise from general meetings.

There are probably more than 2,000 investment clubs in West Germany today and often these clubs send representatives to annual meetings of companies with the aim of obtaining detailed information from the companies. The representative of some of the larger clubs can often be a powerful figure at an annual meeting, representing in some cases a small percentage of the company's total shares. Some investment advisers and investment club representatives have become well-known figures at annual meetings and have caused inconvenience to directors, through the asking of awkward questions. Some companies find that shareholders have clubbed together to establish a group, whose aim is to protect the interests of minority shareholders, and these groups can at times be important forces within a company.

Some of the individuals who have in recent years made reputations for themselves by appearing at numerous annual meetings with long lists of questions ready, have enlivened annual meetings considerably. They have made it quite common for shareholders to ask questions and have thereby converted once boring and uninteresting meetings into events where the directors of a company face real tests and where companies become increasingly transparent.

Today many annual general meetings of large German companies are almost 'capitalist happenings', full of humour, argument and excitement. Special microphones and speaker podiums are set up in halls where meetings of shareholders take place. It is now quite common that annual meetings last six or seven hours and few major companies manage to conclude an annual general meeting in just a morning. Germany's small shareholders take their role as owners of portions of big business seriously. Many annual meetings attract more than a thousand shareholders, who come for an assortment of reasons, ranging from general interest to the desire to get a small free lunch, to the desire to seize the opportunity of speaking for a few minutes to a huge audience, to the simple motive of ego boosting that results from playing a small role in the decision taking process in a huge industrial company.*

Apart from the amusing aspects, the frills and often idiotic speeches, general meetings are developing in a way in West Germany now that is bringing about greater control of large company affairs, through the use, by skilled operators, of all the laws regarding the rights of shareholders, outlined in the regulations governing publicly quoted companies. If the term 'shareholder democracy' has any meaning, then it probably is meant to refer to just the sort of situations commonly seen now in general meetings in West Germany. Small shareholders are increasingly becoming aware of their rights and major changes are resulting. One of the most important events in recent years in this context, which clearly shows just how much power well-organised groups of small shareholders can have, concerned the merger between Auto Union and NSU.

NSU AG of Neckarsulme was a medium-sized highly individualistic automobile manufacturer, which by the mid-1960s was not in a position, due to lack of capital and marketing experts, to compete effectively with the giants of the world car business. Its shares were widely distributed, but the largest single holding of around 26 per cent was held by the Israel

---

* I shall never forget the time when a shareholder rose in an annual meeting to point out to the Aufsichtsrat members that they were the mere servants of the general meeting and should show proper respect. Some of the speeches made at annual meetings are utterly absurd and I recall once at Volkswagen that lengthy speeches were made on such odd subjects as the role of the Red Cross in the first world war and the efficiency of aircraft builders in Germany in the last world war.

British Bank of Tel Aviv. This bank firmly believed that NSU was a potential gold mine on account of NSU's ownership of the revolutionary Wankel engine patents.*

In the late 1960s Volkswagenwerk was keen to expand its subsidiary, Auto Union and looked for existing car plants that it could buy. NSU was an especially attractive proposition for VW, for like Audi, it was based in South Germany, it had skilled labour and an impressive research and development department. VW was also interested in the Wankel engine. NSU at this time was meeting increasingly poor demand for many of its ageing products and its Ro80 Wankel-engined car, which was the first rotary-engined car ever mass produced, was meeting with a poor reception on acount of substantial teething problems with the engine. The chief directors of the company realised that it would be difficult to remain independent for much longer and believed that a marriage with Auto Union could be a perfect solution to company problems, while ensuring that the NSU name remained alive.

NSU directors were keen to ensure that the company maintained its identity and they would probably have opposed a direct take-over offer from Volkswagen, which would have meant NSU being completely swallowed by a huge giant. VW proposed a merger between Audi and NSU in Spring 1969 and it seemed that VW would be content to have slightly more than 50 per cent of the shares in the new joint company. Many of the

---

* The Wankel rotary engine is rapidly becoming a highly popular engine used by motor-cycle, motor-boat and motor-car manufacturers. Most of the leading car makers in the world have licences to use and develop the engine. It was invented by Felix Wankel and he and his partner, Ernst Hutzenlaub, set up Wankel GmbH. The inventors needed capital to develop their idea and NSU provided this and established special technical divisions to exploit the engine and improve it. An arrangement was made whereby Wankel GmbH held 40 per cent of the patent rights while NSU held the remaining 60 per cent. This arrangement was slightly altered when the Curtis Wright Corporation did a deal whereby it obtained 10 per cent of all income arising from licences on the engine given to companies in North America. In late 1971 the inventors of the engine sold Wankel GmbH to the British company, Lonrho Ltd. The world interest in the Wankel engine has gathered momentum in recent years and Audi experts suggested in late 1972 that by the 1980s more than 25 per cent of all cars in the world will have Wankel engines. The biggest break-through came in late 1970 with a Wankel agreement with General Motors worth over 50,000,000 dollars.

NSU shareholders did not share the enthusiasm of the NSU Vorstand for the marriage, fearing that in time VW would swallow NSU, that VW would take all the potential future rich profits of the Wankel for itself and that many of NSU's brilliant designing ideas would be cast aside, in favour of the more conservative approach of Audi.

With more than 25 per cent of the NSU shares, the Israel British Bank was in a position to block the merger, for a merger needs approval of more than 75 per cent of a company's shareholders to go ahead. The Israeli bank gave its blessing to the merger only after it had received a number of assurances in writing from VW that guaranteed the continuing development of certain NSU projects, that ensured the independence of the merged company's management from rule by VW, and after special arrangements had been made to give NSU shareholders a guarantee that they would receive part of the profits made on every licensing agreement covering the Wankel engine. Special Wankel shares were created with listing on every German stock exchange, and all holders of NSU shares were given the special shares, with the dividends to be paid to holders of these shares dependent on income from Wankel licensing agreements.

In the year that followed the merger, Volkswagenwerk bought more than 10 per cent of the Audi NSU shares from the Dresdner Bank in a private deal and bought additional shares on the market. By the time of the 1970 Audi NSU annual general meeting full control rested with Volkswagen, who now held just over 76 per cent of the Audi NSU shares. The only other shareholder of any size was the Israel British Bank, which claimed to represent 13 per cent of the Audi NSU issued capital.

The annual meeting lasted a record time of sixteen and a half hours. The meeting developed into a straight fight between Volkswagen as the majority shareholder and the minority shareholders. The latter, led brilliantly by Dr Louis Ertl, a Munich lawyer hired by the Israel British Bank, maintained that Volkswagen had cunningly tricked the shareholders into agreeing to a merger between Auto Union and NSU. The Israeli bank maintained that many of the written assurances given by VW at the time of the merger had been broken. Further, the annual Audi NSU report showed the company to be in a precarious financial position and accusations were made that the books had been rigged to force the share price down, so that Volkswagen could buy the outstanding shares on the cheap.

Bearing in mind the laws governing an Aktiengesellschaft and the fact that VW owned more than three-quarters of the Audi NSU share capital, it may be thought that the protests of the minority shareholders served little purpose. The Israel British Bank took a different view and sought to force Volkswagen into such a tight corner that VW would have no option other than to make a generous offer for the outstanding Audi NSU shares. Dr Ertl put over one hundred questions to the Aufsichtsrat of Audi with the clear intention of taking the Aufsichtsrat to court, should one question of the vast total not be answered satisfactorily. Dr Ertl knew full well that court proceedings could greatly damage the reputation of Volkswagen and prove awkward for the Audi directors. The Audi directors were forced to reveal a vast amount of detailed information, including the full text of a highly confidential contract and there remained, at most, three minor questions that had not been answered fairly.

Rarely before have the affairs of a German public company been so opened to public scrutiny and rarely have company directors been forced to account for all their decisions with such clarity. The failure to answer a couple of minor questions was used as the pretext by the Israel British Bank to threaten legal action against the Audi directors. Further, the minority share-holders voted in favour of appointing special auditors and in an effort to save its reputation, Volkswagen had little choice other than to support this motion.

By Spring 1971 the legal actions by the Israel British Bank resulting from the annual meeting had not got to the courts, but the increasing danger of open court debate on the Audi affair, plus a good deal of damaging press criticism, which was only adding to Volkswagen's troubles,* resulted in the rumour spreading that Volkswagen was about to give way and make a generous offer for the outstanding Audi NSU shares. In April 1971 Volkswagen announced that it was ready to exchange one VW ordinary share for two-and-a-half Audi NSU shares. At this time, the VW shares on the bourse were around DM 200·50, while the Audi shares, aided by speculation of a generous VW

---

* 1971 was possibly the worst year for profits in VW's history.

offer, were at about DM 249·50. The VW offer effectively placed a value on the Audi shares of about DM 80. Unsurprisingly, the Israel British Bank announced that the terms were unsatisfactory and that it would continue its fight.

Meanwhile, most of the original Vorstand members of NSU had lost their positions on the Audi NSU Vorstand and had been replaced by VW employees. The new chairman of the Audi Vorstand was Herr Rudolf Leiding, who had held many senior positions in VW, including having been chief of Auto Union for a time and he came to Audi from the position of managing director of Volkswagen's large production subsidiary in Brazil. The personality changes in the Audi Vorstand were part of a VW plan to fully integrate Audi NSU into the VW empire and, at the time when VW made its offer for outstanding shares, it drew up a special contract between Audi and itself, which almost totally handed over all powers of control of Audi affairs to VW. With close to 80 per cent of Audi shares in its pocket, VW had little fear of its suggested contract for the full incorporation of Audi NSU into VW, being defeated at the Audi annual meeting.

It was quite obvious that a long, albeit pointless, battle would rage at the annual meeting and the Audi management took the precaution of hiring a hall for two days for the affair.* The meeting in fact lasted a full twenty-seven hours, setting a new record for an annual general meeting of shareholders in this country. The reports of the special auditors appointed at the previous annual meeting showed clearly that VW had been honest in suggesting that NSU had been almost broke at the time of the merger, and showed that Audi NSU survived only because of large subsidies given to it by VW.

Finding dozens of minor legal points and minor technical matters, the Israel British Bank launched an attack that was even more desperate than that mounted in 1970. The meeting proved to be a trial of patience and stamina for the Audi directors, who knew that a court case could be built around any small mistake they made. The Israel British Bank threatened at one point to arrange that more than 10 per cent of the company's shareholders would continually call general meetings and that an attempt would be made to run the company by

* Ironically the hall hired was called the 'Harmonie Halle'.

general meeting. After the meeting the Israel British Bank believed it had sufficient grounds to win a court case against Volkswagen, on the basis that VW had intentionally misled shareholders of NSU about its intentions at the time of the merger in 1969.

It seems surprising that Volkswagen was willing to let its reputation get a hammering in this affair and that it did not seek an early settlement with the minority shareholders. The public at large could not help feeling that there was something wrong with a system that led to such bitterness and where a major company, partly owned by public authorities, was willing to try and pull the wool over the eyes of small shareholders. The Aufsichtsrat of VW was clearly worried about the situation and this affair was an important reason for the dismissal of VW Vorstand chief, Dr Kurt Lotz, in the early autumn of 1971.

Herr Rudolf Leiding replaced Dr Lotz as Vorstand chairman of VW and swiftly brought the Audi NSU affair to an end. In November 1971 Volkswagen made a new offer for the outstanding Audi NSU shares, pricing the shares at DM 226. The offer was immediately accepted by most minority shareholders and the road was clear for the full integration of Audi NSU into the Volkswagen empire. With the acceptance of the offer by minority shareholders the outstanding court actions were abandoned.

The long and bitter saga that surrounded the merger of NSU with Auto Union and resulted in the full absorption of the merged company into the VW group was of vital importance in the development of relationships between minority shareholders and holders of large blocks of shares. This example shows clearly the power that a group can wield in a company when it has more than 25 per cent of a company's shares. It is improbable that special shares would have been issued to NSU shareholders, ensuring an income from Wankel licence profits, had the Israel British Bank not been in a position at the time of the merger to block the merger with its 26 per cent shareholding. This example also shows the full powers that minority shareholders in a company can enjoy and the means whereby minority shareholders can produce considerable problems for majority shareholders.

By the opportunity of asking dozens of questions and the threat of legal action, minority shareholders can exert a measure of influence on the companies that are publicly quoted here. If a group of minority shareholders representing 10 per cent of a company's share capital can organise themselves, then they are in a position to make life highly uncomfortable for company directors by having the opportunity to call shareholder general meetings whenever they like. The minority shareholders in the case of Audi NSU got what they wanted: a high price for their shares and guaranteed income from the Wankel engine. Because of the Audi NSU events it is utterly false to suggest that minority shareholders can exert next to no influence, although such suggestions have often been made and were even more widely made prior to the ending of the Audi NSU affair.

That the Audi NSU affair established many precedents has already become clear, for the representatives of minority shareholder groups have been increasingly more active and more hostile to overpowering holders of large blocks of shares in the recent past. Dr Ertl showed every sign of employing the same tactics as he did in the Audi NSU affair, when representing a group of minority shareholders at the Gebrüder Stollwerk AG annual meeting in December 1972. Countless other examples of aggressive campaigns by other leaders of minority shareholders can now be found.

The increasing aggressiveness of minority shareholders has also resulted in many companies being forced to divulge far more information about their activities now than ever before. The fierce questioning by shareholders of company directors at annual general meetings, has made many company directors suggest that today companies in almost no other country in the world disclose so much information about their activities as German public companies do. Because of the pressures at general meetings, an increasing number of large companies are now voluntarily disclosing more about their activities.

The Audi NSU affair has also contributed in strengthening the case for new legislation. There are demands for greater legal protection of the interests of shareholders who do not hold 25 per cent of a company's issued share capital. There is also strong pressure for the creation of a new Federal authority with similar powers to those enjoyed by the American Securities and

Exchange Commission. The eight German stock exchanges are relatively free to do what they like and are controlled by councils which have powers of a very restricted type. In some countries it is probable that the share dealings in Audi NSU shares would have been suspended after accusations had been made that Volkswagen was rigging the Audi books in order to force the price of the shares down. It is almost certain that some form of investigation would have been held, in some countries, were a company to raise its offer from DM 80 per share to DM 226 per share for outstanding shares within six months, especially when the performance of the company, whose shares are involved, is far from encouraging in this six-month period. In Germany there was no form of public investigation whatever into the Audi NSU affair. Investigations are not covered by the company laws. The courts alone can decide on matters of this nature and then only if civil actions are brought by private individuals or groups.

It seems very likely that the next few years will see a considerable amount of new legislation covering the stock exchanges, disclosure of information by public companies, the rights of minority shareholders and the powers of holders of large blocks of shares. As a result a considerable revolution will have taken place in the way in which large public companies are controlled and owned. The events of the last couple of years have shown that the momentum for reform is gathering pace. It may well be that reforms are not taken alone in this country, but that reforms of bourses and public companies are made in the framework of wide-ranging European Economic Community legislation. However, it seems most likely that new German laws will come earlier than new EEC laws, if only because the present system of public control of the stock exchanges and public companies is a lot more advanced in West Germany than it is in Belgium, France and Italy.

OTHER TYPES OF COMPANIES

The most common form taken by medium-sized private companies is that of the Gesellschaft mit beschränkter Haftung, which translated means company with limited liability and which is generally abbreviated after the company's name by the letters GmbH. This type of company is subject to less rigorous controls than is the Aktiengesellschaft. A GmbH with less than 500 employees need not have an Aufsichtsrat. Directors of a GmbH can take all manner of decisions without there having to be a general meeting of shareholders and without needing to have a lawyer present at board meetings, which is often obligatory in an Aktiengesellschaft. With a few exceptions, the balance sheet of a GmbH need not be set out in such great detail as an Aktiengesellschaft, nor does a GmbH have to publicly disclose so much about its business activities. A GmbH is not obliged under the law to have certain fixed levels of reserves and this regulation and the other less stern controls, make it quite naturally more of a risk to creditors than the Aktiengesellschaft.

Creditors and the general public are to an increasing extent obtaining greater protection against GmbH type of companies and in late 1971, for example, the first of what is likely to be an increasing number of new laws, came into force to increase the amount of information that a GmbH must make known to the public about its business. It is now compulsory for all GmbH companies that fulfil two of three criteria to publish their annual profit and loss accounts. These criteria are annual sales of more than DM 300 million, balance sheet volume of more than DM 150 million and employment of more than 5,000 persons. With the coming into effect of this law such huge concerns as Oetker, Axel Springer, Henkel, Quelle, Hertie, British American Tobacco, IBM, Woolworths, Nestlé, C & A and International Telephone and Telegraph were forced in 1972 to reveal their profits to the public.

A GmbH may not issue shares to the public and the sale of all or part of a GmbH can only be made by means of a fairly complicated legal procedure. To protect creditors, fairly stiff regulations govern the uses to which a GmbH employs its basic capital. A fair number of the largest companies in West Germany are of the GmbH type. These companies, the largest of which is Robert Bosch GmbH, disclose voluntarily almost as much information about their activities as do the large publicly quoted companies and these companies can usually obtain as much capital as they want from the banks and the capital markets, without having to issue shares. One reason why many companies are reluctant to issue shares is that they fear that such an action could result in immense power over the company being obtained by an outside institution, such as a bank.

The GmbH has a more flexible management system at the top than does an Aktiengesellschaft, with the division between Aufsichtsrat and Vorstand not being so pronounced, and this is a further asset. A GmbH can be established by no more than two founders; the law prevents the possibility of just one person establishing a GmbH, but this regulation is usually got around by the founders tending to be in the same family. The GmbH must by law have a general manager, whose name is recorded in association with the company in the official register of companies with the local chamber of commerce. The general manager can be one of the owners of the company, but this need not be the case.

An interesting form of company, adopted by a small number of owners of substantial business groups, as well as a considerable number of owners of small companies, is the Kommanditgesellschaft. In this sort of company the liability for debts is divided, with unlimited liability shouldered by certain individuals, while others have a more limited form of liability. Usually the owners of the company have the unlimited liability, but they are in a position to give or sell a portion of the company's shares to individuals, who will then only become liable for the portion of the company's basic capital that their shares represent. A KG can only exist when at least one director has unlimited liability and at least one other has limited liability. If all directors wanted limited liability then they would have to adopt either the AG or GmbH company form, while, if all directors were willing to take unlimited liability, they could adopt the most common company form, the unlimited company, known as the Offene Handelsgesellschaft.

The advantage of a KG over a GmbH is simply that its credit status is greater in view of at least one director having unlimited liability for the company's affairs. The KG structure can offer some tax advantages to directors and the rules regarding disclosure of information in a GmbH do not apply to a KG. In 1960 about 143 of the largest companies in West Germany were of the KG form. The way in which a director pays for the shares that give him limited liability is at the discretion of the seller.

Often the owner of a KG gives shares to trusted senior executives to reward them for services to the company and to ensure that they do not leave the company for a rival. A KG must bear the name of those of its owners with unlimited liability and hence such well-known KG companies as Friedrich Flick KG or Neckermann Grundstücks KG, tell one immediately who the company's chief owners are. The same rule regarding names applies to the Offene Handelsgesellschaft.

THE CHANGING CONTROL PATTERN

Just how great the changes in the control and ownership system of large German companies is going to be cannot be forecast. Substantial changes are certain and their effects not only contribute to the general wide-ranging transformation of German industrial society, but are also likely to effect the development of foreign portfolio investment in this country. In the very near future the insider information system that presently exists is likely to be changed. Currently, even journalists are informed of a large company's results many days in advance of the general public being allowed to obtain the vital company information, and journalists are usually the last of the experts to know what is happening in companies.*

That large German companies will of their own accord become more willing to disclose vital information is likely to be one result of the trend now by large companies to greatly expand their foreign investments. To obtain capital for large multi-national expansion German companies will increasingly make efforts to raise money abroad and a number of companies in Germany are already preparing to bring their accounting systems into line with United States and British requirements,

---

* A good number of German companies appear at times not to have discovered the telephone or the telex and most companies embargo press releases and company reports. Volkswagen, for example, often gives journalists vital information on its affairs under the condition that the information is not published until more than a week after it has been given to the press. By this means, journalists themselves become 'insiders' in West Germany. That bankers, stock market analysts and journalists are all informed about company affairs well in advance of the general public, places the general public as a whole at a distinct disadvantage in dealings on the German bourses. Major changes towards a fairer system are likely.

in order to seek share quotations on Wall Street and the London Stock Exchange. British and American disclosure rules tend to be stiffer than German regulations, and improvements in German company reporting are likely through the efforts to get foreign listings.

A substantial disadvantage to buying and selling on German bourses is the narrowness of the markets. West Germany has stock exchanges in Frankfurt, Düsseldorf, Munich, Hamburg, West Berlin, Hanover, Stuttgart and Bremen and the first two of these alone account for possibly more than 80 per cent of all the German bourse business. The total volume of all these exchanges is barely one-quarter that of the London stock market alone, and one consequence is that the sale or purchase of a modest amount of shares in Germany can of itself have an impact on the bourse trend. The smallness of the markets is a serious disadvantage for investors and efforts are now being made here to make share purchasing more popular among the general public.

The Germans, possibly fearful of a repetition of the 1920s stock market crises and mindful of major bankruptcies during the Weimar era, tend to place savings on deposits with banks rather than venture into the share markets. The banks naturally earn more on deposits than they do on commissions from buying and selling shares for clients and thus a situation exists where the country's stockbrokers do little to encourage participation in the bourses. This has aroused strong criticism and in the recent past the banks have been modestly increasing their efforts to inform the general public as to just how the bourses operate.

The spectacular demise of Investment Overseas Services in 1970 further discouraged the affluent German public from participation on the bourses. For many Germans the purchasing of IOS funds was the first contact with the stock markets; IOS had over one million German clients and most of these clients lost heavily when IOS fell apart. The IOS affair did, however, have one beneficial effect for German investors. The Federal Supervisory Credit Authority in West Berlin started a thorough investigation into the operations of all off-shore mutual funds, with strong backing from the Bonn Government. The result was that following the collapse of IOS more than one hundred foreign mutual funds were forced to stop selling in West

Germany. This was the start of some degree of effective supervision and control of private enterprise operations in the mutual fund business in this country.

It is likely that the bourses will expand gradually through greater public participation, which will be aided by new legislation governing the stock markets, the banks, holders of large blocks of shares, the use of insider information and the rights of minority shareholders. These laws may have the effect of strengthening the degree of independence of the Vorstand and the powers of minority shareholders, while weakening the effective power that large institutional holders of blocks of shares can wield through their holding of Aufsichtsrat positions.

The two-tier system has been outlined in this chapter and it is by no means a system that can easily be recommended. It has the chief faults of leading to confusion in top management and slowing down the decision-taking process. It is a system, however, that has certain merits, especially with regard to finding a position for employee representatives within the management decision-taking process and this is a theme discussed in the next chapter. New cartel laws are likely to restrict the ability of large institutions to push through major mergers and take-overs behind the scenes and this will produce further curbs on the powers of major shareholders. New EEC private sector legislation will also add to the changing structure here.

This chapter has sought to describe the main types of company forms, how shareholders control their companies, the relationship that exists between minority shareholders, supervisory board directors and executive board directors. It has also sought to point out some of the most important changes and new trends in this area, which can count among the most important basic developments in changing Germany's pattern of business life in the 1970s.

Statistics

According to the Federal Statistics Office there were a total of 2,295 Aktiengesellschaft-type companies in existence in Germany at the end of 1971. This total includes 152 companies in the raw material industries, 954 in the major manufacturing sectors, 393 banks and insurance companies and over 1,000 commercial enterprises of all types from retailers to export agency companies. The total registered basic capital of all these companies was DM 60,562·4 million. There was a total of 52 AG-type companies with a basic capital each of over DM 250 million. At the end of 1971 there was a total of 88,483 GmbH-type companies, with the vast majority having a basic capital of less than DM 20,000. Further details are given in Appendix 1, outlining the general trends of the major industrial sectors.

3 Personnel Management and Industrial Relations

The last few years have seen the worst strikes in West German post-war history. More frequent and more damaging strikes are highly probable, reflecting a major change in the relationship between managers and the managed in large companies. The German trade unions are now on the point of obtaining more direct influence in the industrial decision-taking process than unions in any other Western country have gained, and the German unions are very clearly becoming much more militant and a much more potent political force.

One of the most important developments in the 1972 federal election campaign was the total abandonment by the unions of earlier neutral positions and their total commitment to the Social Democratic Party. As a just reward, the Social Democrats will now push through legislation increasing the direct industrial influence of the unions and just how radical this legislation will be, depends in large measure on the success of the Free Democrats, who are the junior partners in the Bonn coalition Government, in restraining the radical enthusiasm of the Social Democrats.

German managers are quite rightly worried about these developments and their anxieties about trade union policies are increasing at a swift pace. This is something which foreigners are, in large measure, unaware of and the view remains widespread, that German trade unions are docile and timid organisations with German workers being hard workers, with no interest in ever going on strike. Today these views have no foundation in reality. These are views that describe an earlier situation, not the situation in the 1970s. The determination of German trade unions to use their excellent organisations, strong financial reserves and large public support, to obtain great political and industrial power, will be one of the most important characteristics of industrial Germany in the decade ahead.

It is largely true that German trade unions were relatively weak in the 1950s and 1960s and this country's brilliant strike-free record tends to underline this. Only tiny Luxemburg can boast of a better strike-free record in the past twenty-five years than West Germany, in the European Economic Community. The leaders of German unions were slow to learn just how powerful they really could be. They were often out-talked and out-flanked by employers, who time and again convinced the unions that high wage demands and strikes would lead to recessions and severe unemployment.

The post-war German trade unions had a number of special problems, which have only been completely solved in the recent past. The unions had difficulty in mustering public support among a population that remembered how little help unions had been in the periods of mass unemployment in the Weimar Republic, among people who saw the rebuilding of an industrially strong Germany as the chief priority and who viewed strikes with disdain, and among a people fearful of communism who wanted to have little to do with organisations tainted in any way with socialist ideas. These were prevailing public attitudes in the 1950s. In addition, the men who struggled to rebuild the trade unions after the war had to start from scratch and had no traditions to lean upon. Hitler had made trade unions illegal in 1933 and many of the most outstanding German trade union leaders of the pre-war era were dead in 1945.*

The trade union organisers rapidly set about creating new modern unions after the last war. Unions were built on broadly defined industrial lines, so that just one union was formed for all employees in the chemical, paper and ceramics industries, while another single union was formed for all workers in the iron, steel, metal working, engineering, automobile and machine tool industries. A total of sixteen major unions were set up, which

* Germany has one of the oldest trade union and social democratic traditions and histories. The unions in 1946 could look back with pride on over one hundred years of major German contributions to the development of socialist thought, but this all helped little in 1946. The German people were more interested in getting a job and money in 1946 than hearing about Rosa Luxemburg. The union leaders in 1946 lacked any type of organisation and this was their first difficult task. Trade unionism in Germany had been brutally outlawed in the 12 years of Nazism and rebuilding union organisations was a huge task in the immediate post-war period.

between them covered almost every area of employment and which joined together in a national association, the Deutsche Gewerkschaftsbund, DGB.

The union leaders saw their chief task as that of establishing a degree of security of employment for German workers, providing workers with adequate incomes and a degree of self-respect. There was little time in the early years to do anything else other than recruit members and build organisations. The unions were in the main too weak to organise major strikes, or major political campaigns.

It has largely been due to these factors that Germany has been able to boast of such a good strike-free record. The figures are clearly impressive and make German union members look like tame little school children compared to the tough men of Italy, America or Britain. Based on an annual average of the years 1968, 1969 and 1970, figures compiled by the I.G. Metall trade union, show that days lost due to strikes in this country was a mere 400,000, which compares with losses of 4·3 million days a year in France, 10·5 million in Japan, 22·5 million in Britain, 65·3 million in Italy and 154 million in the United States.

The trade unions have been aided in strengthening their position in recent years through the growing respectability of the Social Democratic Party and the easing of tension between East and West. The trends of employment have also been a significant factor in bolstering the power and confidence of the trade unions. On average, there were about 200,000 registered vacant jobs in 1958 against 680,000 unemployed persons. The situation changed swiftly and by 1960 there was a greater number of vacant jobs than people out of work. One year later, serious labour market tension had come to the fore, with just 150,000 unemployed against 536,100 registered open jobs. Another swift change took place during the recession with there being three times as many unemployed as vacant jobs, in late 1966. The people hardest hit by the recession were foreigners, who had come to Germany earlier at a time when industry was crying out for labour. In the first quarter of 1967 West Germany's labour force consisted of 300,000 fewer foreign workers than one year before, there were 600,000 people looking for jobs and some 100,000 employees were on short-time. It was only after this period, when another radical swing took place, that greater confidence about the future likelihood of secure employment established itself. In recent years there have almost always been at least twice as many vacant jobs as people unemployed, despite massive inflows of immigrant workers. In such conditions, the trade unions have flourished as never before, being in a position to exploit the tight labour market and being backed by vast numbers of workers, confident that their jobs will not be lost through increasing pressure on employers for better conditions of employment.

People in West Germany today, basking in prosperity and immense affluence, simply do not believe that a serious depression and heavy unemployment can swiftly develop. They know full well that the first people to lose jobs in a recession are the immigrant workers, and the existence of more than 2·5 million temporary foreign workers here acts as a comfortable cushion against the unemployment of German citizens. The belief in job security is most prevalent among the young, who do not share the memories of older generations of massive inflation and unemployment in the 1920s and in the immediate post-war period. A number of political observers believe that the substantial defeat of the Christian Democrats in the November 1972 federal elections, reflects diminishing fears of existing prosperity being undermined, for the Christian Democrats chose the prospect of galloping inflation as their main election theme. But to some extent this fear is still in existence and acts as a brake on the most militant and radical trade unionists.

As pointed out in the first chapter of this book, many trade union leaders felt that they had been taken for a ride in the late 1960s in agreeing to modest wage rises, at a time when industrial profits were soaring at a faster pace than for many years. This was the main factor in prompting the unions to take a tough stand for large wage increases in 1970 and 1971. Tough resistance by employers was met by strikes in 1971, notably a long strike at Deutsche Lufthansa early in the year, a series of 'lightning strikes' in the spring at many chemical companies and the worst strike in post-war history in the engineering industry, at the end of the year.

The unions in recent years have shed themselves of many of their earlier inhibitions and fears. They have obtained increasing support in Bonn, through the coming to power of the Social Democrats. They have strengthened their direct influence in politics and today there are over 240 members of DGB unions with seats in the Bundestag. The unions are clearly more willing to use strike action than ever before, as the strikes in 1971 so clearly show. The unions have come to realise that employers will always warn of depressions and high unemployment in the weeks prior to wage negotiations and the unions have come to take little notice of these warnings, for they have been made too often.

The unions have been further strengthened by attracting highly qualified experts to their ranks, who can read balance sheets and understand industrial problems as well as the best of managers. The unions are also being led in large measure now by a younger generation of well-educated men, who have travelled widely and learnt a great deal about industrial relations, negotiating tactics and strikes, from the militant union leaders in other countries. The men who rebuilt the unions after the war and who saw their jobs in close relation to the national interests of rebuilding a powerful industrial country, have largely been replaced by men who pay scant regard to the national interest, but whose sole interests concern increasing the power, influence and well-being of German workers.

WORKER CO-DETERMINATION

To a large degree the unions have gained expertise in matters concerning company accounts and management affairs through gaining a greater measure of influence in the industrial decision-taking process than unions in other countries have managed to obtain. It is the further demands of the unions for even greater influence in the decision-taking process in industry that so terrifies managers and company owners in West Germany now. These demands, which are supported by the Social Democrats, threaten to give the unions greater power in industry than company owners have. The unions want to hold just as many Aufsichtsrat seats in a company as the shareholders possess and in the opinion of owners of industry, 'if the unions continue to exploit the tense labour market situation and in addition obtained co-determination, then shareholders and directors of business would not be even partners with the unions, but thoroughly dominated and controlled by them.'*

The German unions have precisely formulated the exact type of position they would like to have in industry. The main aim is to have total parity with company owners in Aufsichtsrats and a direct union appointee in a company's Vorstand. The West German worker co-determination aims, known as Mitbestimmung, have aroused considerable interest abroad. A mild version of the system has won support in the Commission of the European Economic Community, which in late 1972 announced that it favours the introduction of a form of Mitbestimmung in all large European companies.

The German trade union ideas are fairly clear. The unions demand that a parity co-determination system should be introduced in all large companies. They define large companies as businesses which fulfil two of three criteria: employing more than 2,000 people, having a total turnover in excess of DM 300 million and having a balance-sheet volume of more than DM 150 million. In such companies the Aufsichtsrat should be evenly split between representatives of the employees and representatives of the shareholders, and the employees should have sole right to appoint that Vorstand member whose responsibilities cover social and personnel matters.

The employee representatives on the supervisory board of directors should be elected by a works council, which in turn is elected by all company employees. The worker representatives on the Aufsichtsrat should not only be drawn from within the company, so that they can include trade unionists with a broad knowledge of industrial problems and with experience in more than just one specific company. The typical Aufsichtsrat, envisaged by the unions, would consist in a very large company of 21 members, with ten appointed by the works council, ten elected by the shareholders and the chairman appointed as a 'neutral man' by mutual consent of the two sides in the supervisory board. The worker representatives would alone appoint

* Quote by Herr Otto Wolff von Amerongen, the owner of a large steel company and President of the Chambers of Commerce Federation of West Germany. The quote is taken from an interview conducted by the author with Herr von Amerongen and printed in the *The Times*, 16 December 1972.

one of the Vorstand members, whose full responsibilities would cover all matters concerning productivity, wages, industrial training, security against industrial accidents, pensions, social security and other matters relevant to general conditions of employment.

Should such a system be adopted across the country, then the unions would be in a position to feel certain that no major corporate decisions are taken without their knowledge. The unions maintain that Vorstand members would be forced to consider the best interests of employees on a parity with considering how to serve the best interests of the shareholders. As Vorstands are meant to share collective responsibility and as one Vorstand member would be an employee's appointee, the unions believe that they would be fully and continually informed of every action taken or contemplated by the Vorstands of large companies.

Should this sort of system be introduced, then the unions would be in a position, through their Vorstand representation, to have an influence on every aspect of day-to-day management and they would be in a position to effectively block almost any decision they disapproved of, through their strong position in company Aufsichtsrats. In practice the unions could have the greatest measure of power on Aufsichtsrats, even if the 'neutral man' tends to vote in the main with the shareholder representatives. The theory is that employee representatives on Aufsichtsrats will always have identical goals and because they will all know each other well, they will be in a position, prior to Aufsichtsrat meetings, to plan tactics and motions for these meetings. In contrast, the shareholder representatives are unlikely to be such a unified group, nor are they likely to be as well organised among themselves as the employee representatives will be.

As owners of industry point out, there is a danger that employees will come to dominate the companies they work for, pushing owners into a minor position. There are genuine fears that the Mitbestimmung system will lead to a swift erosion of the free enterprise system and prove to be a major step on the road to the full take-over of industry by organised groups of workers. It is argued that this system will greatly impair the efficiency of managers, by slowing down the decision-taking process and almost totally abandoning the entrepreneur's opportunity to take risks. Urgent decisions could be delayed through forced consultation with the unions, leading to strong advantages being obtained by rival foreign companies, that do not have a co-determination system of this kind. Further, it is suggested that foreign companies would be reluctant to build subsidiaries in Germany for fear of their enterprises being too restricted by the unions and that foreign and domestic financial institutions will be reluctant to give capital to German companies, because of fears that, through trade union restraints, these companies will not be able to be internationally competitive. It is highly probable that the introduction of Mitbestimmung throughout German industry could weaken the managerial and financial stability of German companies and lead to serious crises on German stock exchanges.

Many foreign trade unionists are also not in favour of the aims, in this regard, of the German trade unions. It is often pointed out that by taking Aufsichtsrat positions, union members make themselves immediately responsible for management decisions and become quasi-employers. The results could be that union leaders are forced to compromise too often and that, with all the benefits that they would enjoy as directors, they would become estranged from rank and file workers.

The prospect of the trade unions obtaining full Mitbestimmung is now a very real one. The trade unions have already had considerable success in this sphere and it is worth sketching the history and development of this concept, to show how far the German unions have come towards realising their aims, how the system works in practice and why it has taken the form that German trade unions now advocate.

The concept of worker participation is an old one, with models of various types dating back well into the last century to the time of Robert Owen. The German trade unions achieved a degree of co-determination in industry in the Weimar Republic, but it mainly centred on unions having the right to be informed and consulted by managers on matters concerning personnel affairs. But the unions enjoyed little influence in the decision-taking process. The general outline of the modern Mitbestimmung concept had already become an important part of German trade union programmes by the end of the 1920s.

Mitbestimmung was immediately taken up as a major demand by the newly formed unions after the war and has remained one of their top goals ever since.

The unions argue that in modern society the worker has little idea of the real point of his employment; he is dominated and surrounded and often replaced by machinery. The worker figures as a mere number to employers, he rarely knows the suppliers of the company he works for or the purchasers of his output. The worker in large modern factories has no scope for personal initiative, nor has he much influence on the type of work he does in the future. The unions maintain that the Mitbestimmung concept can change the situation, giving employees greater benefits of all kinds, securer employment, greater self-respect and increased direct influence over what they do and what way their careers develop. The unions believe that Mitbestimmung offers greater prospects in these areas than does industrial nationalisation, for this latter concept merely replaces private bosses by bosses imposed by the State, without substantially altering the position or influence of employees.

Apart from these basic reasons, the unions also saw an important political justification for their Mitbestimmung demands after the war. They argued that the existing industrial system gave managers and bosses immense power to determine not just the lives of their employees, but also the strength and success of elected governments. This political power could easily be misused, said the unions, who pointed out that industrial owners during the Weimar period had undermined democracy and contributed in great measure to the collapse of Weimar and the subsequent rise of Hitler. Further, it was argued that Hitler only managed to achieve such great power and wreck and destroy so much, through the active encouragement of powerful leaders of industry. The unions in 1946 were determined to check the political power of industrialists and ensure that misuses of political power by the owners of industry did not recur. The Mitbestimmung system was seen as an ideal checking method and was supported in large measure by the victors of the 1939–45 war, especially by the British.

The Allies shared the opinions of the unions that industrialists had obtained too much influence and misused their influence to destroy democracy, encourage totalitarianism and war. The chief targets of such accusations after the war were the bosses of the vast German coal and steel industries. The iron, steel and coal industries, directed by such tycoons as Krupp and Flick, were seen as the bastions of industrial might and were the first to be attacked by the unions and the Allies. The unions believed that if they managed to get Mitbestimmung introduced in these industries, then they would have little difficulty in getting their system widely adopted throughout German industry. It was reasoned that the iron, steel and coal industries were the most important industries in the country and were likely to maintain their top positions. The unions made a serious mistake here, for post-war Germany has seen modern industries, such as mechanical engineering, automobile manufacture and electronics, grow at a swift pace, while iron, steel and coal industries have declined substantially in significance.

By 1947 a number of steel companies had introduced worker co-determination systems and the Mitbestimmung system was adopted by 25 leading iron, steel and coal companies by 1951. The trade unions brought immense pressure on the young Government of the Federal Republic for legislation on Mitbestimmung. The first aim was for laws establishing the system in just the iron, steel and coal industries. By 1950 the influence of the British in determining the structure of German industry had declined considerably from the position of immense power held immediately after the war. This was just one reason why the unions found immense difficulties in securing their aims. Other important reasons included the rapid regaining of self-confidence of the owners of industry,* the emergence of a strong conservative government under Konrad Adenauer and Ludwig Erhard, which strongly believed in the free enterprise system, which believed that free enterprise should be given free rein in a period when the first priority was rebuilding a crippled industrial country and which had little sympathy for trade union ideas. The view put forward by business leaders, that Mitbestimmung would produce a much slower industrial recovery than would otherwise be the case, carried much weight in Bonn.

The unions threatened major strikes and after a tough fight

* Krupp and others had all been released from prison by late 1951.

they finally won the first round. On 25 May 1951, the Mit-bestimmungsgesetz passed through Parliament. This introduced the worker co-determination system that the unions wanted in the iron, steel and coal industries. In these industries the employee representatives held just as many seats on the Auf-sichtsrat as did the representatives of shareholders and a Vorstand member in charge of all social and personnel matters was elected alone by the employees. The unions believed that with the passing of this law, more Mitbestimmung laws for other industries could be pushed through.

The resistance to Mitbestimmung was becoming too strong, however. The unions had a host of other problems and weak public support. The Social Democrats were a weak party. The Allies had swiftly reduced their direct intervention in the German legal and industrial system. The owners of industry and managers had established associations and federations that were becoming increasingly powerful political pressure groups. A number of laws followed the 1951 law, but none went nearly so far as the first Mitbestimmungsgesetz.

A further law ensuring that the 1951 law applied to all holding companies in the iron, steel and coal industry was passed in 1956, which ensured that owners of these industries could find no ways around the laws. Taken together, the 1951 and 1956 laws have given the unions that represent workers in these industries, the Industriegewerkschaft Metall and the Industriegewerkschaft Bergbau und Energie, considerable power in determing the shape and structure of the iron, steel and coal industries. These laws have given the unions the chance to gain experience of the practical application of their co-determination concepts. This experience has convinced all German unions that this type of co-determination can produce major benefits for employees and as a result, in recent years, the unions have made the realisation of such a system across Germany their chief priority.

In 1952, as a compromise, the Bundestag passed the Betriebs-verfassungsgesetz, which affected all major companies in the country. This law gave employees the right to appoint one-third of the members of the Aufsichtsrat of large companies. The law contained no provision for the appointment by employees alone of a Vorstand member. The law established works councils in all large companies and gave them considerable rights regarding information about Vorstand plans and consultation by the Vorstand on a number of important aspects of company affairs. This law was expanded in January 1971, to give the works councils even more influence with the passing of a new Betriebsverfassungsgesetz. The Social Democrats wanted to introduce full Mitbestimmung, but the Free Democrats held them back and the new 1971 law was the resulting compromise.

This new law ensured that employers gave works councils reasons for redundancies, which could be protested against and contested in the courts. In effect, the 1971 law made it difficult for companies to decide matters in the personnel sector without full consultation with the works councils and, without a measure of support being reached by these councils, the managers had little chance of seeing their plans realised efficiently. This law forces Vorstands to carefully consider the welfare of their employees in all the decisions they take. The law, however, does not go nearly as far as the 1951 Mitbestimmung law and by no means satisfies the unions. In 1955, a law was passed giving a moderate amount of influence to employee representatives in public authorities and in the civil service. This law, the Personalvertretungsgesetz, did not go nearly as far with regard to union influence in the public sector, as the 1952 Betriebsverfassungsgesetz had gone in the private sector.

Employees in the iron, steel and coal industries have clearly benefited through the introduction of a co-determination system. The coal industry has been in financial chaos for many years and heavy unemployment has not resulted solely because of the large measure of power enjoyed by the unions in the iron, steel and coal companies. Redundancies in these industries have been made, but the men hit have received large cash sums. The pension systems in these industries are better from an employee's viewpoint than in most other industries. Young men made redundant in these industries have been given excellent opportunities to be retrained and found other employment. The reduction in the scale of the German coal industry has been done in a highly humane way with few miners being in a position to complain of unfair treatment.*

* It can be argued, however, that these were consequences of Germany's huge industrial boom and the shortage of labour in many young industries,

The various worker participation laws have given union leaders the opportunity to be active in all aspects of company affairs and have forced employers and employee representatives to meet more often, get to know each other better, get used to solving problems together, and all this has helped build up a healthy industrial relations system. Many strikes have been averted on account of union leaders knowing company directors well and knowing a company's financial position well enough to know what sort of wage rises a company can afford. There have, for example, been no major strikes in the iron and steel industry in Germany in the period 1929–72.

There is no evidence to prove that the existence of Mitbestimmung has made the German iron, steel and coal industries less efficient than the same sort of industries in other countries, which do not have a similar system of worker co-determination. The delays that may arise in view of the need for detailed discussion between managers and union leaders on items of major importance are probably offset by the fact that the co-determination system has the merit that once a decision has been reached, managers know full well that the realising of the agreed project can be precisely planned, without fear of delays due to industrial disputes on the matter involved.

The unions have shown no desire to extend their influence beyond the lines set by their co-determination models, despite the fact that in some industries the system has been operating for over twenty years. This would tend to weaken the basis of those arguments by industrialists that suggest that the present union Mitbestimmung plans are only a first step in the direction of planned take-over of industry by the unions. There is no evidence whatever to support the claim that the unions have secretly got plans for increasing their direct influence in the decision-taking process in industry once Mitbestimmung has been adopted throughout German industry.

The Mitbestimmung system has clear disadvantages in the modern framework of industrial society. While nations hang on to concepts of nationality and continually plan policies

---

rather than due to the Mitbestimmung system. In other countries miners have often been made redundant on fair terms and with good pensions without Mitbestimmung existing.

on the basis of national frontiers, industry thinks and acts multinationally. The West German steel companies could find it exceptionally difficult to merge with companies in other countries, because of the existence here of Mitbestimmung. The German unions, once they have obtained Mitbestimmung, will not give it up. They will not allow their influence to be decreased through a merger of a German company under the system, with a non-German company that does not have the system. If the partner company is not willing to accept the Mitbestimmung system, then the German unions will block any merger attempt. At the moment there is increasing evidence that many German companies will have to merge with foreign companies in order to obtain a size that can ensure their remaining competitive in a society increasingly dominated by giant multinational industrial enterprises. The merger in 1972 between the Hoesch steel company of Dortmund and the Dutch Hoogovens company, was vetoed by the German unions until the Dutch agreed to a full worker co-determination system being introduced into the new merged company.

The consequences for German industry should other countries not introduce Mitbestimmung could be grave. There is little chance that worker co-determination systems of the German type will be introduced in such countries as the United States, Britain and France. The EEC Commission will meet immense opposition by some Common Market member countries to its own worker-co-determination ideas, with the British certain to argue that EEC Commission ideas are too radical and the Germans arguing that the EEC Commission suggestions are not sufficiently radical. German companies on the whole have vast international sales networks, but very small foreign investment holdings. German companies are in many ways not in a position to compete alone with such international giants as IBM, ITT, GEC, General Motors, Ford, and German companies have too little capital to finance the massive research investments that international competition will demand. German companies will increasingly be forced into international mergers or joint co-operation agreements and the existence of co-determination here may put many foreign companies off choosing German partners.

German trade unions already enjoy possibly more power in

the board rooms of major companies than unions do in other Western countries. It would be quite inaccurate to suggest that German unions do not have such a great impact on industrial life as unions in some other countries do, simply on the basis of strike figures. It is a purely subjective argument as to whether the trade union concept of co-determination is good for a society or not. As a personal opinion, it would appear that the system tends to limit managerial efficiency and, at the same time, tends to widen the gulf between union leaders and rank and file union members. The system is far from perfect and can bring great hardship to the industry of this country, if Germany alone finds that it is introducing the system, while other countries reject it. There is every reason for business leaders in this country to fear the widespread introduction of Mitbestimmung, in that it will almost certainly reduce their power. However, in the advanced age of industrialisation in which we now live, it is certainly important that democracy be spared the tests that severe strife between social classes can produce and, to some extent, the Mitbestimmung system bridges the gap, in that it places direct responsibility in companies for the welfare of employees on the shoulders of the elected leaders of these employees.

STRIKES AND WAGE NEGOTIATIONS

The opportunities that unions have to strike is limited by well-defined industrial relations laws. While the British trade unions are fighting with vigour to oppose legislation that governs their freedom to call strikes, the German unions fully accept and respect the modern code that exists here. That strikes, when they take place, can do much more damage than strikes in other countries usually do, has nothing to do with the laws, but solely concerns the trade union structure. With just sixteen unions representing all German workers, a strike by just one union can often be equal to a major national strike. The I.G. Metall trade union is the largest single free trade union in Europe with over two million members. This union represents more than four million workers in wage negotiations and were it to call a national strike, almost every industry in the country would be immediately crippled.

Aware of the consequences for the whole economy, the unions

are desperately reluctant to call national strikes. It is recognised that a national strike of just a few days, by one of the major unions, could do immense damage to the whole economy. As a rule, the unions decide to restrict strikes to certain regions, using these regional strikes as test cases to resolve national disputes. The unions are fully aware that their public standing and support could swiftly be weakened by holding national strikes; they also recognise that regional strikes are much cheaper to finance. But the unions are of such a size that even regional strikes can have immense effects on the country as a whole.

The I.G. Metall strike in Baden-Württemberg in 1971 lasted eighteen days and directly involved some 500,000 workers. In the latter stages of the strike there was not one mechanical engineering or automobile company in the country that had not suffered production losses. The closure of engineering and electrical companies in Baden-Württemberg led to sharp supply problems in allied industries across the country. Volkswagenwerk AG, for example, was forced to close all its plants, employing more than 100,000 people, because of strikes at vital electrical equipment suppliers in Stuttgart.

All employees in this country must sign wage contracts and strikes are illegal during the period when a contract is in force. This sharply reduces the possibility of frequent or unexpected strikes. Unofficial strikes during wage contract periods can result in heavy fines being imposed on the unions. The trade unions strongly discourage unofficial strikes and their respect for the law prevents them taking strike action in solidarity with strikers in another country. If British workers at Ford factories went on strike, the Ford management might well try to increase production in Ford plants in Germany. The Ford workers in Germany could refuse to do overtime, but they could not refuse to work at all to strengthen the case of the British Ford workers. The German laws almost totally make thoughts of joint multinational strike action impossible. Trade unions have often got together to discuss striking at the plants of a multinational company in several countries at the same time. The only time that could be chosen to get German co-operation could be after a wage contract has expired and before a new contract has been concluded. At best German unions can show solidarity with unions in other countries, who are striking, by sending cables of sympathy and by refusing additional work.

The Germans clearly tend to like good organisation, discipline and strong leadership and the unions in their structure and mode of operations reflect this. The German unions are vast, highly structured organisations with the leaders holding almost supreme power. The unions are so organised that power is restricted to a small group of national leaders. Factory shop stewards and local regional union leaders are given little opportunity or scope to take individual action without first consulting the national leaders. If wage contracts in a certain industry in a certain region expired the local union officials of the industry would consult closely with their national executive about the sort of demands they should make for new contracts, and they would take no action of any kind without gaining prior approval from the national executive.

Once a wage contract expires the relevant unions and employers start negotiations on a new contract. After a period of time, usually just a couple of weeks, but sometimes longer, the two sides declare that the negotiations are not making progress and that they have been officially terminated. A 'cooling off' period of at least 21 days then starts, during which the union has no power to call a strike. During this period efforts are generally made by one of the two sides to get informal negotiations started. These informal contacts can lead to the start of some form of arbitration talks. In these talks both sides usually agree on appointing some respected figure, often a local politician or judge, to mediate between the two sides.

Should the arbitration talks get nowhere and the 21 days elapse, then the union can call a strike. But such a call can only be made after all trade union members in the dispute are balloted and if the strike vote gains more than a 75 per cent majority for strike action. Such ballots are a pure formality, for once a union's national executive suggests a strike, then the rank and file members almost always give massive support for strike action. For example, more than 90 per cent of the I.G. Metall members in the Ruhr iron and steel industry took part in a strike vote in December 1972 and with the union calling for a strike, the members voted 96·9 per cent in favour of strike action.

Arranging a strike vote usually takes a few days and once the vote has been concluded, the union's executive in the region where the strike vote was held meets to decide on the date when the strike should be started. The regional executive fixes a date and then seeks approval for its decision from the union's national executive. This whole procedure takes several more days and due to this and the other formalities, strikes can at best be held a minimum of four-and-a-half to five weeks after wage contracts have expired. Usually the strike takes place even longer after the expiration of contracts, for the unions tend to space out the various stages leading to a strike, in order to give plenty of room for new negotiations to be held. Often a settlement is finally reached within 24 hours of a strike starting. This has become an almost ritual procedure, with both sides seemingly playing through meaningless rounds of talks until just a few days before a strike, when serious talks start and end swiftly with a settlement.

However, should a strike start, it can be countered by a lock-out. The trade unions claim that lock-outs are illegal, but their case has never been proved. The employers use lock-outs to make subsidising a strike more costly for a union, but this tactic has recently misfired, with federal authorities concluding that locked out workers are in the same position as unemployed people and can therefore claim unemployment pay. Another reason for lock-outs is to pressure union leaders from below. Many workers are not union members, but are just as hard hit by lock-outs as union members and employers hope that these non-union workers will start to bring pressure on their union colleagues to return to work.

The union may start a strike at isolated plants in a region, rather than at all factories involved in the dispute at the same time. Employers tend to counter with lock-outs across the region as a whole and the lock-outs tend to speed up arbitration. Should official arbitration get nowhere, then it can be officially declared as a failure and the neutral mediator can return to a more peaceful existence. There is still scope for new arbitration to start should this be desired by both the employers and the unions. By this time the situation will have become a major national issue, for strikes are not frequent here and protracted strikes, as has been pointed out earlier, can have grave effects on all types of industry across the country. Substantial pressure will be brought on both parties in the dispute by other unions, other employers' associations and by the press and politicians, to resolve the dispute swiftly. Under these circumstances the two sides will almost certainly agree to a new round of arbitration and choose, as the neutral chairman, a man of even greater distinction than the first chairman of the arbitration talks. Should these arbitration talks appear to get nowhere, the unions can add pressure, by holding strike ballots in other regions and threatening a national strike. So far such a national strike has never taken place, but the threat of one developing was very real in the I.G. Metall dispute at the end of 1971.

The wage negotiating procedure is tortuous and gives ample opportunity for lengthy negotiations to be held, prior to a strike being started. Common sense has almost always prevailed and few strikes have taken place. One of the most important aspects of the procedure is the total neutrality in disputes of governments, whether regional or federal. All the major political parties take the view that the settlement of wage contracts is a matter solely for the contract partners. This view falls in closely with the basic ideas of the free market economic system, allowing market forces free of State control to play themselves out. Both Ludwig Erhard and Karl Schiller acted as mediators in major disputes while they were at the top of the Bonn Economics Ministry, but their intervention was at the invitation of both contract partners and their role was strictly that of neutral chairman in arbitration. In the 1971 I.G. Metall dispute, the Federal Chancellor, Herr Brandt, called both sides to Bonn for a meeting. He made no attempt to suggest what sort of solution to the dispute the Government desired, but attempted only to persuade both sides to end the dispute swiftly among themselves in the national interest.

As inflation becomes an increasingly serious problem in West Germany and as the unions show themselves increasingly willing to strike for high wage demands, the Federal Government is finding itself forced to exert ever growing pressure on the unions to accept moderate rises in the national interest. The total neutrality of politicians in disputes may well be entirely abandoned in the not too distant future, as the politicians come to believe that their direct intervention is essential if serious strikes and highly inflationary wage settlements are to be avoided. Following the imposition of wage and price controls in the United States in August 1971 and in Britain in late 1972, there has been increasing discussion in Germany about adopting similar measures. The leading politicians have all spoken out against such controls, stating bluntly that such controls would mean the ending of the free market system in the wages sector and force politicians into an interventionist position in all disputes. However, it seems likely that politicians will come to intervene in disputes more frequently and that as a result, the wage negotiating procedure will in coming years go through a period of substantial change.

The present industrial relations code, as far as it affects wage settlements, is fine in a country with little inflation and where the unions, bearing the national interest in mind, are most hesitant to strike and produce major national disruptions of industry, through protracted regional strikes. At the moment the system is going through a testing period. The 'cooling off' period tends to serve little purpose, for the serious negotiations increasingly seem to start after strike ballots have been held. With unions more determined than ever to achieve a fairer distribution of income through continually high wage rises, and quite ready to strike for their demands, the situation has become acutely tense. Wage contracts are usually made for periods of only one year. Germany may well be moving into an era where significant strikes arise in many industries every year, when wage contracts are being negotiated. Such a situation could do immense damage to German industry and may well give rise to calls, by politicians, for legislation on an entirely new industrial relations code.

TRADE UNION ORGANISATION

West Germany has sixteen main trade unions linked together in the DGB. The individual unions each have their own national head offices and national executive committees. Each of these national head offices tends to be a large and modern building, housing teams of publicity experts, economists, statisticians, experts on all manner of national and international political and social questions. The unions also have central offices in each of the main regions of the country, which have their own regional executive committees. The main work of the unions is in the factories themselves, where the organisation of the unions tends to be very similar from one industry to another. In each department of a factory the unions have members, who are elected by their work mates and known as 'trusted men' (Vertrauensleute).

There tend to be few full-time trade union employees outside the national and regional head offices, although the key men in factories get time to do necessary union business, which is mostly paid for by employers. The 'trusted men' either make up the works councils or elect the works councils, as well as electing the chief officials of the union at regional and national level. The unions aim at having one 'trusted man' for a maximum of 20 employees and as such a large number of elected men could not form an effective committee, they usually elect among themselves the main union committee within a factory. This main committee may have a series of sub-committees, responsible for specific matters, such as the welfare and organisation of apprentices, the organisation of temporary foreign workers and for different sections of a company, such as administration, production in machine rooms or problems of workers on conveyor belts.

The unions tend to have a large number of special rules governing the election of 'trusted men'. The unions make considerable efforts to train the 'trusted men' well and the central regional and national union organisations keep fairly close supervision of the activities of the 'trusted men', in the individual factories. The result is that the 'trusted men', by and large, do not have anything like the sort of independence that British shop stewards have and the union organisations are so structured that almost all important decisions are left entirely to regional and national executive committees.

Apart from the DGB unions, there are special trade unions for salaried workers, which have their own well-organised structures. According to 1970 Federal Statistics Office figures, there was a total of 22·2 million employees in West Germany, comprising 12·5 million wage earners, 7·8 million salary earners and 1·9 million civil servants. The total membership of the

DGB was 6,870,000 or 29·7 per cent of the total number of employees. This DGB total comprised 5,089,000 wage earners, 986,000 salary earners and 638,000 civil servants. The largest single trade union was the I.G. Metall, with close to 2·25 million members, which was close to half the total number of employees in the industries covered by this union.

Union membership trends show that gradually more employees in the country are joining unions. Union membership is not compulsory in any trade or industry and any attempt at compulsion is illegal. The Deutsche Angestellten-Gewerkschaft with 485,000 members is the leading independent trade union for salaried people. The Union der Leitenden Angestellten represents some 300,000 of the country's most senior salaried employees and is in many respects more like an organisation for business leaders and top managers, than a real trade union in the normally accepted sense.

MANAGEMENT PERSONNEL ATTITUDES

Tight discipline and good organisation are hallmarks not only of trade unionism in this country, but also of the way managers treat and promote administrative personnel. Loyalty and status are factors stressed keenly with good results in most companies. A pyramid culminating in the Vorstand can be clearly seen in many large companies, defining with precision, on a titles basis, the various steps to the top. Each step is characterised in the major companies by a title, salary scale and set number of fringe benefits. The system works well, because Germans have a certain love of order and senior employees have a continual firm idea of exactly what their seniority involves and what their chances are of further promotion. The detailed systems vary considerably from one company to the next, but the basic concept, dependent on clearly defined positions of varying degrees of senority, with each position being clearly formulated, is found in most large enterprises. The systems employed here are possibly more rigid than those that exist in other countries and few people are as title and status conscious as the Germans, which helps the system here to function smoothly.

As an example, one could choose a large bank, whose promotion system would probably be of the following type. A young university graduate of about 25 would enter a bank for general training. After a certain training period his future will be fairly clearly outlined by the bank's personnel department. The young graduate may have so impressed, that he is placed on a fast promotion stream, in which case, he is likely today to spend a short time in a large branch of the bank before being sent abroad for a few years, where he will early on be given substantial testing responsibilities, which will show his superiors just how far he can go in the bank's senior management. More normal is that after general training the young banker will get a junior administrative position in one of the bank's larger domestic branches. Here he will be given some sort of title and have an annual income of around DM 24,000.

Depending on his ability and relations with his immediate superiors, the young banker can after some time expect to become general manager in a department of the branch he is working in. This will carry an improvement in salary of possibly DM 6,000 a year and a more important-sounding title. The next step up could be to one of the senior positions in a large branch or a relatively important position in the bank's head office and the obtaining of the 'Prokurist' title, which means that he is in a position to represent his employer in the signing of contracts and has a full power of attorney, in a range of matters of importance given to him by his employer. At this stage his salary could be anything up to double his starting salary.

The next position may be that of head of a large department in one of the bank's main branches or head of the day-to-day affairs of a head office department and our man will get a salary of anything up to about DM 60,000 and the title of 'department director'. From here, if the man is outstanding, he may become general manager of an important branch or be given large head office responsibilities and a salary of up to DM 80,000 a year. The man who managed to go on the fast stream and gained international experience can expect, on returning to the bank's head office, to be on this general manager level or on the department director level. The next step is one that only a select few ever manage to make. Here the man is given one of the key departments of the bank and has at most one or two superiors. His salary will almost certainly be above

DM 100,000. This example naturally only relates to the largest of the German banking institutions and while the promotion system is similar in smaller banks, the salary level is subtantially lower.

The really large banks sometimes have three or four people above the stage just mentioned, but below Vorstand level. These people have the title 'Generalbevollmächtigte', which means a man with general power of attorney over all bank matters. Usually these men have a special role in a large bank, either as the bank's chief economist or chief expert on international monetary matters or some such similar type of responsibility. In some banks this position does not exist and instead the banks have a number of deputy Vorstand members, while in other institutions, both these general managers and deputy Vorstand men exist. The salary range for men at the General-bevollmächtigte level and at Vorstand level can be anything from DM 200,000 to DM 600,000 a year in the very large banks.

Each position on the scale is accompanied by a set of fringe benefits, covering expenses, cars, chauffeurs, office furnishings and a host of other matters. This illustration shows in a simple form, excluding a host of intermediate positions, the career scale in large banks, and similar other models exist in all other large German businesses. Titles mean an awful lot, especially to the wives of employees, who often insist on being called 'Frau Direktor' if their husbands have reached the position of department director in their companies. The particular position and title that one holds is also of great importance in internal office relationships. Respect is always shown in the most formal of ways to one's superiors. Customs are such, that it is exceptionally rare for a man to have the courage to invite his immediate senior colleague out for a drink or home for dinner or to address him in the friendly 'du' form, rather than the more formal 'Sie' form and this goes so far as to cover men who may work in the same office together for many years. German executives never address their colleagues on a first name basis and it is generally expected that the more junior you are, the earlier you get to work and the later you leave your office, for in the respect system, it is just not done for a man to get to work later than his immediate superior.

This formal and rigid system is slowly breaking down, due largely to German executives travelling widely and coming frequently into contact with more easy-going American customs. The formality at times seems absurd, but it is a part of the general system and enables large companies to maintain smooth operating hierarchies. Men in the systems in operation largely depend for promotion on the promotion of their senior colleagues or through senior colleagues dying or retiring. The only reason why such a rigid system has not produced major problems is that most German companies have been expanding at such a rapid pace over the last two decades, that it has been no problem to promote people on to better salary levels and give them more impressive titles at a swift pace.

Loyalty to one's employer is of vital importance in gaining promotion in most companies. People who have changed jobs frequently and increased their status rapidly by these means, often find that at a certain point they are forced to settle down with one company if they want to ever reach really senior positions. It is difficult to find many Vorstand members in large companies who have not been with their companies for more than a dozen years, prior to reaching the top management level. The Vorstand of the Deutsche Bank serves as a good illustration of this. This bank has a large Vorstand and in 1972 the following were the key men: Herr Christians took eighteen years of employment with the Deutsche Bank to get to the Vorstand, Herr Ehret made the Vorstand after nineteen years with the bank, while it took twenty years for both Herr Mertin and Herr Feith and twenty-two years for Herr Kleffel. Four other Vorstand members had been with the bank for between ten and seventeen years before getting on to the executive management board. Only two men, Herr Guth and Herr Herrhausen came directly on to the bank's Vorstand from other companies and both these men have, in their own way, had exceptionally brilliant careers. In very few companies can one find Vorstand members who were attracted into top positions from other companies.

The idea that a man could join the senior ranks of a large company from another company and get to the Vorstand in four or five years is virtually unheard of. The system has major faults and changes are slowly developing. The chief drawback of the German system is that a man works his way up slowly to the top of his company and when he reaches the Vorstand, he has barely any experience whatever of how other companies are organised or managed and he is too prone to take over the methods and views of his former superiors, who may well have been inefficient managers or men with little idea of modern management techniques.

Some top German managers now openly admit that the efficiency of many managers leaves much to be desired. The lack of mobility of personnel between large companies, between the banks and industry and between the public and private sectors, often results in companies getting few new ideas and becoming conservatively managed. Dr Juergen Krackow, the former Vorstand chairman of AG Weser and Krupp, stated in an interview with *The Times* in autumn 1972 that in many German companies today the major problem is that there is too little questioning of business strategies and management methods. He suggested that many companies are still active in spheres which they should have long ago given up or radically reorganised. As an example, he said that he was chosen to head AG Weser, the Krupp shipbuilding subsidiary, by the then Krupp Vorstand chief, Herr Günter Vogelsang, just because he had had no previous experience in this industry and Weser desperately needed a competent manager from outside to radically reorganise the company and approach shipbuilding without emotional ideas, or age-old concepts of how ships should be constructed.

Dr Krackow claimed that such basic questions as 'Is it still worthwhile for Weser to build a wide range of ships?' had not been posed in the company for years, despite rising losses. He said the management had formerly been so involved, for so many years, in going about their business in a certain traditional way, that they had failed to recognise the changing international situation of shipbuilding and the need to adopt modern and sophisticated management ideas. The lack of mobility of managers from one company to another and the rigid promotion system, do clearly work at times against innovation and can often lead to poor management.

In Germany this is a problem of particular importance. The sharp profit declines in a vast number of German companies in

1970 and 1971 were partly due to managers being slow to adapt to modern business conditions, being slow to realise many of the basic changes in their industrial environment that are highlighted in this book. 1972 saw a vast number of companies start wide-ranging consolidation and rationalisation programmes and saw profits climb, even though sales continued in many cases to fall. The rationalisation could in many cases have been started earlier and in some cases it came only after large board room changes. German companies expanded profits and sales so fast in the last two decades, that managers believed in many cases, that they had found formulas that would never have to be changed. Managers in many cases were ill prepared for the slump in 1970 and 1971, due largely to their being oblivious to a changing environment and to the need for continual questioning of their strategies and management methods.

One of the greatest absurdities in large companies is the length of time that managers spend in their offices. With a sense of pride, managers often tell how they work an average of ten or twelve hours a day, six days a week, on company business. It is, however, probably impossible for a man to concentrate with all his energy for much more than six hours a day on a continual basis. Deutsche Bank Aufsichtsrat chairman, Hermann J Abs, once told me that he had not had a proper holiday since 1956 and VW's Vorstand chief, Rudolf Leiding, is reputed to have worked an average of more than ten hours a day, seven days a week, in the first eighteen months of his VW chairmanship. A cynic might suggest that German top executives are forced to work long hours, because they are slow to grasp things. The truth, however, is that many German managers have no idea how to delegate work, they use out-dated management systems that are unsuited to running vast companies, and their rigid personnel systems are not flexible enough to push fresh ideas and new business methods through.

The rather formal relationship that exists among senior executives in large companies does not produce great bonds of trust and many men fear that projects will be ruined if responsibilities are given to junior colleagues. A number of prominent German Management consultants have told me that they continually find that senior executives have little idea how to apportion their time or delegate work and that many Vorstand members in large companies are so involved in matters that they can easily delegate, that they have little time to look at the general business situation and the medium-term outlook for their companies. One basic cause is that many firms have grown so fast from small units into large enterprises, that the executives in top positions have in many cases not managed to make the transition from being heads of small and medium companies, to the top managers of large international enterprises. Many of the men running Germany's biggest companies today have no experience outside just one company or just one industry and they have stuck to the same management ideas in their companies that have grown to ten times the size that they were just fifteen or so years ago.

Changes in the inflexible management systems and personnel promotion systems in many companies are overdue. German managers cannot hope to keep their companies internationally competitive, unless they themselves adopt modern outlooks and methods. Young people in Germany, as in other countries, are demanding more responsibility and swifter promotion. These demands are forcing changes in the German management system. Many young people here are challenging the old promotion systems, that demanded, for example, that even middle ranking staff in a company's public relations office should have university doctorates. Young people are in many companies opposing the title-orientated systems, especially in cases where prestigious sounding titles are sometimes a substitute for high rates of pay.

The young men entering German industry today have often travelled more widely than their elders. They have grown up in a society which has become increasingly more prosperous and they are not prepared to go through the exceedingly tough early business experiences that many of their fathers had to go through. It was often the case in pre-war Germany that a young graduate entering industry would find that much of the first year of his employment would be spent in being little more than a tea boy or messenger. The young industry entrants in the 1970s are not prepared to tolerate such treatment; they want responsibility and job satisfaction at a young age. The labour market is so tight and the shortage of skilled men is so acute, that companies cannot afford to pass up the opportunity of recruiting bright young men. Companies that have tried to continue the old tough approach to young industry entrants have in recent years met with considerable difficulties from apprentices and young graduates. The young graduates, in particular, are so often able to get interesting jobs with foreign-owned companies here and abroad, that German companies must compete for this talent with a more modern approach if they wish to remain strong.

Very slowly German companies are adapting. They are gradually becoming more open to new management ideas and to giving young men responsibilities at an early stage in their careers. Many companies, to show how modern they are, have one man in his late 30s on the Vorstand.* Women are slowly being given better opportunities in industry, although the pace of progress is still very gradual. While changes are taking place, it will still be a long time before one encounters a young German executive who calls his colleagues by their christian names, who has worked for several companies in a range of different types of businesses and who works a normal British standard eight-hour day.

THE LABOUR MARKET

A major force bringing about change in the structure of German industry is the acute tightness of the labour market. The shortage of labour has strengthened the hands of the trade unions and forced managers to make as much use as possible of modern machinery. In recent years the number of unemployed has rarely been above 1·5 per cent of the labour force and the number of registered vacant jobs has almost always been more than double the total number of persons unemployed. A fairly clear picture of the development of the labour market is shown by the following table, where the situation in September (to choose a month at random) in the last eight years is outlined:

* The idea of young Vorstand members is something like the token gesture in some large American companies of having a black person on the board of directors. In 1971 the Deutsche Bank caused something of a sensation with the appointment of a woman to the bank's Aufsichtsrat.

TABLE 3.1

Year (Sep)	No. unemployed	%	No. vacant jobs
1972	194,660	0·9	593,611
1971	146,740	0·7	645,405
1970	97,338	0·5	811,515
1969	100,477	0·5	832,597
1968	174,467	0·8	609,459
1967	341,078	1·6	335,743
1966	112,726	0·5	536,105
1965	84,974	0·4	699,729

(Figures published by the Federal Employment Bureau, Nürnberg.)

The tightness of the labour market in recent years has been a direct cause of the swift acceleration in industrial unit of production wage-costs. The official Federal Bank index for these costs was started in 1962. In the first few years only a modest rise was seen, due partly to the recession and partly to some unions agreeing to 18 month wage contracts after the recession. With 1962 set as the base year at 100, the index had reached 118 by the start of 1969. By the end of 1970 the index had reached 135 and climbed more than another ten points in the next two years. The result, as Herr Hans-Gunther Sohl, President of the West German Confederation of Industry, put it once, was that wage costs per unit of production rose faster in the first years of the 1970s in this country than in any other West European industrial country. In fact, as Dr Kurt Hansen, Vorstand chief of Bayer AG pointed out at the end of 1972, unit production costs in major industrial areas in West Germany were now just as high as in certain major industrial areas of the United States.*

To offset the extreme labour shortage employers have been forced to make high overtime payments and seek workers from

* Speaking at a press conference at the Bayer head offices in Leverkusen, Dr Hansen gave a detailed account of a survey that had been made by company experts comparing wage costs at Leverkusen with wage costs at a chemical company in Charleston, United States. The survey showed clearly, when fully taking into consideration social benefits, holidays, working hours and other factors, that unit labour costs of production were almost exactly at the same level in the two places and rising more swiftly in Leverkusen.

abroad. As the labour market tension has increased, so the efforts have increased to attract foreigners to work in this country. By mid-1972 there were about 3·4 million foreigners registered as temporary residents in this country. This total comprised 1,908,000 men, 970,000 women and 561,000 children. The Federal Employment Bureau announced at the end of the third quarter of 1972 that the total number of registered foreign workers in the country equalled 10·8 per cent of the German labour force or 2,352,000 persons.

The largest contingent of these foreign workers, most of whom remain little more than four years in this country, comes from less developed areas of Europe. At the end of September, 1972, there were 511,600 Turks, which equals 21·8 per cent of all the registered foreign workers. In addition, at this time, there were 474,900 Jugoslavs, 426,400 Italians, 270,200 Greeks, 184,200 Spaniards, 66,000 Portuguese and many thousands of people from other countries, including over 20,000 North Africans. The number of British people employed in Germany is relatively small and they tend to be mainly employed in British subsidiaries. A number of German companies had bad experiences with workers from Scotland, who returned home swiftly on discovering that they were expected to work harder and live less comfortably than they had been used to. Almost all the Americans employed in West Germany are employed at executive level in American subsidiaries or attached to U.S. military ventures.

In addition to the registered volume of foreign workers there are probably many thousands of foreigners in this country who are employed on an illegal basis. These foreigners are working for generally small German companies without work permits and experts have estimated that there could be well over 200,000 of these illegals. The normal procedure for recruiting foreign workers is by placing an application with a regional office of the Federal Employment Bureau. This organisation has close contacts with a large number of similar organisations in other countries and arranges labour permits and visas. Some unscrupulous individuals have gone on their own initiative to such countries as Jugoslavia and Turkey and recruited people there, with the aim of bringing them illegally into West Germany for large commissions from German employers, who see this as a means of cutting social security costs from their wage bills.

Some companies, employing large numbers of foreign workers, appear at times to have few scruples regarding the treatment of their employees. Many foreign workers have been treated little better than slaves, by employers who have viewed these workers in the same category as imported raw materials. These foreign workers have often been paid poorly, charged vast sums for sleeping in confined quarters or in terrible conditions in barrack-type company-owned establishments. The exploitation of foreign workers is a matter of serious concern to the German authorities, who are increasingly becoming deeply alarmed by the strains on all manner of social services produced by the rapidly increasing number of immigrants.

Attempts are often made by employers to integrate the foreign workers, educate them in the German language and in German customs. The cost of looking after, teaching and integrating foreign workers can be most considerable to employers. To reduce the cost many firms insist on taking foreign workers from just one country, rather than facing the problem of dealing with a work force made up of numerous nationalities. Volkswagen, for example, tried for a long time to employ only foreign workers of Italian origin. Almost all the immigrant workers are totally unskilled and the ever-growing shortage of workers is, in the areas where at least semi-skilled persons are needed, becoming acutely serious.

The vast majority of the temporary foreign workers live in the major industrial regions. According to official figures in the autumn of 1972 there were 971,000 foreigners of the total of 3,400,000 living in North Rhine Westphalia, with 793,000 living in Baden-Württemberg, followed by 545,000 in Bavaria, 397,000 in Hesse, 219,000 in Lower Saxony, 151,000 in West Berlin and 111,000 in Hamburg. The construction industry probably employs more foreign workers than any other industry, with fully one-third of the industry's total work force, or 410,000 people, being of foreign citizenship in September 1972, according to a West German Construction Industry Federation survey.

The vast number of immigrant workers poses problems for the trade unions. The unions are seeking to enrol the foreign workers as members, seeking to train and educate them, seeking to organise them through such methods as the publication of newspapers in foreign languages. The unions have a deep fear that foreign trade unions will seek to gain influence in this country through the immigrant workers. There has already been some evidence of militant Italian communist unions trying to organise Italian workers in this country. Such developments could undermine the trade union system here and add to existing problems in the industrial relations field. This fear has made the German unions increase their efforts to pay special attention to the welfare and education of immigrant workers.

The foreign workers are a highly mobile labour force, acting in times of recession as a cushion against high unemployment of Germans. In the mid-1960s, during the recession, some 300,000 immigrant workers are estimated to have returned to their countries of origin. The foreign workers also distort the German balance of payments picture, for the Germans would have a most substantial surplus if their own work force was sufficiently large for the needs of industry. According to Federal Bank statistics it appears that foreign workers in Germany send home about DM 500 million on average per month to their countries of origin.

West Germany does not have private employment agencies. Despite the philosophy of the free market economy, the country's political leaders have long taken the view that private agencies do more harm than good, enriching themselves at the expense of both employers and employees. There are a small number of private agencies supplying purely temporary office staff and several management consultants specialise in the recruiting of senior executive personnel. The main means of finding staff if one is an employer, or finding a job if one is unemployed, is through local government labour exchanges or by newspaper advertisements. The leading newspapers have scores of pages each week devoted to employment opportunities.

The local labour exchange system, expertly run by the Federal Bureau of Employment, works as well as the labour market situation permits. Employers tend to rely most heavily on newspaper advertisements, simply because this is the only means of directly attracting employees with jobs, who may care to switch employment. The acute shortage of all types of labour makes the task of the local exchanges exceptionally difficult. The Federal Bureau is also responsible for the payment of unemployment benefits, which can amount to more than 50 per cent of an unemployed person's former earnings. The Bureau provides the key statistics on the labour market, it channels the requests for labour by firms in both the German and foreign labour forces. It is also in many respects a leader of international agencies in developing improved systems of integrating and handling migrant workers.

The tasks of the Federal Bureau are going to become harder. It is quite likely that West Germany will shortly have three million immigrant workers and the total could well rise to four million, without new immigration restrictions, by the end of 1975. The Bonn Government is determined to check the inflow, fearing chaos in social services and dangers to domestic security, that can be the result of millions of virtually uncontrolled immigrants. This security aspect came dramatically to the fore after the terrorist slaying of Israeli sportsmen at the Munich Olympic Games in 1972. The terrorists responsible had been living in Germany for some time and it was discovered that there were a considerable number of Palestinian terrorist organisations based in this country. The Government in Bonn will sooner or later be forced to take decisions on the immigrant worker flow and it recognises full well that limitations could result in a decline in the economic growth rate that Germany could achieve with a larger labour force.

MAINTAINING WORKER LOYALTY

Because of the critical labour market situation an increasing number of companies are being forced into designing schemes to ensure that workers remain loyal. Some of the country's largest employers, such as Siemens AG, give employees shares at special rates. A large number of firms have even more sophisticated systems. Some companies have not only made major efforts to make factories colourful and enjoyable places to work in and have distributed shares, but have also given employees a degree of freedom in setting their own working hours. The range of assorted types of fringe benefits given to employees is vast, with the prime motivation always being to ensure that employees do not move to other companies. One German construction company gives all its employees, including secretaries and telephonists, a new car on joining the company and contributes to the running costs of the vehicle given. A company in publishing in South Germany gives its senior staff the opportunity to purchase land with an interest-free loan at a quarter of the market price, close to the company's head offices and gives additional loans for the building of a house on the cheaply sold land.

A wide range of profit sharing schemes are now in operation and are becoming increasingly popular. Pampus KG, for example, a medium-sized company in the Ruhr, distributes almost all its profits to its employees on a graded scale, to ensure that related to income the lowest paid employees get the relatively highest amount of the share-out. The scheme is so constructed that employees have a direct large financial interest in remaining in Pampus's employ. Even more drastic schemes, involving total profit distribution among employees, with owners only getting a high fixed salary and a percentage of profits on the same basis as employees, have been started. The concept of profit distribution in this country is still in its infancy, but is spreading swiftly. All manner of different types of schemes are being used to ensure that employees remain loyal to their companies. As the labour market becomes increasingly tight, so it is to be expected that these types of fringe benefits and profit distribution systems will become more widespread. Such a development would naturally produce major changes in the basic organisation and structure of businesses in this country.

The next few years will almost certainly see major developments in the industrial relations and personnel management fields, that could radically change the industrial system in West Germany. The shortages of labour not only increase the power of the unions, the need to find methods of ensuring employee loyalty and produce vast additional costs arising from welfare matters concerned with immigrant workers, but also force managers to consider whether expansion here pays at all.

Wages are now rising at a brisk pace in this country and are likely to continue doing so. Many companies are being forced to consider stepping-up the building of new plants in areas where wage costs are lower and labour in plentiful supply. It is clearly more logical to take plant and machinery to places of high unemployment, rather than bring workers hundreds of miles to a strange country. The power and influence of owners of industry is increasingly becoming limited by the growing influence of the trade unions, which will in all probability shortly be given a further boost through new Mitbestimmung laws.

Managers are being forced through changing business circumstances and pressure from young people to change their methods. Germany is slowly becoming a country where outstanding managers will finally have a chance to change companies and industries more frequently, without fear of never being able to reach top managerial positions as a result. An indication in this direction was given with the appointment in late 1969 of one of the Ruhr's great steel managers, Herr Ernst-Wolff Mommsen, to a top job in the Government and his return back to industry three years later.* A further indication was the appointment of Juergen Krackow to AG Weser from a varied background of banking and business, but with no direct experience of shipbuilding. Gradually German companies are coming to respect the graduates of business schools, albeit foreign business schools, and trying to fit these graduates into the rigid promotion system.

The themes outlined in this chapter show important aspects of the major transformation of the industrial scene in this country. The problems in the industrial relations and personnel management spheres that face German managers are immense. Producing better management systems has already forced major board room upheavals in a number of companies in the last couple of years. Further major board room reshuffles in

* Herr Mommsen held many senior positions in the Ruhr, including a top job at Thyssen. In 1969, Herr Helmut Schmidt the Defence Minister appointed Herr Mommsen as State Secretary in his Ministry. When Herr Schmidt became Economics and Finance Minister in July 1972 he appointed Herr Mommsen as chief State Secretary in this Ministry. Herr Mommsen decided at the time of the November 1972 Federal elections to return to industry and became Vorstand chief of Krupp at the start of 1973 at the age of 62.

major companies are likely in the near future, to make way for younger men with more modern management ideas. Most of the largest German companies today are managed at the very top by men over 60 years of age.* These men won their spurs in the reconstruction era and to some extent even before the war; they are not experts, in many cases, at delegating responsibility, at treating trade unionists as board room partners or at casting aside the old formal system of personal relations among company executives. Coping with the changes and the shortages of labour will be challenging and unenviable tasks of ever greater magnitude in this decade.

The developments outlined in this chapter and in the second chapter of this book point clearly to a weakening of influence on companies by the major holders of company shares. The trends that are now clearly discernible, especially the acute shortages of labour, will in all probability force German companies to greatly increase their foreign investment spending. This could have a major impact on the German balance of payments and the economic health of this country. For while industry will promote an increasingly heavy capital outflow, foreign investors may increasingly reduce their purchases of German securities, while foreign companies increasingly become less enthusiastic to establish subsidiaries in this country. These developments will not simply result from the labour shortages and rising wage costs, but also from the fact that, through Mitbestimmung and a host of other matters, it will become increasingly clear that an erosion of the free enterprise system is taking place, in favour of greater socialisation of industry. This trend is supported by the Social Democratic Party Government and is one major factor why the leaders of industry in this country are so deeply opposed to Herr Brandt's administration.

* Very recently important changes have been made at the top of some large companies, producing much younger managing directors. Some of these changes are noted in the descriptions of companies in Appendix 2.

4 Marketing at Home and Abroad

Brilliant sales records have been achieved by West German companies over the last two decades, through the skilled marketing of high quality products at competitive prices. The competitiveness of German industry has recently been sharply eroded by currency factors and the swift rise in wage costs. The quality of the products offered for sale remains high, but selling these products is becoming increasingly more difficult. German managers are now being forced to devise radically new marketing strategies to cope with the situation.

Through the explosion in wage costs in recent years the industrial costs of production in this country are now higher than in most other industrial countries. Currency factors, however, have been the chief causes of the swift transition from a once intensely competitive industry, to an industry forced to struggle desperately to maintain high foreign sales. In the short period from 1970 to mid-1973 the Deutsche Mark increased in value by over 35 per cent in terms of the U.S. dollar, by close to 30 per cent in terms of the British pound and by more than 12 per cent in terms of the currencies of France, Belgium and the Netherlands. The extent of the increase is far greater if one goes back slightly earlier to consider the unilateral German revaluation in 1969 and the earlier French and British de-valuations.*

The ability of this country to maintain a rate of inflation of well below the average international level swiftly eroded the ill effects on the industry of this country of the 1961 Deutsche Mark revaluation. But the 1969 and 1971 revaluations will not be eroded easily. Germany will never again be allowed to

* These comments on rates are based on the comparison of 1970 parities with values quoted on the exchange markets on 22 June 1973. The increases and decreases reflect effective exchange-rate changes based on average spot rates.

return to her former position of having a greatly under-valued currency. However much she dislikes the fact, this country today is in the mainstream of international inflation levels and is likely to remain in this position. The increasing integration of the European Economic Community and the rising militancy of German trade unions are factors alone that are likely to prevent this country ever again becoming an island of price stability.

The possibility to again obtain an under-valued Deutsche Mark in terms of other European currencies is further precluded by the European Economic Community's exchange rate arrangements, which, through the operation of a narrow currency band system, force the EEC currencies to be held closely in line with each other. Further, new rules governing the adjustments process are likely to be contained in international monetary reforms, which may well force countries to revalue or devalue swiftly, should their international payments balances veer too greatly from equilibrium.

In addition to these currency considerations, the Germans must reckon with intensified international competition. The new round of negotiations within the General Agreement on Tariffs and Trade will probably result in the EEC becoming a less protectionist block. Further, the Japanese are now showing every indication of increasing their efforts to penetrate European markets. This is a direct result of the reduction of Japanese sales opportunities in the United States, following the sharp revaluation of the Japanese Yen at the end of 1971 and recent trade negotiations held between Washington and Tokyo. The 1973 currency changes have strengthened this trend.

The outlook for German sales is not altogether a black one, as new opportunities are coming to the fore. German companies now have better chances than ever before of selling in Eastern Europe, as a direct result of Herr Brandt's foreign policies since 1969. Bonn has concluded several new trade treaties with East European countries and the Russians, in particular, are showing increased determination to advance their industrial development through greater purchases of Western technical equipment and know-how. At the same time new sales opportunities are opening for West German companies with Red China. The leaders of the largest country of the world opened diplomatic relations with this country in 1972 and followed this move with the signing of a bilateral trade treaty and the sending to Germany of numerous high-powered trade missions.

The industrial development of much of the 'Third World' also provides new chances for the Germans, who in the past have largely neglected the under-developed nations. The Germans stand to make particularly good gains in parts of Africa and Latin America. The governments in these areas have recently expressed increasing interest in purchasing German products and some have left no doubt that they prefer to do business with this country than with the sometimes more politically suspect Americans. But achieving large sales in the developing countries and the communist countries depends on international competitiveness and the Germans are now finding it most difficult to come to terms with their weaker international position.

The prospect of possibly slower foreign sales development is a major worry for the Bonn Government and managers here. Few countries are so dependent on foreign sales as this one. Apart from Japan, no other major country can boast of such an export-intensive industry as West Germany. For example, the automobile industry here exports more than 60 per cent of its output, while the engineering industry exports half of its large production volume and the chemicals industry exports over 35 per cent of its production.

For an assortment of reasons the Germans have been forced over the last two decades to make greater efforts than, for example, the British, French or Americans, to sell their products abroad. German companies have in great measure not had the finance necessary to establish foreign-based production subsidiaries and have been almost totally dependent on home-based production to account for foreign sales. To reconstruct industry at a substantial pace and maintain a high rate of growth in the 1950s, it was essential to produce far more than the home market alone could consume. The early recognition of this made many German managers aware of the need to spend heavily on promoting their products abroad.

While such giant companies as Ford, General Motors, Unilever, Shell, British Petroleum, General Electric, Imperial Chemical Industries and DuPont were rapidly building up foreign-based production subsidiaries in the 1950s, the leading

German companies had to content themselves with seeking to establish, from scratch, extensive international sales and service networks. The pattern of German international sales and of the structure of German industry itself over the last two decades has largely been determined by the fact that on account of losing most of their foreign assets and capital reserves in the last war, companies here were financially too weak in the 1950s to invest heavily abroad and were forced to concentrate on high volume exporting to ensure rapid growth.

In almost all cases the foreign sales drives were developed with long-term aims in mind. Unlike some companies in Britain, France and the United States, the view was rarely to be heard here that exports were mainly to be promoted with vigour at times of declining home demand, or at such times when foreign devaluations or revaluations offered especially great opportunities for making large profits through foreign sales.* A large number of companies here in the 1950s were prepared to invest heavily in building up foreign sales operations and were willing to wait some time before export sales produced healthy profits.

Many companies made detailed market research surveys and carefully constructed efficient foreign sales organisations prior to making strong offensives in foreign markets. This has been an approach that has produced good results. There is nothing radical or especial about it and yet, in the early 1950s, there were few non-German firms preparing foreign sales campaigns in such detail and depth. The foreign-based sales networks have been well supported by special export divisions at company head offices in West Germany. The net result of the detailed preparations was often that the salesmen of a German product abroad could impress customers with his knowledge of their needs, assure punctual delivery and offer a competitively priced product, supported by an efficient after-sales service organisation.

To the utter dismay of the Germans the Japanese appear to have learnt a great deal from the Germans about the organisation of effective foreign sales campaigns. In a number of cases, companies here sold products abroad at a loss to build up a sizeable market share and a good reputation. In many cases such methods resulted eventually in high turnover and good

* See comments on British Leyland in Chapter 7.

profits. For many companies selling abroad was more important than selling in the home market. The immense thoroughness of the preparation of foreign sales drives has clearly been the most outstanding feature of German marketing in the last two decades. The Germans, at first, largely concentrated their efforts in those countries closest at hand and they devoted much of their efforts to continually looking for gaps in foreign markets and, if necessary, many manufacturers were prepared to tailor-make goods for specific foreign markets. The Germans spent heavily on ensuring that their products were always technically competitive with those of the best of foreign rivals.

The Germans have prepared foreign advertising campaigns with meticulous care and, unlike some American companies, they have generally made use of the leading national agencies in the countries they aimed to sell in, rather than use German companies to advertise on foreign sales campaigns. The skill of carefully choosing the best foreign advertising agencies has possibly been best demonstrated by Volkswagen in the United States. This company hired a top New York agency that prepared a campaign quite different to that used by VW in its domestic market. In West Germany the VW 'Beetle' was long promoted as a first choice car to all classes, especially to lower income groups. In the United States the 'Beetle' was strongly promoted as a second family car and aimed, with effect, at young executives, students and academics and people who would be tempted to buy on the basis that the product in question was distinctly different to the sort of automobiles being offered by Detroit.

The German marketing men abroad have had their task made easier by the willingness of German companies to spend lavishly, in various ways, on large foreign advertising campaigns. In addition, the salesmen have been greatly aided by the substantial weight given by German companies to design, research and development. To some extent the last war was a benefit in producing a wide variety of new technology that post-war industry could take advantage of. After the war many German companies started on a modern technological footing. This country has long had a high reputation for craftsmanship and high precision products, and great attention was given after the war to ensure that this reputation was maintained.

The great marketing drives did not all meet with success. Some managers simply cast profit considerations to the wind in their desire to rapidly boost foreign sales figures. The concentration on turnover alone, which still today can be detected among some top executives, produced serious problems for a number of sizeable German concerns. To some extent this was the chief trouble at Krupp. This company brilliantly achieved high volume sales in Eastern Europe, but many of the contracts were of a barter nature, leaving Krupp to try and sell products it had little knowledge of and, more seriously, many of the contracts involved generous credit terms. By 1967 Krupp found itself in the midst of a major liquidity crisis and was saved from bankruptcy only through a major rescue operation organised by the Federal Government and the large banks. The crisis resulted from Krupp losing all sight of profit levels and its credit position in its aim to continually boost sales.

A fact widely appreciated by all Germans involved in foreign selling is that it is much easier to lose a large share of a foreign market, than to build up such a large share. Having spent vast sums in penetrating foreign markets in the 1950s and 1960s, German companies were determined not to lose their strong foreign market positions as a result of the 1969 revaluation of the Deutsche Mark. Most German companies cut profit margins on foreign sales after the revaluation to ensure that they did not lose foreign market shares. In some cases companies showed themselves willing to take losses on foreign sales. Most exporters believed that, as in the past, the domestic inflation rate would continue well below foreign average inflation levels and that opportunities would swiftly come about to lift profit margins to former high levels. To some extent the gamble involved in taking losses on exports paid off. The Germans maintained an exceptionally high level of foreign sales in 1970, despite the revaluation. Company profits fell sharply in 1970, but at the start of 1971 expectations were high of substantial profit improvements. The decision by the Bonn Government to float the German currency in May 1971 effectively shattered hopes of a return to 1969 profit levels. If the actual volume of German foreign sales has not declined in the recent past, this is primarily a result of German companies contenting themselves with much narrower profit margins on exports. In addition, the widespread cyclical upswing in international economic activity in much of the Western World, which started to become visible in 1972, has stimulated foreign demand for a wide variety of German products.*

NEW SALES STRATEGIES

The basic preparations for large foreign sales offensives were largely completed in the 1950s, at least as far as Western Europe and North America are concerned. The 1960s saw tremendous increases in foreign sales volumes and one of the chief tasks for the present decade is ensuring that the large foreign market shares that have been established are not lost. In the early days the Germans had to struggle to get into foreign markets and had to be more competitive than their more established foreign rivals. In the present decade the chief challenge is to ensure that, at least, they are just as competitive as their foreign rivals. Thus, there is a distinct change of emphasis in the aims of German foreign marketing today and further changes are coming about through the increased domination of international trade by giant international and multinational concerns.

This has been fully grasped by German managers and is a major cause of the increasing pace of industrial concentration here. A considerable number of the leading industries here now are dominated by just a handful of companies. The only independent car manufacturers here now are Volkswagenwerk AG, Daimler-Benz AG, Porsche and Bayerische Motoren Werke AG (BMW). The other major car companies, Ford and Adam Opel are both wholly owned U.S. subsidiaries. Such companies as Borgward, Glas, Auto Union, Lloyd and NSU have either been forced into liquidation by the tough competition or been swallowed by one of the giant companies. The German chemical industry is dominated by a very small number of independent companies today. Total annual domestic turnover of the industry is around DM 55,000

---

* The full causes for the profit declines in 1970 and 1971 are outlined in the first three chapters of this book, while the following chapter gives some details on the extent of the profit falls. The currency factors had different effects on the foreign sales of different industries and these are discussed in Chapter 7 and in Appendix 1 and Appendix 2.

million, with most of this accounted for by Hoechst, Bayer, BASF and to a lesser extent, Veba and Henkel. No other independent chemical company here has an annual turnover in excess of DM 1,500 million, with large shareholdings in most medium-size chemical concerns held by one or other of the giants. With the exception of the mechanical engineering industry, giant companies dominate most of the leading industries here and their relative power increases as the concentration pace appears to accelerate.

But even some of the German giants appear small when compared to the leading American concerns. Siemens is a highly diversified electrical products manufacturer and while large in total, some of its sections are small by comparison with American companies. Because of their relative smallness compared to leading multinational companies, many of even the largest German companies are now being forced to consider mergers or close joint ventures with foreign companies. Agfa-Gevaert is one of the largest photographic equipment manufacturers in the world, yet just one-fifth the size of Eastman Kodak. Had the German Agfa not merged with the Belgian Gevaert, it seems likely that international competitive pressures would have either forced Agfa into another merger or out of business.

Siemens is the largest German owned manufacturer of computers, but International Business Machines has something like 70 per cent of the Continental European computer market and Siemens, despite its size, could not hope to continue producing competitive products on its own in face of IBM. To try and remain competitive Siemens concluded a detailed co-operation agreement in the computer sector in 1972 with Philips of Holland and Compagnie Internationale pour L'Informatique (CII) of France. Just as the Agfa merger with Gevaert has produced a radical change in Agfa's marketing approach, so the international agreement concluded by Siemens has changed the way in which this company sells its computers. Siemens no longer needs its own computer products sales force in France and the Netherlands and whereas Siemens before only offered a narrow range of computers for sale, it can now offer a more extensive programme, involving CII and Philips equipment.

German companies will increasingly be forced for market competitive reasons to participate in international mergers and joint ventures. These developments are bound to have a radical effect on company sales approaches. In a few cases German companies have sought to strengthen their sales opportunities by participating in illegal cartels. A number of major cartel agreements were uncovered by the Federal Cartel Office in 1972 and reflect the growing pressures on German companies that are involved in maintaining high foreign sales.*

DIFFERENT TYPES OF MARKETING APPROACHES

The comments made here so far tend to blur the strong differences that exist in marketing methods from one industry to another. These great differences can best be illustrated by a detailed look at two quite different types of industries. Good contrasting examples are the automobile and mechanical engineering industries, which differ greatly from each other in the types of products they sell, the types of people they sell to and in their basic industrial structures.

The mechanical engineering industry consists of about 5,500 companies, employing about 1·2 million people. The largest sector of the industry is concerned with machine tools output and accounts for about 10 per cent of the mechanical engineering industry's total sales. The industry as a whole can be divided up into more than thirty sections, with some, such as machine tools, exporting about 50 per cent of total output, while others, such as the sectors concerned with safes and treasury installations, exporting less than 6 per cent of total output.

The mechanical engineering industry is the largest manufacturing industry, in terms of labour, in this country, yet only five companies within it have sales of more than DM 1,000 million. These companies are Gutehoffnungshütte AG, which is highly diversified into many engineering sectors and which largely owns Maschinenfabrik August Nürnberg (MAN), which itself is a large engineering concern. The other major companies are Klöckner Humbold Deutz AG, Demag AG† and

---

* See Chapters 6 and 7 for more details on mergers and cartels.

† Mannesmann AG gained majority control of Demag in summer, 1973.

the largely British-owned Babcock & Wilcox AG and the American controlled ZF-Borg-Warner GmbH.*

The other truly large manufacturers of engineering products tend to be the steel companies, all of whom have rapidly diversified in recent years into a wide range of sophisticated mechanical engineering activities. However, by and large this is an industry of small and medium-sized companies and naturally the sales methods in the industry vary considerably, dependent upon the size of the companies. Many companies are simply too small to support full-time foreign sales organisations of their own and most companies are represented in foreign markets by import agents and free-lance salesmen, many of whom represent several German companies in different engineering sections at the same time. Surprisingly, many of the small engineering companies, which tend to be largely concentrated in Baden-Württemberg, Bavaria and the Ruhr, account for most of their sales from exports.

The machine tools sector with its 500 manufacturers includes some 200 companies active in other sectors of mechanical engineering as well. This sector has been one of the strong growth industries of post-war Germany and many of the companies are relatively small and highly specialised, privately owned concerns. To some extent the machine tool manufacturers are representative in their sales strategies of most small and medium-sized German manufacturers. One of the strengths in recent years of the machine tool makers has been their ability to spot swiftly the need for new types of machinery for newly developing industries. And these machine tool makers, partly because of their smallness, which allows some flexibility in products made, have been sufficiently adaptable to make very special types of machine tools at competitive prices. In many cases the reputations of these small companies have spread around the globe in an accidental fashion, without heavy product promotion being made. In most companies, budgets are so slim that promotion has been restricted

* Much of the statistical information concerning the mechanical engineering industry that is mentioned in this chapter is based on publications and material specially prepared for the author by the industry's national association – the VDMA – Verein Deutscher Maschinenbau-Anstalten e.V.

to participation in some trade fairs and advertisements in domestic and foreign trade journals.

The German machine tool makers have often scored well in international competition, because they have managed to package and design their products more attractively than their rivals. The British machine tool industry still tends, on the whole, to make its fine products look complex and dirty, while the Germans manage often to produce tools that are just as good as similar British products, but which externally look more advanced and more attractive. The simple fact is that German manufacturers have long paid immense attention to marketing requirements in designing their products, knowing full well that products with a streamlined and modern external appearance sell better than complicated-looking products. The developer of German machine tools has often an eye on the opportunity of increasing the sales of the products he designs by giving his product clear and sharp lines. It may well be that this approach results in some product sophistication being abandoned in favour of better external appearance, but if this is the case, the German industry does not appear to have suffered as a result.

The German machine tool makers have managed to maintain high sales development by adapting quickly to market needs, by packaging and designing their products attractively and by ensuring that they keep well up with the latest international technical improvements. The fact that many of the companies are small is in some respects an asset, for it allows them to do the small-volume highly-specialised type of work that would be uneconomic for large concerns.

The larger concerns have built up strong domestic and foreign sales organisations and have spent lavishly on all types of product promotion. Some of the major companies, notably GHH, have built up well-integrated machinery and mechanical engineering empires, that are in a position to offer a customer an almost complete programme of engineering installations for equipping a new plant. This ability, combined with a close relationship that exists between many mechanical engineering companies, has enabled companies in this industry to swiftly build consortia capable of fulfilling large and varied projects, and this has won many German companies a large number of huge orders. German engineering consortia are currently involved in major projects in several places, including areas of South-East Asia, South America and Eastern Europe.

The German mechanical engineering industry is the largest industry of its kind in Western Europe, but the competition within the industry is ferocious and many of the smaller companies are finding it particularly difficult to keep pace, in view of the wages explosion and the revaluations. Furthermore, over the years the bitter competition has forced many smaller companies into mergers or out of business and in the thirteen years to mid-1972 there were 113 mergers involving medium and large sized companies in this industry. The economic downturn in the first three years of this decade, involving a sharp decline in demand for capital goods, resulted in a large number of company closures in this industry. The trend towards automation and mass production, coupled with the increasing shortage of labour, is adding to the difficulties of many machine tool makers and makes the prospect in the near future of many more mergers, most likely. However, the ability to adapt quickly, the need for specialised tool makers, the flexibility that allows the production of tailor-made goods and shrewd marketing techniques are likely to ensure that a large number of small companies in this industry survive.

The following table gives an indication of the size of the industry in terms of sales and the importance of exports. The figures are from the VDMA. Probably the most interesting aspect of the figures is the way in which exports have increased from less than one-third of total sales in 1956, to about half of total sales today. The volume of imports to Germany has risen rapidly and in percentage terms, at a faster pace than the export growth. Yet the real surplus in Germany's favour of machinery exports over imports, tends to increase in size from year to year.

TABLE 4.1

Year	(Sales in million Deutsche Marks) Total Sales	Exports	Imports
1956	16,945	5,867	883
1960	24,405	9,285	2,127
1964	33,920	14,039	3,433
1968	40,036	21,136	5,085
1971	61,170	29,062	9,421

From the following figures it can be seen that Western Europe and the United States play a particularly important role in the foreign sales of this industry and in view of the currency realignments and the temporary 1971 U.S. import surcharge, it can be understood why this industry was hit particularly hard. The following figures show the main countries where German machinery industry products are sold and the main countries that sell machinery products to West Germany:

TABLE 4.2

Country	1971 Exports from Germany in mln DMs	1971 Imports to Germany in mln DMs
France	4,023	1,857
Italy	2,477	1,258
Netherlands	2,095	748
United States	2,002	1,658
Belgium–Luxemburg	1,619	439
Switzerland	1,501	813
Britain	1,489	886

The German automobile industry consists of just a handful of companies, in contrast to the multitude of assorted types of companies in the mechanical engineering industry. The marketing styles of these two major German industries are quite different because of this and, because by the nature of the products made, the mechanical engineering industry sells to other industries, while the car industry sells directly to the general public. A brief look at the different marketing approaches of the main German car manufacturers shows that great differences in styles exist between the various companies and tends to illustrate, to some extent, the ingenuity of German salesmen and some of the present difficulties.

Two of the major car manufacturers are foreign-owned, while the remainder are completely under German ownership. Fordwerke AG of Cologne is the largest foreign subsidiary of Ford of America and has manufacturing plants directly under its own control in the Ruhr, the Saar and at Genk in Belgium.

Adam Opel AG is the rapidly expanding General Motors subsidiary, which is GM's chief European company and has plants in Rüsselsheim near Frankfurt, in Bochum and Kaiserslauten, as well as assembly plants in Denmark, Belgium and Switzerland. Both these American subsidiaries are well established in the German market and as export orientated as their chief German rivals.

Ford of America's network of production and assembly plants across Europe has in recent years been closely tied together into a well integrated pan-European organisation and this development has greatly altered the marketing strategy of Fordwerke in Cologne. This German company largely produces the same range of products as its British sister company and these two subsidiaries rarely rival each other in third markets. The European General Motors organisation is not as tightly integrated as the Ford network. A clear trend towards integration and greater overall supervision of General Motors activities in Europe, however, is now visible. Opel does seek to sell its cars in Britain and has enjoyed considerable success in this market, while Opel's British sister company, Vauxhall, has generally steered clear of the intensely competitive German market. An indication of the closer integration of the GM European units is the recent decision by Opel to market British-made Bedford commercial vehicles through the Opel sales organisation in Europe. The Bedford vehicles are being considerably modified to come into line with Continental laws and tastes.

The great success enjoyed by both Opel and Ford in the West German market itself is due largely to these companies being even more alert than some of their German rivals to changes in tastes and requirements among the German car-buying public. Both Ford and Opel have had sufficient financial backing to have permitted them to take losses and narrow profit margins for a considerable period. They have offered Germans a real alternative to the small and medium-sized cars produced by Volkswagenwerk, at highly competitive prices. The standard of engineering at these companies was for long superior to that of VW, which for many years, until the very recent past, relied heavily on old concepts. These two American subsidiaries recognised earlier than some of their German rivals that the spreading of affluence would lead to a considerable expansion of the market for medium-sized cars and for sporty versions of small cars. The main efforts of Ford and Opel have been in these car categories and have met with increasing success.

Vast expense has been involved in the developing of medium-priced sports-saloon cars, such as the Ford Capri and the Opel Manta and on modern medium-sized saloon cars, such as the Ford Taunus series and the Opel Rekord series. These models, because of their modern design, technical strengths and modest pricing, have won rich acclaim in West Germany and in other European markets. The slowness of VW to recognise that medium-sized cars were swiftly becoming the major sector of the German car market and the launching of new models by Opel, resulted in 1972, in Opel out-selling VW in this country for most of the year. This was the first time since the start of VW after the war, that VW had failed to maintain its market lead in this country.

The whole emphasis of the Opel and Ford strategy in West Germany has been to offer an alternative to the more conservative German cars and to continually produce new models, that would appeal in increasing measure to those Germans, who after years of always driving a VW 'Beetle', wanted something else. The Ford and Opel campaigns have probably involved even greater advertising spending than the campaigns of their chief German rivals. These companies have been significantly aided in foreign sales by the long-established and strong Ford and GM sales and service organisations around the world. These organisations are far older, and in many respects financially stronger, than the foreign organisations that German manufacturers have been able to build up.

Few car companies in the world have such good export records as have the three main German-owned car makers, VW, Daimler-Benz and Bayerische Motoren Werke (BMW). The success of these companies in international markets has largely been the result of painstaking efforts to establish excellent sales and service networks, which in many cases have been of superior quality to the organisations built by foreign rivals. While the British Leyland Motor Corporation has changed its mind frequently on how to approach the Continental market and has still not managed to obtain a significant market share or shatter an old image of unreliable servicing in many of Europe's largest markets, the Germans have built brilliantly managed and powerful sales and service organisations in Britain and in most other West European countries. The Germans have not sought to attack all markets at the same time, but have carefully built up one market after another. Such an approach has produced rich rewards. The German car makers started their foreign sales drives in the richer neighbouring countries – France, Belgium, Holland, Austria and Switzerland. On the whole, other markets were only given special attention, once large market shares in these neighbouring markets had been secured.

In these neighbouring markets, which in the main are within the European Economic Community, the Germans largely used the same sales approach that they used in their home market. Highly detailed work was put in to establish good dealership networks, adequate and reliable service organisations and well-supplied spare parts depots. These efforts were supported by heavy advertising, which in the case of VW, Daimler-Benz and BMW, largely stressed the technical excellence of the products being offered and the reliable service that was available. Still today, when these companies are well established in most European markets, the themes of advertising are similar to those of several years ago. Daimler-Benz still seeks to stress the engineering skills that go into a Mercedes car and aim to convince the public that a Mercedes is the last word in automobile technology and sedate luxury. BMW promotes its products by stressing the quality of BMW engineering and the swift acceleration and performance of BMW cars. VW has mainly emphasised the price-worthiness of its products, their reliability, and VW is probably the only car maker in the world that benefits by stressing the advantages of an old design, which through sheer longevity has proved its merit.

In the recent past the Germans have paid increasing attention to the Italian market, seeking to benefit from the rising affluence in Italy and exploiting the existence of a vast number of temporary Italian immigrant workers in Germany, to aid the promotion and familiarisation of German products in Italy itself. Labour problems in Italian car factories have been a significant help to the Germans. Further, the Germans have sought to provide the Italian public with real alternatives in each class to the Fiat, Alfa and Lancia. The strong recent

German push into the Italian car market has forced Italian manufacturers to produce more varied ranges and fresher models. The familiarity of German cars in Italy was also aided by the vast number of Germans going on vacation each year to Italian resorts. These German tourists alone provided a need for the establishment of German car service centres in Italy and provided a basis for strong promotion drives in the Italian market. This is a market where the Germans are likely to considerably increase their penetration in coming years.

In Britain, the Germans scored by recognising that the quality of many British products left much to be desired. The quality and reliability of their products have been a main feature of the German campaign to get a strong foothold in the British market. The entry of Britain into the European Economic Community was a strong spur to the Germans to invest heavily in Britain in establishing sales and service organisations, to be in a position to capture a large part of the British market as soon as the tariff walls between Britain and the Common Market fell. German manufacturers have felt certain since the mid-1960s that British entry into the EEC was only a question of time and the Germans have greatly increased their efforts in Britain since that time.

The VW campaign in Britain was that well tried in other markets, stressing cheapness and reliability. BMW and Daimler-Benz took another approach. Mercedes cars have been sold in Britain as purely top quality products and at one time they were even suggested as a real alternative to Rolls Royce cars. The launching of the hideous Mercedes 600 was partly involved in this campaign to strengthen the image of the company, as the makers of the finest cars in the world. While in many markets Mercedes has stressed that it is worth waiting for their products and that demand is so great that delivery dates can only be set many months after orders have been made, in Britain an opposite approach was made. Recognising the continual delivery delays that Jaguar has, Mercedes has sought to keep dealers in Britain well supplied, so that purchasers can almost take immediate delivery of a Mercedes on signing a purchasing agreement. Mercedes has in many respects appealed in Britain to snobs and priced itself accordingly. Many of the smaller Mercedes cars are not promoted in Britain, and Mercedes has met with considerable success in the British market. BMW has taken more pains in Britain to emphasise the sporting quality of its products and its large saloon cars are not promoted as strongly as in some markets. The top BMW sports cars have been fiercely marketed by the company in Britain, at high prices. Few objective Germans would think of comparing a BMW with a Ferrari or Aston Martin, but in Britain BMW has chosen such comparisons and met with success in its campaigns.

The United States has been another major market where the German car industry has registered notable successes. The Mercedes image is similar in the U.S. to that promoted by Daimler-Benz in Britain. The appeal is greatly to the rich with a desire for something different. Many Americans would certainly be deeply shocked to learn that most German taxis are Mercedes cars and that there are a number of Mercedes models that retail in Germany at lower prices than some European Ford models. BMW, which has been so successful since almost inventing the concept of medium-priced saloon cars with sports car performance, has been doing well in the United States market with a varied range of models. Porsche has also been registering good sales figures in the United States, partly because its sales organisation in the United States is tied together with the extensive VW of America organisation.

The Volkswagen campaign in the United States, which has been discussed earlier in this chapter, has been quite different to the approach the company has taken in almost all other markets. But so brilliant have VW sales in the United States been that VW's drive into the American market probably can count among the top ranks of foreign car-selling stories that have ever been written. The success in the United States was largely due to firm leadership and the adoption of American management and selling methods by Carl Hahn, who became head of Volkswagen of American in the late 1950s. Hahn's achievement was such that at the age of 36, in 1964, he was recalled to VW head offices in Wolfsburg and made the company's Vorstand member in charge of sales. Hahn's selling methods have only been questioned recently as the company's domestic sales have started to fall. The new VW Vorstand chief Herr Rudolf Leiding, has different management and mode, ideas to Hahn and the result was that after several arguments Hahn, one of the most brilliant car salesmen around, was fired from VW in late November 1972.*

The following table shows the development of West German car sales and exports in the main foreign markets. The figures show clearly how strong sales growth has recently been in Britain and Italy. The figures also show clearly that German car salesmen have until now largely neglected areas outside Western Europe and North America. South America is somewhat of an exception with VW having established a vast production subsidiary in Brazil, with current annual output of about 250,000 units a year. Daimler-Benz also has an important production facility in Brazil. At the moment these are the only

TABLE 4.3

| Importing country | *Years with figures relating to unit sales* | | | |
	1962	*1964*	*1968*	*1971*
France	57,199	105,332	115,466	167,948
Belgium–Luxembourg	82,295	110,826	128,310	132,084
Netherlands	63,925	109,468	121,456	122,700
Italy	67,877	73,964	108,141	210,131
Britain	22,254	37,768	34,960	104,109
All Europe†	647,182	875,136	900,417	1,153,778
Africa	61,856	86,788	87,065	79,117
Asia	35,556	53,963	65,440	63,520
United States	258,431	369,489	743,951	872,215
North and South Americas	338,970	456,524	846,702	967,153
Rest of the World	7,929	14,393	19,405	28,513
Total German exports	1,101,822	1,498,964	1,919,754	2,293,005
Exports as a percentage of total German car output and sales	48·6%	51·5%	61·8%	57·6%

* Carl Hahn was appointed managing director of West Germany's largest tyre manufacturer, Continental Gummi-werke AG, in spring, 1973.
† Includes both east and west Europe.

major foreign-based production facilities owned by German car makers. With the exception of a number of foreign-based assembly plants, all non-German car sales by German car makers result from exports from German plants.

The table opposite is based on statistics compiled by the West German Automobile Federation (VDA).

The figures show clearly the dynamic pace of export sales over the last decade. That the percentage of total cars exported of all German cars sold in 1971 declined from more than 60 per cent, was partly due to the Deutsche Mark revaluations and the imposition in August 1971 of a 10 per cent import surcharge by the United States. Volkswagen was forced to introduce short-time and close some plants for short periods in early 1972 as a result of a swift decline in sales to the United States. While the surcharge was a special factor, there is good reason to believe that the high growth rates in the United States of German car sales, which was seen in the last decade, will not be maintained. The dollar devaluation and Deutsche Mark revaluation, coupled with such factors as the growing penetration of the U.S. market by the Japanese, the introduction by Detroit of small cars and the declining novelty in the United States of the 'Beetle' are all important factors behind this prediction. Mercedes and BMW are likely to continue enjoying success in the United States, but VW has recognised that an entirely new approach to the U.S. market is needed.

But for West Germany's largest company the problems in the U.S. market are only the tip of the iceberg. VW has been forced to recognise that its model and marketing strategy is in many respects out-dated. The problems facing VW are enormous. That this is widely realised at the company and is partly reflected by the sacking of Kurt Lotz, Werner Holste and Carl Hahn from the VW Vorstand within the 18 months to the end of 1972. VW needs a new image and a new approach and has started out in a new direction under the new management of Rudolf Leiding. The key to VW's future success lies largely with the development of new models and with the adoption of sales strategies largely similar to those of Ford and Opel. The company is now striving to build a wide range of models, from a car smaller than the 'Beetle' to the luxury top class of the market. It seems likely that in the next few years VW will offer a range of small cars, including the 'Beetle'; a series of medium-sized cars, depending largely on the Audi models, and the NSU Ro80 Wankel car at the top end of the range. The company is striving to ensure that its image of producing reliable products, supported by cheap and efficient service networks is maintained. At the same time it is trying to cultivate a new modern image to show that its engineering is as advanced as that of any other car producer.

The investments needed to bring about these changes will be vast. VW, however, is confident of success in maintaining high sales in all European and North American markets. At the same time the company by no means considers the famed 'Beetle' as obsolete. This car is still being produced at a rate of more than 5,000 units a day. It is likely that VW will make a far greater effort in the future to get into the new markets of the developing countries and that the 'Beetle' will play a key role here. At the same time the company realises that many developing countries are unwilling to allow a high volume of imports and, in consequence, VW is preparing to expand its production in Brazil, its assembly facilities in Mexico and South-East Asia and open new assembly plants in Africa.

The first phase of VW's build-up as a leading international car maker has been completed. The company now has a formidable market share in many of the markets of the richest countries of the world. The next step is to penetrate all markets and this will involve building more foreign plants and a wider range of more modern models. BMW and Daimler-Benz are not in the same boat as VW in this context. Both these companies have continually produced exciting new models and for them the main interest is to continue expanding sales and market shares in Western Europe and the United States and continuing in large measure to neglect the Third World.

BMW is slowly seeking a fuller integration of its European sales network. It now considers the European Economic Community area as a single large domestic market and hopes in coming years to do away with import agents in Europe and with wholesalers, and to supply all dealers in the EEC directly from Munich. This is an adventurous path that many other car makers will watch with interest. The merit of the plan is that it provides higher profit margins for retailers and for the company, by cutting out middlemen. It also will involve the devising of advertising and promotion campaigns that can be launched throughout the EEC at the same time.

Unlike VW, both BMW and Daimler-Benz know that demand for their products is likely to increase as affluence spreads. Both these companies are active in sections of the car market where buyers are not nearly as price conscious as they are in the VW class. As a result, BMW and Mercedes have had it easier than VW in terms of increasing prices to offset the wages escalation and revaluations of the recent past. By and large, Mercedes and BMW will stick to the promotion formulas that in the past have brought rich rewards, while VW is being forced to adopt a totally new style of operations.

MARKETING PROBLEMS IN OTHER SECTORS

The basic changes in Germany's competitive position in the recent past are forcing other industries than just the mechanical engineering and automobile industries, to devise new marketing strategies. Increasingly, German companies are stressing the qualities of their products, rather than the prices, in the hope that customers may be willing to accept German goods at slightly higher cost than similar goods made in other countries, on the basis that German goods are of superior quality. Most industries are increasing their efforts to exploit new markets and to penetrate the developing countries, which in the past have largely been neglected, as full attention has been concentrated on Western Europe and North America.

Currency and cost factors have forced major changes in many companies other than just VW. For example, Bayer AG has felt forced to turn its marketing strategy for synthetic fibres on to a totally new path. Bayer lost heavily on its vast synthetic fibres output in 1971, due to wages and revaluation factors and to general excess world supply of fibres. Bayer has spent fortunes, like its chief international rivals, in promoting a range of special fibre products, with each product having a distinct brand name. As profits fell swiftly, Bayer concluded that it could no longer continue the individual promotion of dozens of separate types of fibre products. To achieve major savings in advertising expenditure, Bayer decided in late 1972 to abandon its product names, except for the specially successful 'Dralon'. The company started to promote all its fibres under the single brand name of 'Bayer Fibres'.

Through casting aside the individual promotion of special fibres, Bayer could in 1972 cut its synthetic fibre advertising budget to 40 per cent of the level of spending set in 1969. The risk of abandoning product names that had taken years to promote, was forced by the narrower profit margins that Bayer had to come to terms with. Bayer was convinced that as new special fibres were invented, so the advertising budget in the fibres sector would become so widespread that the individual product campaigns would become ineffective and the total advertising budget would reach vast dimensions. This radically new approach, which may well be followed by other fibre manufacturers, was the result of Bayer's weakened international position. Many other industries have been forced to find other means to cut their overhead costs to compensate for the rapid decline in the international competitiveness of their products.

The German shipbuilding industry was almost rendered a cripple as a result of the wages explosion and revaluations that produced a situation where its products were too highly priced. The owners of the shipbuilding companies begged the Bonn Government for aid to bolster their international competitiveness. The high rates of interest that prevailed here in 1970 and 1971 made it most expensive for domestic shipping companies to borrow in Germany. The imposition of exchange controls and cheaper foreign interest rates, made it more attractive for German shipping companies in 1972 to borrow abroad and place orders abroad. These interest-rate factors, coupled with the more general economic considerations, resulted in German shipbuilders receiving almost no new orders in the first nine months of 1972.

Two of the main shareholders in the country's largest shipbuilding company, Howaldtswerke-Deutsche Werft, were keen to sell, believing that the shipbuilding industry here could never return to a position of profitable and effective international competitiveness. These shareholders, AEG-Telefunken and Gutehoffnungshütte, found great difficulty in finding a buyer for their HDW shares. An agreement was finally reached through the intervention of public authorities and control of

HDW in 1972 moved 25 per cent into the hands of the State of Schleswig-Holstein and 75 per cent into the ownership of the wholly nationalised Salzgitter AG steel company. In addition, the Federal Government gave approval for HDW to start negotiations with its chief rival, Blohm und Voss, which is largely owned by Thyssen, to find means of co-operating, in order to bring about a wide-ranging rationalisation of the shipbuilding industry. Special Government subsidies were given in 1972 to the shipbuilding industry and to shipping companies. As far as marketing is concerned, most of the efforts of the shipbuilders turned from going out to win orders, to strengthening a lobby in Brussels and in Bonn for greater subsidies and greater protection against the Japanese industry. Blohm und Voss and HDW concluded a co-operation agreement, which will lead to some reduction in the size of the shipbuilding industry, but will probably improve its efficiency. In other industries, the weakened competitive position led to mergers and co-operation pacts and to strong lobbying in Bonn for special subsidies. Some companies resorted to the establishment of cartels within Germany to protect the home market from increasingly competitive foreign rivals. This latter move strengthened pressure in Bonn from some quarters for new and tougher cartel laws.

The development of the German camera industry is yet another example of changes that have been produced through the weakening of this country's competitive position. The Japanese, in particular, and the East Germans, have gained a strong foothold in the German camera market and in the international markets that were once dominated by German products. While the makers of lower priced cameras, such as Agfa, have found ways to survive and have in large measure not been troubled by Japanese competition, the German manufacturers of more expensive amateur photographic equipment have experienced a major crisis. For many years many people were prepared to pay more for German, than for Japanese, quality amateur photographic equipment, due largely to the brilliant international reputations of such names as Rollei, Voigtländer and Zeiss.

But in many respects it was a losing battle for the Germans, for the Japanese increasingly produced excellent products. The

Deutsche Mark revaluation of 1969 was the last straw for the high quality German camera makers. The price difference between German and Japanese equipment became simply too large. Zeiss notched up high losses of its own, while Voigtländer, which Zeiss had tried to rescue shortly before, continued to amass vast deficits. Rollei had the foresight to recognise the trend and set about establishing manufacturing facilities in Singapore. Today Rollei only has research and sophisticated professional equipment manufacturing facilities left in West Germany, while its amateur products are fully made with the use of cheap labour in Singapore.

Zeiss has almost totally given up the manufacture of cameras. The company managed in 1972 to get special State loans and is concentrating on special optical and professional photographic lenses. Zeiss has also concluded a licensing agreement with Rollei, covering the output of lenses and shutters in Singapore. Voigtländer was only saved from being completely closed, by local government aid, supported by aid from Rollei and the trade union owned Bank für Gemeinwirtschaft. The Voigtländer plant is being radically reduced in size and will be mainly used to make products for Rollei and it seems most unlikely that cameras bearing the famous Voigtländer brand name will ever be made again.

The currency and costs upheaval at the start of the 1970s has clearly forced some companies to change their approach to manufacturing and marketing as the above examples have shown. Some companies are riding out the storm, confident that happier times will again appear and spending, at the same time, great efforts in seeking soft loans and subsidies from public authorities. Some companies are moving into more expensive product sectors and into the manufacture of more sophisticated and specialised products. This latter development is as much to do with the recent currency and costs factors, as with the increasing Japanese penetration of the German market and markets where the Germans were once strong. For example, almost all German electrical companies have given up manufacturing small radios because of Japanese competition, and some companies have been forced to radically cut output of black and white televisions, because of the rapid domination of this market by the Japanese.

THE DOMESTIC MARKET

All the factors outlined so far in this chapter are having a profound effect on the domestic market. Foreign companies are swiftly seeking to take full advantage of their stronger competitive position vis-à-vis the Germans, by penetrating the German market. The growth of imports to West Germany is now faster than the expansion of exports and this trend is likely to continue. It will still, however, be some time before Germany finds that she has a balance of trade deficit. If the pace of import growth has recently been sluggish, then this is largely due to the sharp economic downturn in 1970, 1971 and much of 1972, which forced German companies to severely cut their purchases of capital goods.

After the 1969 and 1971 revaluations, many foreign companies took immediate advantage of the currency changes to increase profit margins by maintaining prices. This resulted for short periods in higher earnings in the German market, but did not result in foreign companies increasing their market shares here. However, a good number of foreign companies used the revaluations as an opportunity to gain a strong share of the rich German market and in consequence, boosted sales considerably by not increasing profit margins. This policy resulted in notable successes in certain sectors, ranging from the sale of automobiles and ships to steel and coal. It is significant, in fact, that while sharp foreign price increases were a main cause of high German inflation in 1971, foreign prices were to some extent a break on inflation in mid-1972. Between the start of 1972 (thus immediately after the international currency realignment) and August 1972, there was barely any increase whatever in the average level of prices of imported products that entered West Germany. The result was a sharp rise in the volume of imports.

There are still few industrial sectors where Germany imports anything like the amount it exports. To some extent this is due to many foreign companies having large subsidiaries based in Germany and thereby supplying the German market from within, rather than through exporting from outside the country. DuPont, Monsanto, Imperial Chemical Industries all have plants of substantial size in West Germany and this helps to account for the fact that total annual German chemical imports are little more than half the volume of total German chemical exports. IBM has vast operations in Germany, from which it not only satisfies the German domestic market, but also a number of important foreign markets. The same applies in other product sectors to such companies as Unilever, Ford, General Motors, Borg Warner, International Telephone and Telegraph and a host of other international giants with major German subsidiaries.

In most product sectors competition within the German market is exceptionally tough. British and Japanese car manufacturers have long, for example, concentrated their export energies on other markets than West Germany, because of the bitterness of the domestic German automobile market. Similar policies resulting from tough market conditions here have been adopted by foreign manufacturers of electrical, chemical, engineering and steel products. The first chapter of this book

TABLE 4.4

The Overall Trade Situation

	1969	1970	1971	1972
German Exports (in Mln DMs)	113·6	125·3	136·0	149·0
German Imports (in Mln DMs)	98·0	109·6	120·1	128·8

TABLE 4.5

Percentage Share of Product Categories in German Trade

	Exports				Imports			
	1969	1970	1971	1972	1969	1970	1971	1972
Food industry	3·2	3·5	3·7	4·0	19·7	19·1	19·0	19·4
Trade and industry of which:	96·2	95·9	95·7	95·4	79·1	79·6	79·6	79·4
Raw materials	2·7	2·5	2·4	2·3	14·8	13·5	13·2	12·3
Semi-finished goods	7·8	7·6	7·7	7·0	17·1	16·1	13·6	12·8
Finished goods of which:	85·7	85·8	85·6	86·1	47·2	50·0	52·8	54·3
Primary goods	18·6	18·4	17·6	17·4	16·1	15·5	15·6	16·1
Fully finished	67·1	67·4	68·0	68·8	31·1	34·5	37·2	38·2

detailed the main countries with which Germany conducts trade and the tables opposite, based on official Government statistics, give a general break-down of trade on a product basis. The figures show clearly how imports in the recent past have expanded at a slightly faster pace than exports. Details of imports and exports of main industrial sectors are given in Appendix 1.

Retailing in West Germany has proved to be too competitive for a number of foreign companies that have sought to enter the market and it remains largely in the hands of German companies alone. The most notable exception is the Dutch Brenninkmeyer group, whose C & A stores across the Federal Republic account for between 15 per cent and 20 per cent of all textile retail sales in this country. British American Tobacco has recently become another notable exception, having acquired 25 per cent of the Horten department stores group, in a deal with the founder of the group, Helmut Horten, at the end of 1971. By and large foreign companies have failed to enter the retail business, with such companies as Sears Roebuck having concluded, after a deep study, that the German market was too tight to produce reasonable profits.

The large department store and chain store groups play an exceptionally important role in retailing in West Germany. The mail order business has enjoyed more success here, measured on its share of the total retail market business, than mail order business in any other country has achieved. The major department store and mail order groups have today entered almost every section of retailing, from food, household appliances, furniture and all manner of clothing, to insurance, travel and, in some instances, petrol and car servicing.

The retailing trade is becoming increasingly competitive and a substantial concentration process is taking place. Between 1962 and the end of 1971 a total of 90,000 retail companies closed.* More than 50 per cent of the closures were in the food business. At the end of 1971 there were 382,500 retailing companies in this country, employing about 2·3 million people and recording a combined total annual turnover of DM 205,000 million. Sales

* Figures outlined in the context of retailing here are largely based on a statistical survey made by the Commerzbank AG and published in November 1972.

have almost doubled in the last decade and the increase in 1971
alone was over 10 per cent.

Retailing is a business sector largely dominated by large
concerns. In 1962 more than 84 per cent of all retail companies
had annual sales of less than DM 250,000 and they accounted
between them for 31·5 per cent of all German retail sales. By
1970, a considerable change had taken place, with the number
of retail companies with sales of less than DM 250,000 being
modestly reduced to 71·2 per cent, but with these small companies now accounting between them for just 16·4 per cent of all
retail turnover. The development is all the more striking when
one looks at the major companies. In 1962 just 0·1 per cent of all
retail companies had annual sales in excess of DM 100 million
and this increased to 0·2 per cent by 1970. In 1962, this small
number of giant retail companies, accounted for 14·8 per cent
of all retail sales, but their share increased to 22·3 per cent by the
end of the last decade.

The increasingly tough competition produced by the rapidly
expanding large retail groups is forcing a greater number of
closures of retail companies than openings. The country's retail
business association, the Hauptgemeinschaft des Deutschen Einzelhandels, estimates that in coming years about 4·5 per cent
of all existing retail companies will close each year, while the
number of new companies opening in retailing each year will
equal about 2 per cent of all existing retail companies. Germany
is to a large extent not a country of specialist retail chain stores.
A number of food, clothing and shoe companies have specialised stores in most towns but, by and large, there are few large
chain store groups that specialise in a narrow range of products.
Instead, the department store groups tend to dominate the
scene. Such companies as Kaufhof, Karstadt, Horten, Hertie
and Neckermann have large stores selling vast ranges of assorted
products, from food to furniture and stationery to cosmetics, in
most towns and cities. The exceptions are such companies as the
Tengelmann food company, Salamander shoe company, Photo-
Quelle which has photographic equipment retailing outlets
across the country and is the largest company of its kind in
Europe, Wienerwald restaurants, Möbel Mann and Möbel
Hess in furniture, and C & A and a few similarly large rivals in
clothing.

The techniques of sales are also increasingly sophisticated and here the German retailers are in many respects ahead of other Europeans. About 80 per cent of all West German food shops use self-service systems, compared to about 65 per cent in the Netherlands, 50 per cent in Belgium, 30 per cent in France and barely 5 per cent in Italy. The large stores and the shops belonging to the chain groups tend to be modern and spacious. The mail order companies use sophisticated packaging and sorting methods and spend lavishly on promotion. The mail order catalogues sent out by the large groups, such as Quelle and Neckermann, twice yearly, cost about eight marks each copy to produce and post.

The retail companies do most of their advertising through the newspapers. Bonn governments have largely opposed advertising on television and as a result, short special advertising programmes lasting just a few minutes per day are transmitted on the television here. Other promotion methods include cinema advertising and door-to-door circulation of well-produced brochures of all types. Out of town shopping centres are slowly growing up across Germany. This development is most gradual and experiences have differed widely, with some of these centres proving to be highly successful, while others have been costly failures.

Wholesaling in Germany is largely similar to that seen in other countries. Most manufacturers use wholesalers, whose organisations tend to be largely regionally based. The cash-and-carry system is widespread and highly successful, but there are few truly large companies in this sector of business. For the purchasing directors of large retail groups, for the salesmen of manufacturing companies and for wholesalers, the trade fair has a special significance in this country.

TRADE FAIRS AND GENERAL CONCLUSION

Few countries can boast of such vast and numerous trade fairs as this one. The significance of the trade fair in the marketing strategies of German salesmen is probably greater than in the sales strategies of foreign salesmen. But the big German industrial trade fairs have an importance that goes beyond selling alone. The trade fairs are the occasion for the presentation of this country's industrial might, in a manner that can only impress the foreign businessman and that can only boost the confidence of the German in his opinion of his country's industrial strength. The giant pavilions on the fair grounds of all of Germany's largest cities are, for short periods, the meeting places of businessmen from all over the world and of laymen, who understand little about the machinery and assorted products set out on glittering stands before them, but who spend hours examining the assorted wares of hundreds of international companies.

Ministers from Bonn are always on hand to open the most important trade fairs and to use the opportunity of addressing leading businessmen to praise the skills of German industry. The foreign businessman, who knows little about this country's economic problems, but who visits the trade fairs here, must go home convinced that Germany continues to enjoy an 'Economic Miracle'. The hundreds of thousands of ordinary Germans, who just visit the fairs out of curiosity, must take away with them impressions that can only convince them that the prosperity of their country and the technological advance of this country's industry, is steaming ahead. In some countries only the large car and boat shows really attract the general public in large numbers. In Germany, the general public shows a fervent interest in all the large list of fairs, even the ones specialising in the most technical of products.

The range of annual trade fairs here is great. The most important include the huge annual Hanover Fair, which attracts more than 500,000 visitors in the ten days that it is on and which is really a large number of trade fairs rolled into one, with such diverse industries as chemicals, electricals, machinery and consumer goods all having their own special exhibition halls. In Hanover, room is even available to allow such giant companies as Thyssen, Krupp, Mannesmann, Salzgitter and a number of others to have their own large pavilions. The spring and autumn consumer goods fairs in Frankfurt-am-Main are probably the largest fairs of their kind held annually in the world. Internationally large fairs dealing with toys, food, home furnishings, books, optics, sports goods, men's wear, women's textiles, children's clothes, television and kitchens are held each year, as well as dozens of others. In their own right each of these fairs is of major international importance. Publishers, literary agents and writers from all over the world meet annually at the Frankfurt Book Fair, just as people involved in the toy business, from around the globe, go to the Nürnberg Toy Fair each year.

The managers of the trade fairs started early in seeking to make their fairs of major international significance. The Hanover Fair was started in 1947 and has become the largest investment goods fair each year in Europe, attracting currently more than 5,500 exhibitors from more than 40 countries. The fair is staged on 460,000 square metres of exhibition ground. In an average year there may be more than 60 important trade fairs in Germany, with Hanover, Frankfurt, Cologne, Düsseldorf, Hamburg, Munich and West Berlin being the main fair centres.

Apart from boosting confidence in this country's industrial strength among the general public that visits the fairs, it is difficult today to gauge clearly just what purpose these fairs really serve. Ostensibly, fairs should provide facilities for customers to make deals with manufacturers. This was the prime purpose of fairs after the last war, but this function has now become relatively unimportant. Only the public relations chiefs of some companies have the audacity to suggest that multi-million dollar deals are negotiated and signed on the trade fair stands. For publicity purposes some major deals that have been fully negotiated prior to a fair, are signed at the fair. The motor industry, in particular, enjoys this type of publicity stunt by announcing vast deals only minutes after motor shows have been opened.

Fairs today are generally places where manufacturers can make new contacts that can develop into customers. They are places which offer experts in an industry a chance to see what all the leading companies in an industry are offering and what new and novel products are being launched. The trade fair is the opportunity for practising industrial espionage without risks. Here one rival has the chance to see, in a single place, what all his rivals are selling and has a chance to compare international prices.

For small and medium-sized companies the fairs offer the chance of meeting potentially new customers, but this hardly applies to the large well-established companies. A potential Krupp customer, for example, will not first hear of the Krupp company or learn about its products, by passing the Krupp pavilion by accident at the Hanover Fair. However, meeting new possible customers is the main aim of the small and medium-sized companies that exhibit at the fairs and has proved to be a highly successful method of marketing for a vast number of German concerns.

For the large companies, prestige plays a major role in participating in trade fairs. In the early years of the Federal Republic, the trade fairs gave all German companies an excellent opportunity to publicise their products and names. Today, the large well-established companies are so well known that the publicity value of trade fair participation is questionable. And yet the fear of doing damage to one's reputation, by not participating in a major international trade fair, is an important motive for spending lavishly year after year on building vast trade fair stands. The cost of exhibiting at trade fairs is immense, especially as an increasing number of countries are encouraging the launching of new fairs and creating a situation where a trade fair in important products is held from one country to the next almost throughout the year. An increasing number of German companies are now becoming greatly cost-conscious and selective about trade fair participation. Large companies are coming to realise that fairs produce increasingly less return the more internationally well-known a company is and as a result, the larger a company is, the more questionable trade fair participation becomes. The German motor industry voted against the holding of a motor show in Germany in 1970, simply because it believed that there were too many motor shows in the world, that these shows cost a fortune to mount and did little for sales and that the money could be better spent on direct advertising. In 1972 many leading German chemical companies greatly reduced the size of their stands at the Hanover Trade Fair and the day may not be far off when the chemical industry withdraws completely from this fair.

For companies abroad seeking to sell in West Germany there can be no doubt that participation in trade fairs here can be highly beneficial. However, many British companies in recent years have done themselves more damage than good by trying to save money on the furnishing of their stands. The Germans spend lavishly on the design of their trade fair stands and to appear as an equal rival, foreign exhibitors must be prepared to spend equally lavishly. Small and medium-sized German companies continue to become better known internationally by participation in fairs and are likely to continue taking part in all the large exhibitions.

The German fairs have established a brilliant international reputation for themselves, due largely to the flair and skill of the fair organisers. German companies take fairs seriously and spend heavily in participating in fairs around the world. The West Germans have, for example, continually been the largest Western contingent at the huge Leipzig trade fairs, and the German participation at Leipzig has been a major element in boosting West German sales to Eastern Europe. West German stands generally occupy more space at the Leipzig fairs than the stands of all other Western companies put together.

But trade fairs only form part of the sales strategies of German companies, albeit a particularly important part. The great success of German exporters and the toughness of the domestic market has largely been the product of skilled and thorough marketing. These skills should not be under-estimated, even at a time when it is clear that cost factors are substantially weakening the international competitive strength of many German companies. If much of this chapter has been devoted to showering praise on German marketing men, it is because the sales records of German companies have in many cases been brilliant and, time and again, German salesmen have shown themselves capable of beating foreign rivals to major international deals.

The Germans are going to fight desperately hard to maintain the strong market positions that they have developed abroad over the last twenty years. However, in this endeavour managers here are increasingly becoming aware that more radical measures must be taken than simply making minor changes in advertising slogans, or modestly improving the quality of products. The chief priority for most companies is to push through major cost-saving programmes, to pull production costs back to a level where the products of German companies can again sell well, returning high profits, on international

markets. Cuts are being made in advertising budgets and in
expenditure on trade fairs. To compensate for these cuts the
German salesman must find new ways of promoting his products and the search for more economic methods of marketing
is one of the major challenges now facing German businessmen.

But the radical changes that are being forced upon managers
here do not concern cutting costs alone. Even with substantial
cost reductions, German companies will increasingly be unable
to compete with the giant multinational concerns. To effect
really major cuts in development, research and sales costs, an
increasing number of German companies will be forced to
merger with rivals, or conclude wide-ranging co-operation
agreements with rivals. A swifter pace of industrial concentration here will in all probability be one of the most important
basic consequences of the reduction in German industry's
competitiveness.

At the same time, many companies now believe that their
efforts to regain increased competitiveness can only be achieved
by greater direct support of industry by public authorities. An
increasing number of companies are now going cap in hand to
Bonn requesting cheap loans and other special subsidies and
warning that bankruptcy could result if such aid is not forth-
coming. These demands hit directly at the heart of the 'Free
Market Economic System', which successive Bonn governments
have used as their basic philosophy for guiding the economy.

The sharp wage increases of the first few years of this decade
and the currency realignments, pose severe problems for
industries here, if the Bonn Government continues to stick
rigidly to its belief in the fully free interplay of market forces.
In a number of areas, most prominently in the steel, shipbuilding, coal and energy sectors, the Government is going
to be forced to play a great interventionist role. Strong Government grants and subsidies will directly affect the marketing
strategies of companies here and the degree of success that
German salesmen enjoy.

A further major consideration concerns the economic sense of
continuing to supply almost all foreign markets from plants
based in this country. The advantages of production here have
been swiftly eroded in the recent past and may well be even
more swiftly eroded through new reforms in such fields as

industrial relations, cartels and taxation. The higher costs of production and the labour shortages, are making more companies now plan foreign investments, aimed at developing foreign based production subsidiaries. This again is a direct consequence of Germany's weakened competitive international position.

But it would be false to gain the impression from many of the comments made in this chapter that it is now getting much easier for foreign companies to sell their products here. It is still going to be exceedingly difficult to get into this rich market, and German companies have shown often enough that they are prepared to take paper-thin profits to maintain a high level of home market sales. For new companies entering this market an additional difficulty centres on finding good personnel. Top free-lance sales agents now command vast earnings here and frequently the marketing men in German companies are the highest paid employees.

The German market is exceptionally tough and German retail company purchasing managers demand exceptionally high quality products at highly competitive prices. But opportunities for foreign companies do certainly exist here, particularly as consumer spending levels are rising fast and many foreign companies, due to currency factors, are now in a better position to challenge German companies in the German markets. A host of foreign companies have proved, in recent years, that this large market can be a source of rich profits if sufficient time and money is spent on preparing promotion campaigns and organising sales and service networks. The Japanese have, for example, come to dominate large sections of the camera, radio, television and office equipment markets here, just as foreign car makers increased their share of this, Europe's largest car market, from below 22 per cent to close to 28 per cent, between 1970 and the end of 1972.

The structure of German industry is now undergoing great change, due to the pressures caused by the weakening of this country's competitive position. The changes being brought about cover not just the development of new marketing strategies, but a greater concentration of industry, more direct State intervention in industry and the opening of the doors to the German markets to a larger extent than before to foreigners.

5 Investment and Finance

West German companies will increasingly develop foreign-based production subsidiaries to support their already large share of international trade. The expansion of foreign spending may well be the most outstanding characteristic of German industrial investment in coming years. A major consideration for many companies now is the fear of losing foreign market shares as a result of the weakening competitive position of products manufactured here. General domestic and international economic developments, combined with basic changes in the structure of industry in this country, which have been outlined earlier in this book, all suggest that few German companies will manage to achieve similar rates of export growth to those seen in the 1950s and 1960s. In addition, tax and cartel reforms, coupled with the likely prospect of continued labour shortages, no longer make the Federal Republic such an attractive place to expand industrial production as it was in earlier years.

The level of German industrial investment spending abroad is relatively small compared with levels reached by American, British and French companies. The total volume of foreign investment spending in West Germany is greater than the volume of German investment spending abroad. This situation is likely to change considerably as foreign companies become less enthusiastic to invest here, on account of all the factors outlined in previous chapters of this book, and as German companies sharply increase their foreign spending. Historical factors, closely relating to the 1939–45 war, largely account for the relatively small volume of German foreign investment spending to date. Twice this century German companies have utterly lost their foreign holdings and assets through world wars; they were quite naturally hesitant for some time after the last war to build up foreign investments for a third time, for fear of losing them yet again. But even if some companies may have wished to swiftly establish foreign-based production subsidiaries in the 1950s, they would have stood little chance of quickly achieving their goal. The last war destroyed the capital reserves and basic assets of most companies and with the first priority being the rebuilding of strong domestic plants, very few German companies were in a position until the 1960s to finance heavy investment abroad, or claim a high enough credit rating to borrow heavily in foreign markets.

The first two decades of the Federal Republic were devoted to the establishment of strong domestic production plants, supported by highly organised national and international sales organisations. A new phase in the international development of German companies started in the mid-1960s with the growth of foreign-based production subsidiaries. Because this new phase is still quite young it is not surprising that the foreign investment volume of German concerns is still relatively small. One further factor that made managers here hesitant about building large foreign subsidiaries was a basic inferiority complex. German companies sought to make no attempt to promote themselves internationally as powerful giants. Aware of hostility in many countries to anything German, resulting from German activities in the last war, German companies for long sought to establish a generally low foreign profile.

That the possible existence of anti-German feelings was widespread played a definite role in the international strategies of many German companies. As late as the mid-1960s this inferiority complex and awareness of foreign hostility was to be found in almost every German board room. As late as 1964 a clear example of anti-German feeling, affecting business developments, can be found so near to this country, in Belgium. Belgian business executives were reluctant at first to allow the merger of Gevaert with the German Agfa company, for purely nationalistic reasons. The final agreement on the merger was only reached when the Germans gave assurances that the direction of all plants in Belgium would be run by Belgians and that the senior management personnel of the merged company, as well as the basic capital, would remain at least 50 per cent in Belgian hands.

Today, German companies largely have a higher international credit standing than ever before and are sufficiently strong to venture forth on major foreign expansion programmes.

In addition, here and abroad the memories of the last war are fading and German businessmen now meet a generally good reception abroad, which has strengthened their confidence with regard to boosting the international images of their companies. The next two sections of this chapter seek to describe in brief and general form the scope of international investment spending, in as far as it directly affects this country and the trends of domestic industrial investment here.

Compared with American and British company foreign spending the total of German industrial foreign spending is small. According to German Government estimates the volume of German industrial investment abroad in the twenty years to the end of 1971 totalled DM 23,800 million, against a spending volume abroad in the ten years to the end of 1970 of about DM 283,000 million by United States companies and DM 76,000 million by British companies. The production volume of foreign-based U.S. company subsidiaries is now about four times as great as the volume of U.S. exports of goods, while the output volume of German foreign-based subsidiaries is little more than 15 per cent of the total volume of German exports of manufactured products.

In a survey published in October 1972, the Bonn Economics and Finance Ministry stated that German foreign investment spending between 1952 and mid-1972 totalled DM 24,985·2 million. The recording of foreign company spending levels in this country only officially started in September 1961, which is unfortunate, in view of the high level of British and American investment here in the 1950s. However, according to the Economics and Finance Ministry the volume of foreign company investments here amounted to DM 27,571·9 million between September 1961 and mid-1972.

A break-down of these figures shows considerable differences in the pattern and volume of this foreign investment. German companies have invested more in France so far than in any other country, with a spending volume of DM 2,795·6 million. As is the case in so many other countries, the German chemical industry has so far been the heaviest investor in France, accounting for about 20 per cent of the total spending volume. Other chief investors, accounting individually for between 8 per cent and 10 per cent of the total, are the steel, electrical, mechanical engineering, metal working and construction industries.

The German investment total so far in Belgium and Luxemburg is a formidable DM 2,757 million. The chemical industry accounts for about 28 per cent of this, largely due to the construction of major plants by such companies as Degussa, Bayer and BASF, in the Antwerp area. The automobile industry accounts for a further 28 per cent of this total, but significantly this is mostly represented by heavy spending in North Belgium by Fordwerke of Cologne and Adam Opel of Rüsselsheim, near Frankfurt, which respectively are wholly owned subsidiaries of Ford and General Motors of the United States.

The German investment totals in Switzerland and Canada are large and yet of a quite different nature to investments in other countries. The total for Switzerland is DM 2,706·9 million, with a substantial amount invested in property and with 66 per cent accounted for by the creation of special financial holding companies. Tax advantages have been the chief incentive for the creation of these holding companies, but the introduction of a double taxation agreement between West Germany and Switzerland, at the start of 1972, may well result in a slowing down of German investment in Switzerland. The German investment total in Canada is DM 2,017·9 million, with some DM 848 million involved in holding companies, again for tax reasons, and a further DM 378 million is invested in real estate.

The German chemical industry accounts for 33 per cent of the total investment volume of DM 1,315·3 million in the Netherlands. The increasing number of mergers and co-operation agreements between Dutch and German companies in the aviation, chemical, steel and electronics industries, may well lead to a substantial rise in German investment in the Netherlands in coming years. German companies of assorted types are now looking for suitable coastal places for the establishment of production plants and, apart from North Germany itself, the Netherlands and Belgium still offer German firms good chances and may, as a result, obtain a significant portion of the high German investment volume planned for coming years.

The tourist potential of Spain is attracting an increasing amount of German investment in real estate, hotels and restaurants, which together may shortly exceed the investment volume in this country of the chemical industry, which is currently DM 242 million of the total volume of DM 1,245·1 million. Such German car makers as Daimler-Benz and Volkswagen are also building up significant investments in Spain. Austria has so far been the recipient of a similar volume of investment spending to Spain, with a wide variety of companies having significant Austrian subsidiaries. In Italy, the German investment total is DM 935·7 million, chiefly accounted for by the engineering, chemical, electrical and food industries.

The German investment total in Great Britain is a relatively modest DM 733·4 million. A number of major German companies, such as Hoechst and Grundig, have been attracted to make large investments in Northern Ireland and the general development of German industrial investments in Britain may well grow substantially, now that Britain is a member of the European Economic Community. In general, however, German companies are hesitant about investing in Britain because of fears of British trade unions (which may well be exaggerated) and uncertainty about Britain's future economic development. Close to one-third of the present volume of German investment in Britain is accounted for by the chemical industry, with about DM 200 million represented by insurance and banking companies and about 10 per cent by engineering.

The total volume of German investment spending in the United States, by mid-1972, was DM 2,127 million. About 25 per cent of this was accounted for by the chemical industry, with Hoechst, Bayer and BASF, all rapidly increasing their investment spending volumes in that country now. The electrical industry, most prominently Siemens, accounts for 15 per cent of the total investment volume. The German automobile industry, which is the single greatest exporter of goods from here to the United States, has so far refrained from establishing U.S. based production plants. The rise in overhead costs here, however, which are in some cases reaching unit production cost levels on a par with U.S. levels, is forcing some

German companies to reconsider the way in which they maintain high sales in the United States. The U.S. market may well in future years be supplied by Volkswagen from its growing Mexican and Brazilian plants and possibly by a U.S. based plant.

The volume of U.S. investment spending in West Germany, by mid-1972, was close to ten times as great as German investment in the United States, at DM 120,630·3 million. Oil and petroleum connected companies alone accounted for DM 3,669 million of the total. Partly on account of the weak capital reserves basis of German companies, there are no German companies today with large direct holdings of their own in any large oilfields in the world. The historical factors mentioned earlier in this chapter, that have played a key role in German foreign spending developments, have had their greatest impact in the oil sector, where Germany is almost entirely dependent on foreign companies for her supplies. Here the American concerns, followed by the British and the Dutch, are most prominent.

The American mechanical engineering industry has invested about DM 2,400 million here in the period between late 1961 and mid-1972, while the chemical and automobile industries of the United States have each invested about DM 1,000 million in this period. The investment total of U.S. electrical companies was about DM 809 million. Significantly, a large amount of these totals has been accounted for by a relatively small number of companies, with Ford, General Motors, DuPont, Dow Chemical, International Telephone and Telegraph, International Business Machines and Litton Industries, all springing immediately to mind in this context, alongside the U.S. oil giants.

Swiss industry is more deeply involved in German business than is often realised, with an investment total of DM 3,825·4 million. A large portion of this is accounted for by the six leading industrial companies in Switzerland, with the Basle-based chemical and pharmaceutical companies alone representing DM 648 million of the investment total. Swiss mechanical engineering companies account for DM 385 million of investments here, followed by electrical companies representing DM 330 million and food companies with a total of DM 225 million.

The British come next in line with an investment total of DM 3,037·7 million. Chemical and oil companies respectively account for DM 762 million and DM 700 million, with Imperial Chemical Industries, Shell and British Petroleum, all owning large subsidiaries here. British mechanical engineering companies have invested DM 231 million here and a substantial rise in investment, by this sector, may well develop as a direct result of British entry into the Common Market. A noticeable increase in British investment in property has been seen since late 1972 and this may well be an area of great investment increases in coming years.

The Dutch investment total in Germany was DM 2,682·1 million, while the French and Belgian totals were respectively DM 1,504·6 million and DM 1,711·6 million. Oil, chemical, engineering, electrical and food companies accounted for the major portions of the investment from these three countries. Apart from the countries mentioned here no other country

TABLE 5.1

Investment Spending Totals		
Country	Investments in Germany* (mln DMs)	German Investments Abroad† (mln DMs)
Europe	13,878·0	14,653·6
of which:		
EEC‡	6,260·5	7,803·6
EFTA§	7,532·7	5,215·2
East Bloc	20·7	3·0
other	64·8	1,631·8
Africa	8·6	1,567·6
North and South Americas	13,401·8	7,698·2
Asia	285·5	817·8
Australia and other	1·0	248·0

Source: *Economics and Finance Ministry Survey*, 25 Oct 1972.

* Figures for period Sept 1961 to 30 June 1972.
† Figures for start 1952 to 30 June 1972.
‡ Belgium, Luxembourg, Holland, France, Italy.
§ Britain, Switzerland, Austria, Norway, Portugal, Sweden, Finland, Iceland.

has an investment spending total in Germany of more than DM 500 million, although Canada is swiftly approaching this total.

Few German companies can boast today of owning large international production networks. The chief exceptions, perhaps, are BASF, Bayer, Hoechst, Volkswagenwerk, Siemens, Daimler-Benz and possibly three or four more. Yet none of these companies has anything like the scale of international operations of such major American companies as General Motors, Ford, Chrysler, ITT, IBM, General Electric, Westinghouse or the large U.S. oil concerns. Nor for that matter do the international operations of any German company, measured on the size of foreign investments, bear comparison with such concerns as Royal Dutch Shell, Unilever or British Petroleum.

The majority of German foreign investment spending has been concentrated in the most industrially developed countries of the world and been accounted for by only a few industries. In the 20 years to mid-1972 only five German industries spent more than DM 1,500 million on foreign investments: chemicals DM 5,449·7 million, motor vehicles DM 2,109·5 million, electricals DM 2,840·9 million, mechanical engineering DM 1,806·2 million and iron and steel DM 1,503 million. The chief industries abroad to invest in this country between September 1961 and mid-1972 were: oil with DM 5,258·6 million, chemicals DM 3,063·4 million, mechanical engineering DM 3,562·3 million, motor vehicles DM 1,375·7 million and electricals DM 1,552·6 million.

In coming years West German companies are likely to step up their investment spending in 'developing countries' to a proportion of well above the current volume of barely 30 per cent of all foreign investment. The 'developing countries' offer potentially large markets, but tend to be protectionist, demanding that foreign companies invest locally in order to obtain significant market shares. Many 'developing countries' have their own raw material stocks, plus large and relatively cheap labour resources. To obtain large sales in Africa and South America, in particular, German companies recognise that they must develop manufacturing subsidiaries in these areas and that potentially, such subsidiaries can produce healthy rates of profits and sales growth. In the constant search for new markets and new ways of boosting foreign sales the large German companies are now showing signs of taking greater interest than ever before in the markets of South America and Africa.

It remains questionable whether the swiftly rising pace of German foreign investment spending will be matched by a decline in the rate of growth of domestic investment spending. The overall investment spending volumes of large companies here are now rising significantly, as the economies of most industrial countries appeared in early 1973 to be at the start of a new phase of substantial expansion. Currently, quite a number of German companies are drawing up investment plans calling for a roughly even split between foreign and domestic expenditure. In the main the domestic spending is concentrated on consolidation and rationalisation, while the foreign plans are mainly accented on the establishment of new production subsidiaries. A good number of German managers fear that the pace of production expansion here, in coming years, will not be able to rival possible rates in a good number of foreign areas, due to the growing labour market tension here. In consequence, it is possible to suggest with a good deal of caution that over the next ten years a number of leading German companies may well spend more abroad than in the Federal Republic itself in the expansion of production facilities.

The rise in foreign spending, coupled with a possible decline in the rate of growth of foreign company spending in this country, could quite possibly produce eventual balance of payments difficulties. West Germany may well move permanently into the category of the deficit countries, from its former position as one of the leading surplus countries. The full reasons for this development are discussed briefly in the final chapter of this book, but one significant factor will be the trends of international investment.

DOMESTIC INDUSTRIAL INVESTMENT SPENDING

Sharp differences in investment spending patterns within the Federal Republic can be seen from one industry to another. Generalisations, therefore, must be treated with considerable caution. However, on the whole the rate of real investment development over the last two decades has been most substantial. A significant slow-down has been seen in the recent past as a result of the profits recession of 1970, 1971 and part of 1972, and on account of mounting inflation. For most industrial sectors the record profits achieved in 1968 and 1969 led to 1969 and 1970 becoming years of record investment-spending volume.

According to IFO-Research Institute estimates the average level of industrial investment spending in 1970 equalled six per cent of total turnover, representing a gain of 34 per cent over 1969. The gain seen in 1969 over the previous year was even more dramatic at well over 40 per cent. The industrial investment volume in 1970 averaged out at about DM 3,315 per man employed in industry, which was one of the highest levels achieved in any industrial country. While the investment volume in 1971 showed a nominal advance over 1970, the real totals, taking inflation into consideration, were in all probability below the 1970 levels and the real gain in 1972 was probably less than four per cent.

In terms of turnover the percentage of investment spending by most companies has declined over the last decade. A major factor influencing the trend was the recession in the mid-1960s,

TABLE 5.2

Investment Spending by Major Industries (in mln DMs)		
Industry	1968	1969
Chemicals	3,393	5,042
Foods and Tobacco	2,606	3,114
Mechanical Engineering	2,471	3,634
Construction	2,291	3,068
Motor Vehicles	2,037	2,925
Iron, Steel, Metals	1,861	2,561
Electricals	1,635	2,605
Textiles, Clothing	1,349	1,779
Stone, Earth, Cement	987	1,331
Mining	967	713
Oil, Petroleum	538	834
All industries excluding Water and Electricity: Total	25,070	34,458

Source: Federal Statistics Office

when most companies substantially reduced their investment volumes. To a large extent the investment trends have closely followed the trends of profits and, significantly, most companies have substantially increased their borrowing volumes in recent years. In the case of a considerable number of industries the volume of borrowing has more than trebled in the last ten years. A revealing guide to the general financial situation was produced in 1972 in an analysis of company balance sheets made by the Hoppenstedt Verlag. This showed that earnings as a percentage of sales in the steel industry fell from 2·6 per cent in 1962 to 1·3 per cent in 1966, then rose after the recession to 3·3 per cent in 1969, before falling to just 1·6 per cent in 1971. These average figures are based on the reports of August Thyssen-Hütte, Klöckner, Hoesch and Mannesmann.

On the basis of Bayer, BASF, Hoechst, Schering and Degussa reports, the Hoppenstedt Verlag's study shows that chemical industry profits, as a percentage of total sales, rose from 6·9 per cent to 7·5 per cent between 1962 and 1966 and then declined from 7·5 per cent in 1969 to 5 per cent in 1971. The sharpest decline seen in this ten year period was in the electrical industry. On average, based on the reports of Siemens, AEG-Telefunken and Brown, Boveri of Mannheim, profits declined from 3·7 per cent in 1962 to 3·2 per cent in 1966 and then went on declining from 3·1 per cent in 1969 to just 1·9 per cent in 1971. In all industries, with very few exceptions indeed, profits as a percentage of total sales were substantially down on 1962 levels by 1971.

To maintain substantial investment spending against this background companies have had to increase their borrowing volumes, but even so, few companies have managed to maintain a steady development of investments. While most large companies plan detailed five-year investment programmes, only the chemical industry has really managed to come close to achieving its medium-term investment goals on schedule. Most industries have chopped and changed their investment programmes in line with annual profit developments. The result has often been that companies have maintained highly erratic investment patterns, by cutting expenditure sharply in times of general economic slow-down, and have had to invest swiftly and greatly to expand capacity in line with demand in the boom periods, that have so characterised much of the last twenty years of the country's history.

The chemical industry continued most of its investment plans throughout the recession of the mid-1960s and was, as a result, one of the few industries really in a position to take full advantage of the boom of the late 1960s. The steel industry, by contrast, has continually failed to push through medium-term investment programmes and its investment growth reflects patterns on one extreme within German industry over the last two decades, just as the pattern in the chemical industry reflects the opposite extreme.

TABLE 5.3

Investment Development in the Chemicals and Steel Industries
(in mln DMs)

Year	Chemicals	Steel	Year	Chemicals	Steel
1954	900	950	1963	2,300	1,810
1955	1,300	13,00	1964	2,800	1,520
1956	1,400	1,200	1965	3,800	1,250
1957	1,500	1,320	1966	4,100	1,180
1958	1,600	1,070	1967	3,500	890
1959	1,700	870	1968	3,500	900
1960	2,400	1,130	1969	4,900	1,210
1961	2,700	1,700	1970	5,600	2,380
1962	2,300	1,670	1971	5,300	2,710

Total Chemical Industry investment 1954–1971   52,300
Total Steel Industry investment 1954–1971   24,060

Sources: West German Chemical Industry Federation and European Coal and Steel Community.

The exact break-down of investments from one industry to the next again shows interesting variations regarding the levels of spending per man employed and the percentage that investments take of total turnover volumes. The IFO-Institute, for example, pointed out in a comprehensive study in 1971 that on average, capital goods industries showed a seven per cent rise in investment spending in 1968, followed by a rise of 46 per cent in 1969 and 34 per cent in 1970 and then a provisional decline of two per cent in the following year. All manufacturing industries taken together, however, showed neither a decline nor a rise in spending volume in 1968, followed by rises respectively of 38 per cent and 26 per cent in 1969 and 1970 and a provisional increase of two per cent in 1971.

Even substantial differences can be seen in industries that have many common features, such as the engineering, electrical and metal working industries. One fact that comes out very clearly from all the figures is that the profits recession in 1970 and 1971 was so strong, that exceedingly few industries could even manage a nominal gain in investment spending volume in

TABLE 5.4

Differences in Investment Patterns between Major Industries				
*Electrical Industry**	*1968*	*1969*	*1970*	*1971†*
Gross fixed asset spending (in Mln DMs)	1,480	2,325	2,830	2,640
Percentage change	+6	+57	+22	−7
Investment per employee in DMs	1,580	2,285	2,585	2,475
Investment as percentage of total turnover	4·3	5·5	5·6	4·8
Mechanical Engineering Industry‡				
Gross fixed asset spending (in mln DMs)	1,900	2,735	3,290	3,250
Percentage change	+19	+44	+20	−1
Investment per employee in DMs	1,805	2,425	2,940	2,910
Investment as percentage of total turnover	4·6	5·4	5·8	5·3
Iron, Lead and Metal Goods Industry				
Gross fixed asset spending (in mln DMs)	670	990	1,190	1,200
Percentage change	+6	+48	+20	+1
Investment per employee in DMs	1,715	2,405	2,845	2,890
Investment as percentage of total turnover	4·2	5·2	5·7	5·4

Sources: Investment Test of the IFO-Institute for Economic Research, Munich.

* Excluding computer facilities after 1970
† Provisional figures
‡ Excluding office equipment after 1970

1971 over 1970. Because Germany still managed a rate of real economic growth in the first years of the 1970s, the extent of profit declines and resultant cuts in investment spending has not been widely recognised outside this country. Many industrialists in Germany, however, fear that the rate of real economic growth in the present decade may be substantially below levels seen in the last two decades on account of the cuts in real investment spending volume in 1971, 1972 and part of 1973 in many industries.

LOCATION OF INVESTMENTS-DEVELOPING AREAS

German industry is heavily concentrated in a few key areas and the distribution of industrial investment spending is by no means even, in any respect, across the country as a whole. This has been the case for many years and resulted in some regions being largely neglected and consequently heavily under-developed industrially. Nearly twice as much is invested in the Land of North Rhine Westphalia in any year as in any other area. The Ruhr remains the industrial heart of West Germany and can boast today of not only the old German industries bound up with iron, steel and coal, but large modern giant production plants, concerned with the manufacture of everything from cars to machine tools to chemicals. From a provisional total investment-spending volume of DM 38,521 million in 1970, this area obtained DM 12,819 million, according to Federal Office of Statistics data.

Baden-Württemberg and Bavaria, however, are today the homes of many of Germany's most swiftly expanding technological industries. These are the regions that have shown the swiftest industrial development in recent years, through the growth of a vast number of electrical, electronics, engineering and light capital goods and consumer goods companies. Industrial investment spending in Baden-Württemberg in 1970 was a provisional total of DM 7,006 million, while the Bavarian volume was DM 5,022 million. Other relatively strong areas of industrial development are around Hamburg, in Hesse, Lower Saxony and Rhineland-Palatinate.

But even in the most heavily industrialised regions there are areas crying out for industrial development and a wide variety of all manner of aid programmes exist to develop these areas. The most important development area from a political viewpoint for this country is West Berlin. International and national aid schemes exist to try and persuade companies to establish themselves in West Berlin and thereby strengthen the links between this island in East Germany and the mainland of West Germany. The geographical location of West Berlin makes it a rather unattractive place for companies to locate in and many young people, suffering from the claustrophobia of the city, are moving out to jobs in other parts of the Federal Republic. The greatest single hope for West Berlin's future industrial development lies in the efforts that Herr Brandt has been making since 1969 to normalise relations between the two German states. The transport and basic treaties between West and East Germany, concluded in 1972, may well open the way for greatly improved communications between West Berlin and the rest of West Germany and thereby make West Berlin a more attractive place to invest in.

West Berlin covers an area of about 186 square miles and is West Germany's largest city, with a population of about 2·2 million. There are over 5,000 industrial enterprises in the city, manufacturing a wide range of assorted consumer and capital goods. In the three years 1968, 1969 and 1970 the industrial investment volume in West Berlin was a significant DM 2,700 million. Companies locating in the city can obtain substantial tax-deductable allowances, cheap credits and higher rates of depreciation allowances than exist in other areas of the country. The investment incentives given to companies in West Berlin are, in total, greater than those that can be obtained in any other area of the country. These subsidies are supported by the Berlinhilfegesetz (Berlin Aid Law) of 1964 and the Berlinförderungsgesetz (Berlin Development Law) of 1971.

Substantial investment subsidies of a similar kind to those available in Berlin are given in the areas running along the East German border. The Saar is another special development area, offering substantial incentives, largely because of its present problem of being the home of mainly out-dated industries, such as mining. In addition to these special areas, almost every regional authority in the country offers some sort of incentive to investors. Part of the reason for this is rivalry between regions and the more basic factor, that regional and local governments depend heavily on corporate taxes for their incomes.

Even such exceptionally industrialised regions as North Rhine Westphalia now offer substantial investor aid programmes. In this area, for example, there are more than 90 locations that are considered industrially under-developed, offering special grants to investors of assorted types. A series of laws have been made in the last decade to regulate the incentives and, from the start of 1972, a detailed action programme to help under-developed regions has been in operation, under the joint agreement of the Federal and Land governments.

There are large parts of Lower Saxony, for example, that could greatly benefit from industrial investment and the aid programmes that have been designed in this area have in recent years met with substantial success. The Lower Saxony authorities did not content themselves alone with cheap credits, low land prices and tax allowances, to induce investors to the under-developed areas. A major programme of land reclamation was launched to improve the coast region of Lower Saxony for industrial development. Because of this a number of major companies, such as AKZO of Holland, Dow Chemical and Mobil Oil of the United States, have been attracted to Lower Saxony in the recent past. In Schleswig-Holstein, a vast programme of land reclamation has enticed Bayer to plan a massive production complex, that may grow to the size of Bayer's Leverkusen facilities in the next decade.

It seems quite likely that the growing over-congestion and labour shortages in the main industrial areas will tempt an increasing number of companies to take advantage, in coming years, of the investment incentives given in the developing areas. This suggestion applies with equal validity to German companies as to foreign companies locating plants here. There are still sizeable areas of the country where labour is in good supply and the incentives being offered to companies to locate in the developing areas are highly generous. The freedom that local authorities have here to offer high investment grants may, however, be curbed by European Economic Community decisions on regional policy, which will aim to strengthen the most under-developed areas of Europe, very few of which are to be found in this country. Furthermore, the ambitious plans of such authorities as those in Lower Saxony and Schleswig-Hollstein may well be damped by growing pressures from environmentalists. Authorities in charge of German coastal areas have in the recent past encountered growing public pressure against plans to allow the building in these areas of chemical, energy and oil plants.

INVESTMENT FINANCE

Investments are primarily financed out of depreciation and profits. The tax system, which is currently being reviewed by the Bonn Government, provides varied scales of depreciation possibilities, which depend in great measure on the type of item to be depreciated (varying categories exist differentiating between fixed capital equipment, buildings and mobile equipment, such as commercial vehicles), as well as on the location of the objects to be depreciated (various scales exist depending largely on the local authority tax regulations).

The next main source of investment funds is the banking and capital markets. In the major public bond markets private companies have in recent years found it increasingly difficult to float large issues, as the capital demands of public authorities have risen substantially. In the first nine months of 1972, for example, the only private sector borrowers on the public bond markets here were Volkswagenwerk, RWE, Klöckner-Werke, August Thyssen-Hütte, Gelsenberg, Siemens and the Commerzbank.

In December 1972, the Commerzbank AG, stated that in the first nine months of 1972 the total new issue volume of all bonds, bills and mortgage notes on the public capital market totalled a record DM 40,000 million, against DM 31,000 million in all of 1971. The total volume of long-term straight bond issues for 1972 was DM 12,765 million, after DM 10,517 million in 1971. However, a break-down of this total by borrowers shows clearly how the share of the market for private borrowers is declining. The bond issue total for 1972 comprised 40 per cent foreign DM issues, 44 per cent issues for public authorities, 4 per cent issues for special institutions (which are largely controlled by public authorities) and just 12 per cent for industrial and commercial concerns. In 1971, the private sector accounted for

18 per cent of the new issues, while 40 per cent went to public authorities, 7 per cent was taken by special institutions and 35 per cent of the issue volume was accounted for by foreign DM flotations.

The Federal Government and Federal Bank exert great influence on the coupon levels and new issue volume in the bond market. The Central Capital Market Committee, composed of the representatives of the major credit institutions and the Federal Bank, meets monthly to decide on the issue volume for bonds and priority is almost always given to public authority borrowers. Two kinds of issues exist: the domestic straight or convertible issues, of which the convertible is still a rarity, and the foreign DM issues. The latter, for withholding-tax reasons, are not generally of interest to domestic investors and are almost totally placed abroad (very largely in Switzerland). The foreign DM issues today represent a major component of the total issue volume in the Eurobond market and the coupons and pricing of these issues depend entirely on Euro-currency and money market rates. The Central Capital Market Committee has largely restricted in the recent past the total volume of new DM foreign issues to about DM 300 million to DM 400 million a month. Because of the extreme difficulty of getting an issue floated domestically, some German companies have in the past floated DM foreign issues through their special Luxemburg holding companies. At times the conditions of these issues have been more advantageous to borrowers than have the conditions fixed to purely domestic issues.

The major German banks have played a key role in developing foreign DM issues and, as a result, have figured prominently among leading managers of Eurobonds. The position of the German banks in this international capital market, coupled with the growing financial strength of German companies and their increasing interest in foreign investment, will almost certainly result in German companies becoming much more frequent borrowers in all sections of the Eurobond market. But because of the competition among international companies and organisations to float Eurobonds, it seems likely that raising capital from this source will be restricted to a relatively small number of German companies with particularly high credit ratings.

The purely domestic side of the German bond market functions badly, through the continual desire of public authorities for large volumes of cheap capital. The Federal Bank has attempted time and again to organise the flotation of issues for public sector borrowers on conditions below those expected by investors. The result has often been virtual chaos in the market, as placing difficulties have arisen and as the Federal Bank has sought to assure a good placing by tight restrictions on new issue volume. In December 1972, for example, the bond market was at a standstill as the Federal Bank sought to push through public authority issues with 8 per cent coupons. This 8 per cent level had been held since June 1972, and in the following six months the Bank Rate had been increased from 3 per cent to 4·5 per cent and money market rates had risen sharply. Only after a Bank Rate rise to 5 per cent in January 1973 did the Federal Bank allow coupon rates to move on to 8·5 per cent and open the path, once again, for investors to take an interest in purchasing bonds on the market.

Because of the heavy public sector capital demands, companies are being forced to increase their private borrowing from the banks, or seek to raise capital abroad, or more frequently increase their basic capital levels through the new issue of shares to the public. That only 2,278 companies have publicly distributed shares, with only about a quarter of this total having their shares publicly quoted on the bourses, largely reflects the fears that company owners have of being dominated by the major financial institutions. Some companies have remained private solely because their owners have feared that the large banks could obtain effective control of their companies, should their shares be publicly distributed. This view is swiftly changing now, as companies are continually increasing their bank borrowing volumes, which effectively strengthen the hands of the banks over the borrowers and because companies are finding that their capital needs can only be satisfied by going to the public.

Going public is, however, an expensive business and there are a number of tax advantages to remaining a GmbH type of company, rather than becoming an Aktiengesellschaft. Changes may result from tax reforms and increased controls on the banks, that may result in reductions in the costs of issuing new

shares. But the public at large must first of all come to understand the operations of the bourses, if more companies are to
successfully have their companies floated and if the volume of
new share issues is to increase.

Public interest in the purchase of all manner of securities is
slowly developing, for the reasons largely described in Chapter
Two. The developments on the German bourses in 1972 tend to
illustrate the manner in which companies use the capital
markets and the growth of public interest.* The chief market
factors were the decline in company profits in 1971 and the
increase in public sector demand for capital. The profits trend
forced companies to borrow greatly, and the imposition of
exchange controls forced companies to borrow largely on the
domestic markets alone.

The expansion of commercial bank lending in 1972 was
swifter than in any previous year. The money supply expansion
rate for most of the first half of the year was around an annual
level of 20 per cent; it declined to near 13 per cent in the first
four months of the second half of the year, but then came close
to 16 per cent in the last two months. The exchange controls,
coupled with the increasing stability of the U.S. dollar, also
prompted German companies to repay short-term foreign loans
and roll-over loans into medium and long-term domestic
credits.

However, 1972 also saw a sharp increase in foreign demand
for German securities, largely prompted at first from the continuation of currency speculation and later by such special
factors as British entry into the Common Market – which was
a key incentive for British investment companies to purchase
a large volume of German shares and bonds.

These factors together resulted in a number of records being
set on the German bourses. The developments in 1972 are
significant, because they will in all probability be continued in
coming years. It seems most probable that companies will rely
more heavily on external funds to finance investments and that

---

* The comments made here largely result from interviews by the author
with bankers and leading company executives in late 1972. Furthermore,
much of the information here is based on the annual bourse surveys published by the major banks, especially the Commerzbank book *Rum um die
Börse*.

the public sector will continue substantially increasing its public borrowing level. Furthermore, it seems improbable that the Federal Bank will ease its exchange controls in the near future, with the result that German companies will be forced to largely finance domestic expansion through finance raised in this country alone. (The volume of German company foreign borrowing for use in this country has been estimated by some bankers to have exceeded DM 28,000 million in 1970.)

The longer-term outlook for the capital markets is virtually impossible to forecast. So much will depend on the policies pursued by the Federal Bank and on the degree of radicalism involved in new legislation on such matters as worker co-determination, cartels and tax reform. It does seem clear, however, that German companies will seek to raise most of the funds needed to support their foreign investment programmes in foreign markets. To prepare for this a number of German companies plan to seek quotations for their shares on foreign bourses and intend to make themselves better known to foreign investors. A few German companies sought foreign bourse listings in 1972, including Siemens, AEG-Telefunken and the Commerzbank in Vienna. At the moment only 23 German companies have their shares listed abroad and none has a U.S. quotation. BASF is currently preparing its accounts in line with Securities and Exchange Commission rules and may well be the first German company to be quoted on Wall Street. In many cases German companies have their shares listed on the three Swiss bourses and in Amsterdam and, by the end of 1972, only August Thyssen-Hütte, Bayer, Commerzbank, Hoechst and the KKB Kundenkreditbank had London market listings.

While the longer-term outlook is most uncertain, the next few years should continue to see new records broken in the volume of bond market issues, bourse turnovers and possibly in the number of companies to go public. The average monthly turnover of the eight West German stock markets in 1972 was about DM 2,000 million, which was a new record here, yet still a relatively small volume by comparison with the Wall Street, London and Tokyo markets. The Commerzbank AG figures for 1972, measured on the basis of 422 quoted companies, show that the share market value of these companies, by the end of November 1972, stood at a record level of DM 120,000 million, compared to a level of DM 94,000 million at the end of November 1971. The large rise was mainly due to increases in quoted share prices, rather than through rises in basic share capitals. However, according to Federal Statistics Office figures a total of 1,360 Aktiengesellschaft-type companies raised their basic share capitals in the first half of 1972. The total increase was a record for a six-month period of DM 4,100 million. This brought the total share capital volume of the 2,278 German Aktiengesellschaft-type companies to DM 62,100 million at mid-1972.

The majority of the capital increases were for small sums. Only five major capital rises for amounts of over DM 100 million were made through rights issues in the first two-thirds of 1972. However, a total of 17 major companies gained permission from shareholder general meetings to raise their basic capitals at a future date, to be set by the supervisory and executive boards of these companies, by a combined total of DM 1,049 million. These companies included such leading concerns as August Thyssen-Hütte, Hoechst, BASF, Bayer, Siemens, Kaufhof, Mannesmann and Klöckner.

The growing public interest in securities is well reflected in the recent swift rise in investment in mutual funds. Property funds have increased their total investment assets resulting from sales of share certificates, from just DM 120 million to DM 1,047 million in the period from the end of 1970 to November 1972, according to a Federal Bank survey published in January 1973. The Federal Bank calculates that mutual funds of all types took in more than DM 4,000 million from savers in 1972, which was a greater volume than that taken by the funds in both 1970 and 1971 together. The strong increase in investment in mutual funds by the general public partly reflects rising affluence here and increasing awareness of the stock and share markets, as well as increasing controls on the activities of the funds. The Berlin Supervisory Commission for Credit Business greatly strengthened controls on mutual funds after the Investors Overseas Services crisis of early 1970. This has given greater guarantees of secure investment to the general public, as well as seeing the banning of some 100 off-shore funds from operating in this country.

The fixed interest securities side of the bourses are generally of greater interest to the general public than the share markets. The total value of bonds in circulation at the end of the third quarter of 1972 was DM 212,230 million, producing an annual coupon payment sum to investors of DM 14,074 million. The generally stronger interest by the public in bonds, rather than shares, centres on fears of speculation and uncertain yield returns. To stimulate share interest companies have continually sought to maintain high dividend payments. This objective has been a particularly difficult one to achieve in the recent past, on account of the sharp profit declines in 1970 and 1971 and the urgent need to strengthen reserves for investment purposes. Cuts in dividends in the recent past by many companies have once again made large sections of the general public hesitant about buying shares and greater public interest in the bourses may only come about if companies return to the high dividend levels achieved in 1969 and 1970.

Fearing a general slow-down in economic development and recognising the need in the future to borrow more heavily, German companies are now making strong efforts to strengthen their basic reserves. The problem is complicated, for companies must seek to raise more capital from the public, while at the same time trying to place a greater proportion of profits than before in reserves. To do this companies must persuade shareholders to accept lower dividend levels as the price of ensuring the greater security of their investments. This task is so difficult that many companies tried to avoid attempting it in 1971 and 1972 by maintaining previous dividend levels, even though profits had fallen sharply and in many cases the dividend payments could only be made by fully distributing all net earnings, plus funds from reserves.

According to the Federal Statistics Office the profits of 850 leading companies in this country fell on average by 25 per cent in 1971. The total net earnings of these companies amounted to just DM 4,900 million in 1971 and these companies account between them for close to half of all private company turnover in this country. For the first time in over two decades the average rate of dividend payments fell in 1971, with the average distribution at 11·1 per cent, against 12·9 per cent in the previous year. The total volume of dividend payments made by 1,541 Aktiengesellschaft-type companies in 1971, according to a Federal Statistics Office study, was nine per cent less than in 1970, at DM 5,000 million.

The decline should have been much greater, but many companies preferred to draw on reserves rather than make cuts. But further profit falls in 1971 forced widespread dividend cuts in almost all business sectors in 1972. The Federal Statistics Office figures for 1971 include many medium-sized companies and these were the main ones to cut dividends. The stronger companies held on, but as the Commerzbank AG survey of 422 companies shows, dividends in 1972 by these large companies fell sharply, to an average of 12·6 per cent, representing total distribution of DM 3,600 million, from 14·8 per cent in 1971, representing DM 4,000 million.

Slowly, but surely, German companies are convincing shareholders of the need to accept lower dividends and to subscribe more often for new shares. The German public must start to take greater interest in the bourses, if companies are to raise the capital they will need to finance the ambitious investment programmes that are widely being planned. The banks are now making efforts to make share buying more popular and less is being said these days about the questionable ethics involved in buying shares to make a quick capital gain, rather than buying shares solely to obtain regular high dividends. The capital markets are expanding at a swift pace now and are likely to continue doing so in the medium-term. The existence of tight credit controls and exchange controls, coupled with the increasing difficulty in the private sector of raising cash through new bond issues, may lead to many more companies going public. But these developments must be seen alongside the ambitions of German companies to greatly increase the size of their international operations.

In this latter regard foreign banks are coming to play an increasingly important role in the lives of German companies. The desire of industry to expand abroad has opened new opportunities for foreign banks to do business with German concerns and has forced German banks to become more internationally orientated. The high level of foreign investment in this country in the last decade and its likely continuation, coupled with the great strength of the German currency, has resulted in a massive expansion of foreign banking activity here. Foreign banks have been opening German branches, mainly in Frankfurt-am-Main, the banking capital of the country, at an increasingly swift pace. The aims of these banks are to aid foreign companies investing here, to strengthen their base in the Euro-currency and money markets and to improve contacts with German companies, with the aim of eventually aiding these companies to raise cash for foreign investment.

The pace of foreign banking growth here is most clearly reflected in figures published in a special survey by the Federal Bank in March 1972. At the end of 1960 only thirteen foreign bank branches existed in this country, with a combined business volume of just DM 1,000 million, which equalled 0·4 per cent of the total credit institute business volume in this country. By 1968, the number of foreign bank branches here had increased to 22 and their business volume amounted to DM 6,800 million. By the end of 1971 the total of foreign bank branches had risen to 29, accounting for 1·7 per cent of the country's total banking business volume or DM 15,400 million.

In the recent past an increasing number of German companies have struck close relationships with foreign banks. A main cause was the large difference that arose between domestic interest rates and Euro-dollar rates in 1970, which led many German companies to borrow heavily on a short-term basis in the Euro-markets. To make sure that they do not miss the foreign industrial investment expansion boat, many German banks have in recent years made bold efforts to establish strong international organisations. For many years the banks contented themselves with loose correspondent relationships with foreign banks abroad. Since the late 1960s, however, the German banks have developed a large number of much closer foreign relationships. The Germans have been instrumental in the establishment of many 'international banking clubs' that closely tie international banks together in certain types of operations. These intimate clubs, such as the one formed between the Commerzbank, Crédit Lyonnais and Banco di Roma, are well on the way to becoming highly integrated multinational banking organisations. The formation of these clubs has enabled the German banks to establish good banking bases throughout the world in a short time. To support these clubs many of the banks have opened branches or representative offices in the key international financial centres. German companies have increasingly become sophisticated experts in the operations of international capital and money markets. The international banking community will increasingly find German companies keen to borrow large sums abroad, through all manner of medium and long-term private and public placings. The German banks have placed themselves well in the newly formed 'international banking clubs' to ensure that they, at least, get some portion of the profits involved in the increasing volume of German corporate foreign borrowing.

In the case of medium and small companies, the tightness of the capital markets and the decline in profits are producing increasing dependence on the banks. These companies could find themselves in great difficulties if credit restrictions become so tight, that the banks only have money to lend to their biggest clients. In such a situation the medium and small companies would become even more under the influence of banking control than ever before. This is a major danger and the only hope of this not happening is the possibility that the publicly controlled savings and giro banks will concentrate even more fully on aiding medium and small companies and leave the financing of the big companies to the joint stock and private banks. Should this sort of situation develop even more strongly than is presently the case, then a substantial transformation of the banking scene will come about. Such a transformation, producing a more clearly defined difference in the credit activities of the publicly controlled and the private banks may well be aided by greater controls on the private banks. Much of this, however, still lies in the realm of speculation, for the private banking lobby in Bonn and at the Federal Bank is formidable and the Government has so far kept fairly quiet on the whole subject of banking reform.

There is the danger, nevertheless, that many medium-sized companies will become too greatly controlled by the banks. Bank controls on companies, through the granting of credits, exist in all countries, yet it is particularly dangerous in parts of Continental Europe, including this country, where the banks are also allowed to be major direct shareholders. A conflict of interest can easily arise where a bank, as a major shareholder in a company, can say how and where a company raises its capital. The banks deny that such a conflict ever exists, but the fear that the banks use their position in this way is widespread among the general public and among the owners of medium-sized firms. The medium-sized companies in this country face a growing dilemma over the way they raise capital. Tighter credit restrictions may force these companies to try and go public, while many others will seek to strengthen themselves through merger and through being taken over by large concerns. There are still many thousands of medium-sized companies in this country, but the growing pressures on profits and raising capital may well lead to some shake-out.

This chapter has given a general outline of investment trends and developments involved in raising the finance for investments. The tighter profit margins here, which have come to the fore since the start of this decade and which most business leaders expect to continue, are the most important factor in influencing changes in the way companies finance their investments. Borrowing in all forms is coming to play an increasingly important role in the affairs of companies of all sizes here. At the same time a period is starting of major foreign expansion by German companies. An exciting era in German industrial development is only now really beginning. Ten years from now it may well be that a large number of German companies will be able to boast of sizeable international production organisations. As a result, the names of German companies abroad will become much better known. Apart from Krupp, Thyssen, Volkswagen and Daimler-Benz, few German companies are really well known internationally among the broad general public. In the United States, for example, BASF is virtually solely known as the manufacturer of tape recorder tapes, even though the output of such products barely accounts for five per cent of the company's total sales.

The years ahead are going to become increasingly difficult and challenging for the finance directors of German companies. They will have to become more sophisticated in their national and foreign banking relationships, they will have to convince the general public more often of the security of investing in their companies. Their task will be complicated by possibly severe increases in corporation taxes, reductions in tax-deductable allowances and by tighter credit controls and exchange controls. To a large extent, however, German companies, which in great measure are financially sound and potentially strong, face a massive public relations task. They must convince the national and international banking and investment community of their strengths and to do this, they must use some of the talents they displayed in marketing their products, in finally marketing themselves as companies. At the same time they must seek, as best they can, to convince the Government in Bonn and the Common Market Commission in Brussels, to shelve present plans that could restrict corporate growth. The way these problems will be attacked is outlined in Chapter 6.

6 The Image of Industry, its Organisation and its Aims

The Germans love organisations, associations and federations. In few countries are there so many business organisations as in this one. More than 70 per cent of this country's registered companies are voluntary members of at least one business federation. In many cases the hundreds of assorted types of business associations, federations and confederations duplicate each other's work and appear in some respects as rival bodies. The highly complex manner in which companies are organised in assorted associations contrasts strongly with the manner in which employees are organised, for there are just 16 main trade unions, which are all members of a single national confederation, the Deutscher Gewerkschaftsbund (DGB).

Individually and combined these business associations form a powerful set of political pressure groups and provide valuable services for their members. These associations seek to keep their members well informed on all manner of political, social and economic developments relevant to their businesses, as well as seeking to influence the views of elected authorities and the courts in ways that serve the best interests of their members. Probably the most important national federation is the Deutscher Industrie- und Handelstag (German Federation of Chambers of Commerce), which represents all the chambers of commerce in the country and which derives its strength from laws that demand that all registered companies be members of a chamber of commerce. The DIHT can therefore claim to represent all companies in this country.

The most important federations of manufacturers are members of the Bundesverband der Deutschen Industrie (German Industry Federation). The BDI can fairly claim to speak for industry and in political significance it must be rated almost on a par with the DIHT. The third chief national federation of great importance is the Bundesvereinigung der Deutschen Arbeitgeberverbände (German Federal Confederation of Employers Associations), whose membership is composed of some 800 assorted employers associations and whose main task is to deal with all matters directly relevant to employment and which to a large extent is the direct opponent of the DGB.

In addition, there are a good number of other national federations that exercise substantial influence and the most important of these are the: Verband der Landwirtschafts-kammern (Federation of Chambers of Agriculture), the Deutscher Bauernverband (German Farmers Federation), Bundesverband des Deutschen Gross- und Aussenhandels (Federation of German Wholesalers and Foreign Traders), Hauptgemeinschaft des Deutschen Einzelhandels (Central Federation of German Retailers), Bundesverband Deutscher Banken (German Federation of Banks), Deutscher Sparkassen- und Giroverband (German Savings and Giro Banks Federation), Zentralverband des Deutschen Handwerks (Central Federation of German Crafts), Verband Deutscher Reeder (Federation of German Shippers).

Apart from the chambers of commerce, membership of all business associations is voluntary. A hierarchical system of organisation exists within almost all the national federations. At the base in manufacturing industry, for example, there are hundreds of small associations composed of manufacturers of distinct types of similar products. In some cases, above this level, there are larger associations composed of various smaller associations of manufacturers of roughly similar products. On the next level there are the national product federations that cover whole industrial sectors and a good number of these federations are at the top of the pyramid represented by the BDI. For example, manufacturers of candles are members of the Verband Deutscher Kerzenhersteller, which alongside associations of detergent makers, paint manufacturers and dozens of other associations concerned in specific areas of the chemical industry, is a member of the Verband der Chemischen Industrie, which in turn is a member of the BDI.

Apart from being organised on a branch sector level, many of the national federations are also organised on a regional basis. The BDI and BDA have central organisations in each of the Federal Lands. The DIHT is organised solely on a geographic basis and is composed of more than 80 chambers of commerce scattered across the country. There is probably little need for as many assorted types of business federations as exist in this country and it is probable that the image and aims of companies in Germany would be clearer were a substantial rationalisation of the multitude of associations and federations to take place.

THE MAJOR FEDERATIONS AND THEIR VIEWS

The DIHT, based in Bonn, sees its main tasks as putting forward the views of German business to national and international authorities, ensuring that the general public is kept well informed on business attitudes and providing a wide variety of services for its members. In the latter context, for example, a German company seeking to establish a business in Britain may well use the London office of the DIHT to obtain general information, while, to give another example, a British company seeking a sales agent in a region of West Germany may well go to the chamber of commerce in the region for help in finding the right individual. The DIHT has a full-time staff of 200 in Bonn and its national organisation is sub-divided into eleven specialised sections, each dealing with specific economic, political and social themes, and each headed by a committee of businessmen. Each year it publishes a wide variety of pamphlets and booklets on topical subjects (it distributed a total of 460,000 booklets in 1971). Furthermore, its leaders hold regular press conferences, make hosts of public speeches, appear regularly in television discussions and on average the DIHT issues two or three press releases each week on current controversial issues.

The DIHT has enjoyed a fair measure of success in its publicity efforts in recent years through the strong and aggressive leadership of its president, Herr Otto Wolff von Amerongen, a millionaire Cologne industrialist. The views of the DIHT, published in 1972, give a broad idea of the opinions of business in this country on current economic problems. The leaders of the DIHT complained continually throughout 1972 that the Bonn Government was not doing enough to restore price stability. In February 1972, for example, Herr Otto Wolff von

Amerongen complained bitterly that Bonn was failing to break the increasingly widespread inflation mentality among the people of this country, which, he claimed, could eventually produce an impossible situation for the healthy development of industry. In the same month the DIHT accused the Government of irresponsible management of the budget, stressing that high public spending deficits were adding fuel to the inflation. In the following month the DIHT attacked the trade unions and the Government, and suggested that the basic principles of the free market economy were being abandoned and that essential freedom of action of businessmen, which is needed for healthy economic progress, was being eroded.

Time and again the DIHT in 1972 returned to the inflation theme and consistently criticised the Government for neglecting the issue. The heavy propaganda of the DIHT on this subject became increasingly important as the federal elections in November approached. The leading business organisations here mounted a major series of attacks on Government economic policies in the critical months prior to the elections. The DIHT regularly spoke of a serious crisis in Federal finances. Many of the views put forward by the DIHT and the other leading business federations on economic matters were highly similar to those propagated by the Christian Democrat and Christian Socialist parties. While the business federations claim to be politically independent, their strong attacks on the Government throughout 1972 must have done considerable damage to the Social Democrats in the elections.

But the DIHT, like the other national business organisations, by no means confines its public statements to current economic topics alone. In 1972, for example, the DIHT issued press releases on such diverse topics as the running of the country's postal services, the organisation of trade fairs, environmental problems, European Economic Community integration and problems concerned with development aid for poor countries. On Common Market matters the leading business federations have from the very start been strong supporters of a large and well-integrated European Community. They have long believed that the integration of the economies of Western Europe can produce a large and powerful domestic market, which can form the basis for industry to grow strongly and match the powerful competitive position of the giant American companies, whose major asset has long been their base in a vast domestic market.

For long the leading business federations have been ardent free traders. They have tended to the view that German industry can gain far more from low international tariffs and from the cutting of other obstacles to free trade, than can be gained from protectionist policies. All the main business federations have supported reductions in tariffs on exports from under-developed countries in the belief that such measures, coupled with development aid, can stimulate the economic growth of the Third World and thereby open new markets for German investment and sales and produce securer raw materials supplies. Dozens of statements in the recent past by the DIHT, the BDI and the BDA, have shown quite clearly that there are few differences of opinion between these leading organisations on major matters of economic and social policy and international affairs.

The DIHT sees itself as having the responsibility of representing all types of business in this country in all areas that directly and indirectly effect business life here. The BDI sees itself as the chief representative of manufacturing industry. It was established in 1949 and provided a continuation of the pre-war Reichsverband der Deutschen Industrie. Its successful development in many respects was due to Herr Fritz Berg, who was the head of the organisation for many years until his retirement in 1972, when he was succeeded by Herr Hans-Günther Sohl, who at the time was also head of the country's leading steel company, August-Thyssen Hütte AG.

Some of the chief fears of business leaders in this country were well expressed in a speech in November 1972, by Herr Johann-Friedrich Hünemörder, the head of the BDI's central policy co-ordination committee, who noted that 'we find ourselves today in a phase of increasingly clear confrontation. It is clear from the words of the head of the DGB, Herr Vetter, that the trade unions believe that they have a higher position of importance under the constitution than do other social groups. In fact, following comments made at this year's DGB congress, one must expect that the unions are now prepared to go so far as to place pressure on Parliament through use of political strikes.'

Herr Hünemörder continued that 'in line with the hardening of diverse economic views the DGB has stressed that it wishes to move from the policy of co-operation, that has been evident in the post-war period, to policies of hostility and confrontation. For a long time now all one has heard in the debate on income policies is mention of the need for fairer distributions. A healthy economy is as a result being turned into an arena for ideological tensions, with the prospect of bringing about its ruination'.

The BDI and BDA have increasingly been angered since the coming to power of the Social Democrats in 1969 by the increase of political influence that the trade unions have managed to obtain. The business associations are now increasingly gaining the impression that their importance in Bonn is not being given sufficient attention, after years of enjoying most substantial political influence. They see the Social Democrat Government as paving the way for radical socialism that in the end will result in the nationalisation of all the means of production, of property and of land, and in the imposition of high confiscatory taxes. It is probably fair to say that the business federations have been even slower than the CDU and the CSU to come to terms with the fact that the Social Democrats are currently the most popular political party in this country. The fear of an era of radical socialism dawning and the belief that the trade unions are on a confrontation course and more militant than ever, has persuaded the major national business federations to widen the scope of their activities to all manner of social and political questions, from the narrower framework of primarily economic topics.

In the fiscal policy area the chief associations see their main aim as being the creation of greater possibilities for companies to use their funds for investment purposes and thereby be in a position to strengthen their financial base and competitiveness. The federations are therefore strong supporters of increased tax-deductable business allowances and lower taxes. It is equally unsurprising that they are in the main firm opponents of the Government's tax reform plans. These reforms aim primarily at increasing corporation taxes, widening the scales of incomes and wages taxes to the disadvantage of top income groups, abolishing a great number of tax-deductable allowances and imposing new taxes on land, property and inheritances.

In the corporate law sector the federations see their chief aim as increasing the opportunities that businessmen have to decide alone all matters concerning the development of their enterprises. Thus, as stressed in Chapter 3, the federations are opposed to the Government's plans for greater worker co-determination and are highly reserved about the Government's cartel reform programme. In July 1973 the Government pushed through new cartel laws, establishing for the first time in this country firm powers for the Government and the Federal Cartel Office to prevent mergers and take-overs where these authorities consider there to be monopoly dangers. The new laws state specific sizes of mergers and take-overs that can be subject to investigation and approval by the Federal Cartel Office. The new law is subject to wide interpretation and it is still far too early for it to be clear just how much use the authorities will make of their new powers to slow the pace of industrial concentration. The business federations, while generally accepting the need for some controls on monopolies and oligopolies, fear that the cartel reforms could substantially restrict the healthy development of business competition, rather than increase such competition.

The views of the business federations on worker co-determination, tax reforms and cartel reforms are well known to the Bonn Government. The federations fear that they have failed to persuade the Government of the need to tread cautiously in these reform areas. However, the federations have managed to exert considerable influence on the Free Democrat Party, the junior Bonn coalition partners and have won full support from the CDU and CSU parties. In consequence, it seems quite likely that, in the current legislative period to the end of summer 1976, the Social Democrats will fail to realise their plans for the full introduction of worker co-determination on the lines in existence in the coal and steel industries (see Chapter 3), that less use will actually be made of the new cartel laws, as far as preventing mergers and take-overs is concerned, than the trade unions would have liked and that tax reforms may well be so delayed that they are only partially brought into law.

The leading business federations are all highly concerned with general structural problems in industry. They all support greater aid programmes for the less developed industrial regions of this country. They all are engaged in the planning of detailed programmes relating to labour market questions and industrial training, as well as matters concerning social conditions of employment. Environment questions are becoming increasingly important here, as in most other developed countries. The federations are seeking to persuade the federal and regional authorities to devote more public funds to improving the environment and to give up the present guiding principle of the authorities that 'the polluter pays'. In defence of industry's contribution towards improving the environment the DIHT published a survey in Spring 1972 showing that companies here spent twice as much on all manner of anti-pollution devices in the three years from the start of 1969 to the end of 1971, than they did in the previous three-year period. The total industrial spending volume in the last three-year period was DM 3,100 million.

In view of the exceptionally strong involvement in international trade of German business, the leading national business federations devote a great deal of time and energy to international questions. Each of the major federations has its own international research departments, some have foreign based representative offices and most are in some manner represented in such international organisations as the International Employers Organisation (IOE) in Geneva and the Union des Industries de la Communauté Européenne (UNICE) in Brussels. In several foreign business areas the federal authorities here have come to respect the business federations for their expert knowledge and have often consulted the federations on major international issues. In view of this it was not surprising that the Bonn Government should have appointed such prominent business leaders as Kurt Hansen, Berthold Beitz, Otto Wolff von Amerongen and Alwin Münchmeyer, to its negotiating team to work out avenues of trade expansion with the Russians in 1972.

The leaders of the main national business federations are often invited to present special reports to the Government on topics relevant to business matters and to participate in special parliamentary committees. By these means the federations can seek to influence new legislation and governmental decisions in a manner favourable to business. In most cases the federations most often consulted by the federal authorities are the DIHT, BDI and BDA. The last is the chief representative of German employers and, while being active in almost all areas of social and political affairs, it specialises in matters directly concerned with personnel management and labour relations. The BDA sees its chief tasks as setting general guidelines on employment matters to the individual specialised industrial employers associations. In addition, it seeks to advise employers on tactics in disputes with trade unions, it attempts to co-ordinate employers in negotiations with the trade unions and it strives to reach general agreements with the DGB in the interest of securing a healthy business environment.

On a more basic level the BDA sees its chief task as ensuring that employers have the freedom to settle wage contracts with the trade unions free of State intervention. The BDA, like the DGB, is an ardent opponent of any form of statutory wages and prices controls. In the area of wage negotiations the BDA seeks to ensure that the trade unions do not have any special rights that could place the unions in a more powerful position than employers. The BDA ardently defends the right of employers to mount lock-outs in the face of strikes, despite the view of the DGB that lock-outs should be made illegal. The BDA is in many respects a staunchly conservative body, reflecting the solid capitalist principles of its chief leaders, Herr Otto Friedrich and Herr Martin Schleyer, both of whom were for many years close business associates of Germany's most powerful and dictatorial post-war tycoon, Herr Friedrich Flick. It is no surprise therefore that the BDA, probably more than any other leading national business federation, increasingly utters loud fears about increasing trade union militancy here and mounting dangers of open confrontation with the unions.

The internal organisation of the business federations is in most cases highly similar. In all the national federations attempts are made to ensure that the various business branches represented in the federation are all equally represented in the top policy-making committees of the federation. In the banking sector the Bundesverband Deutscher Banken is the leading national federation and its internal structure serves as a good illustration of the organisation of the major federations. This federation has a total of 306 members, consisting of the three national branch banks (the Deutsche Bank, the Dresdner Bank and the Commerzbank), their three West Berlin subsidiaries, a total of 99 regional based joint stock banks, 138 private banks, 26 foreign banks with branches in this country and 37 specialised banks, mainly mortgage banks. The most important organ in this, as in all the other federations, is the general meeting of members, which is usually held annually. This meeting has the right to dismiss elected officials, but this almost never happens. The next most important body is the central committee, which in the Bankenverband is composed of representatives of all affiliated associations (there are special associations for each of the various types of credit institutions) and by three individuals from each of the main banking groups – the private banks, the regional joint stock banks coupled with the specialist banks and thirdly, the national branch banks.

The main function of the central committee is to elect the federation's executive directors, form special subject subcommittees and elect members to these committees. All elected officials in most business federations hold office for three years. In the Bankenverband the executive committee consists of nine persons, with three being directors of the three national branch banks, three being partners in private banks and three drawn from the regional and specialist banks. This committee elects from its midst a Presidium, consisting of three persons from the three main banking sectors, with one being the President and the others being Vice-Presidents. The Presidium represents the federation on a daily basis and meets from time to time to discuss general policy with the executive committee. The Bankenverband, based in Bonn, has a full-time staff of 80, which is managed by a senior committee of officials, who are directly responsible to the Presidium.

The national federations seek to maintain close contact with their members and, in an effort to ensure that they fairly represent the views of large companies as well as small and medium-sized companies, the federations regularly send detailed questionnaires to their members on a variety of policy matters. These questionnaires are also used for statistical purposes and help the national federations to be expertly informed on trends in business and on planned business developments. While attempts are made to continually present balanced views, it is almost inevitable that the views of the federations are little more than the personal opinions of their chief officers and this is a fault in the system, for often the views of small companies are given little airing as the presidents of the federations are invariably drawn from major concerns.

Apart from the federations of business there are a vast number of special interest associations, whose activities have a direct relevance to companies in this country. These associations, ranging from consumer protection groups to groups of environmentalists are in large measure similarly organised on a regional and national level to the federations described in this chapter so far. An association of particular importance for the financial community, whose influence on legislation can be said to be considerable, is the Arbeitsgemeinschaft der Deutschen Wertpapierbörsen (Association of German Stock Exchanges). This is an association formed on a voluntary basis in 1952 by the country's eight stock exchanges based in Frankfurt, Munich, Hamburg, Düsseldorf, West Berlin, Hanover, Stuttgart and Bremen. The first five exchanges mentioned here are the most important and it was agreed in 1952 that the leadership of the association should rotate every two years among these five bourses. Since the start of 1973 the leadership of the association is held by the Düsseldorf stock exchange, which organises the work of the association and whose president, Dr Zahn, is automatically chairman of the association for two years.

All laws governing the bourses here are made by Parliament and the courts alone can decide matters of dispute concerned with stock market transactions. Further, each of the eight stock exchanges is an independent body subject to the jurisdiction of the Land in which it is based. The association therefore is not in a position to create new rules and regulations governing stock market activities, nor has it any power whatever to dictate to an individual bourse how this bourse should manage its affairs. The association is, however, an important forum for the top officials of the bourses to exchange views on technical questions of operation and to ensure that a degree of co-operation exists between the bourses, which makes it possible for arbitrage business between the bourses to run smoothly. The management committee of the association is composed of the eight heads of the individual bourses, who meet to discuss general problems about once every six months. The association has a number of important sub-committees that study means of improving the technical efficiency of the bourses, that seek to educate the general public about the security markets and make the bourses more attractive and that seek to influence the views of the Bonn authorities and the authorities in Brussels, on matters concerning the operations of the bourses and questions of European Community harmonisation of stock exchanges.

In conjunction with the Bankenverband and the major business federations the association of stock exchanges plays an important role in seeking to ensure that the Bonn Government does not intervene too greatly in the security markets, that these markets can function well in the best interests of private enterprise and that the main operators on the bourses, which are chiefly the banks, maintain a great degree of influence on the way in which dealings in stocks and shares are organised and controlled here.

PUBLIC RELATIONS, PRESENTING VIEWS AND PRIVATE LOBBYING

All the national business federations fully appreciate that their aims can be sponsored only with the assistance of expert media specialists. All the federations have highly competent public relations departments. These departments are often split into several sections, specialising in internal information for federation members, relations with public authorities, contacts with the press, radio and television and contacts with the universities. Some of the federations have their own advertisement and film divisions, which aim to sponsor a general good image of the business sectors they represent by means of newspaper and magazine advertising, by means of organising special industry stands at international trade fairs and by means of educating the general public and school children about modern business through making special types of documentary films.

Communications with the universities has played an important role for many of the business federations, who have sought to do their own research and support university research on matters concerned with the role of business in modern society, its desirable aims and functions. Much of the work done in this context by the leading business federations has been of a high academic standard. The major federations sought to co-ordinate their basic research and in 1951 created the Deutsches Industrie-institut for this purpose. The chief aims of this organisation are to make clear to the general public the position of private enter-prise in modern society, to study deeply new problems affecting business and its environment and to generally support the public relations efforts of the individual major industry and employers federations.

The publicity campaigns continually mounted by the leading national business federations receive strong support from the country's largest companies. The degree of open support given by individual companies to controversial political campaigns mounted by the federations depends largely on the personality of the top directors of the individual companies. For example, while the leading directors of such huge companies as Siemens, Bosch, Hoechst and Volkswagen remained relatively silent about general economic and political trends in the months prior to the 1972 federal elections, the leaders of such com-panies as Bayer, Thyssen, Daimler-Benz and some of the major banks used press conferences they mounted to discuss their individual business problems, as a means of joining the leaders of the business federations in strong criticism of the Bonn Government's economic policies.

The public relations divisions of the major companies in this country can claim an equal degree of expertise to the similar type of departments within the business federations. The main leading companies spend heavily on public relations and the business leaders of this country are still strikingly aware of the existence of broad suspicion of businessmen among the general public. To some extent this suspicion can be traced back to the 1930s where it was clear that powerful business leaders used their positions to aid the Nazis in taking power and later in preparing this country for war. But even more fundamental is a general uneasiness here about profit. Hard work and efficiency are highly respected, yet discussions about profits and claims by individuals of making large profits are for many people here, as elsewhere on the Continent, somehow distasteful and vulgar.

The image of the rich being a class that has profited from the hard labour of lower classes is still widespread. It is an image which the trade unions continue to spread. And it was no surprise that the business community should have taken strong exception to some of the phrases used by Herr Vetter, the head of the DGB, at the DGB's 1972 congress, where such comments as 'we are no longer prepared to take merely the crumbs that fall from the tables of the governors' were to be heard.

It is on account of these attitudes that the large companies and the business federations strive at great expense to explain to the general public their aims, their views on the position of business in modern society and seek to improve the general image of private enterprise. The federations do this through advertisements, the publication of hosts of booklets, the making of films and by publicly taking a stand on all manner of political issues. The private companies seek the same goals by primarily trying to show the public that they are in no way secretive organisations and that all their activities can be publicly examined. To this end the major companies regularly hold press conferences, frequently issue press releases on all manner of new business developments, publish comprehensive and well-designed annual reports and their directors frequently make public speeches on all manner of business subjects. The sum result is that German business seeks to bend over backwards to present an image of honesty and, in so doing, the major companies of this country reveal a good deal more about their activities than do companies in most other major industrial countries.

While this most considerable effort in private company public relations is largely aimed at boosting a company's products and strengthening its image, so that it can more easily raise capital from the public, the awareness of the need to boost the general image of big business and industry here is a further significant element in the public relations efforts. Germany's leading businessmen continually seek to present the public with a picture of a businessman who actively supports all manner of social reforms, so long as they do not produce an environment that could stifle individual business initiative. The model businessman, as presented by the business federations and big companies to the general public, is a man who cares deeply about the welfare of his employees and who works exceptionally hard and, in return, is prepared to take only modest remuneration. Just how much top business executives get paid is a topic that is almost taboo as far as public discussion is concerned in this country.

Fearing that any other sort of image may well lead to greater conflicts with the trade unions and produce greater antipathy among the general public to big business, the business federations make immense efforts to promote the image described above and have a considerable distaste for flamboyant entrepreneurs who clearly are out of line with the general picture that is being presented. A man like Dr Anton Ernstberger, chief executive officer of the Bayerische Hypotheken- und Wechsel-Bank, is largely shunned by the business establishment here. Dr Ernstberger has actively bought and sold shares in major brewing companies and produced as a result major changes in the structure of the brewing industry. He has openly spoken about his activities and the success of his strategies and this is the sort of thing that just does not go down well in West Germany. The whole style of Mr Bernard Cornfeld was brash and sharp and for this reason his Investors Overseas Services company was at the very start highly unwelcome in Germany to the leaders of business.

Because of this approach it is probable that a young man with brilliant financial ideas would find it a lot harder here than in some other countries to establish his own company and swiftly become a successful tycoon. In Britain and the United States, for example, such aggressive young business wizards as Jim Slater or Peter Walker of Slater, Walker Ltd., or Jimmy Ling of Ling-Temco-Vought or Saul Steinberg of Leasco, can obtain widespread admiration and acclaim. In West Germany the business community thinks and operates in such a way that such individuals are highly restricted in their opportunities and a major factor is the fear of business leaders that such brilliant young businessmen could do damage to the image of solid respectability that the business federations have sought to create in the last twenty years.

Recognising that at times the various business federations fail to present their views clearly, because of too many federations shouting at the same time, the leading federations consult with each other on major issues on occasion in the so-called Bonn Gemeinschaftsausschuss der Deutschen Gewerblichen Wirtschaft (Joint Committee of German Business). This committee has become particularly important since the creation of the Konzertierte Aktion, the so-called committee of concerted action, which under the chairmanship of the Minister of Economics brings together leaders of the business federations, the trade unions, the Federal Bank and the Government's independent Council of Economic Advisers. It is essential in this forum that the business federations maintain a common front and to ensure that this is the case, the leaders of the federations have increasingly met together to discuss matters of economic and social policy. The Konzertierte Aktion was established by Dr Karl Schiller when he became Minister of Economics in 1966. At the start, in view of the recession, it performed a useful function and aided the Government in designing short-term economic policies, with the assurance that these policies would be given support by the business community and the trade unions.

For the business federations the Konzertierte Aktion is an excellent forum for outlining to the Government and the Federal Bank the economic policy desires of business, and warning the Government of the dangers of pursuing policies that may be contemplated by some politicians or supported by the trade unions. Views differ greatly on the importance that should be attached to the Konzertierte Aktion. Dr Schiller believed that it was an absolutely essential organisation, but he could say little else in view of its being a creation of his own. The present Minister of Finance, Herr Helmut Schmidt, suggested to the author in an interview in early 1973 that the value of the Konzertierte Aktion was often greatly exaggerated. He maintained that it could not be of use in times of major wage disputes, when the relationship between the trade unions and the business federations was particularly highly charged. Further, he suggested that at best it was a useful means of getting a clear exchange of views, but that as its novelty wore off, so its value in producing better harmony between the two rival sides of industry declined.

Individual company directors are often not content to allow the business federations alone to lobby the national and regional political authorities. The major companies ensure that they maintain close contacts with leading politicians and like the business federations, they seek to keep well informed on possible Government plans, by maintaining contacts with well-placed civil servants. Major private initiatives of a lobbying nature rarely come into the open, although they almost certainly exist in good number. One such instance, which gives an indication of how private individuals seek to exert influence on the Government, came to light in early 1973. Herr Sohl, in his capacity as head of Thyssen, rather than in his position as head of the BDI, wrote a detailed letter on 18 December 1972 to the Finance Minister, Herr Schmidt and the Economics Minister, Herr Friderichs, demanding changes in the Government's coal policies.

The German steel companies were formerly the chief owners of the coal mines of the Ruhr, but in 1968 they consolidated their coal interests in a new company, Ruhrkohle AG. This company in recent years has amassed vast financial losses, which the steel companies have in large measure been forced to subsidise. To strengthen the sales of the company the Government does not allow the steel companies to buy foreign coking coal. The price of Ruhr coking coal in 1972 was well above international levels and the steel companies were losing heavily in international competition, largely because their overhead costs were simply too high. Herr Sohl demanded in his letter that the steel companies should be allowed to buy coking coal abroad as a means of strengthening the competitiveness of the German steel industry.

Herr Sohl suggested in his letter that Thyssen might have to cut its domestic investment plans and boost its foreign investments if the Government did not change its coke policies. Beyond this he called for a major rationalisation of the coal industry with large public spending to finally alleviate the burden of keeping the coal mines going that the steel companies had to carry. Herr Sohl's letter was leaked to the press by people in the steel industry in January 1973, after it was clear that the Government was not going to make a quick reply. The letter, when published, caused a major public debate on German energy policies. The Minister of Economics was forced to make a public statement on the issue and said that he was not prepared to devote funds *ad infinitum* to supporting an inefficient coal industry. The Federal Chancellor felt bound, in view of the publicity that the Sohl letter attracted, to state that the creation of a new general energy policy was a chief Government priority.

While the steel industry had to continue buying domestic coke, the Sohl letter had the effect of forcing the Government to get off the fence and take a stand on the whole subject of subsidies for the coal industry. At the same time the letter, by being carefully leaked and by being drawn up by Herr Sohl in close co-operation with other steel industry leaders, did draw attention to the special financial difficulties of the steel industry here. In many respects the Sohl letter achieved a great deal and many of its suggestions may well be incorporated into the Government's energy industry programme.

It is primarily through actions such as this, through business leaders being active in the Konzertierte Aktion and on Government committees, through business leaders developing close private contacts with politicians and through skilled use of the mass media, that the business lobby in the country works. This lobby is skilled, highly efficient and can claim many successes. But currently the business federations are finding it more difficult than ever to influence Government, as the trade unions become more adept at exercising political influence and as they receive a warm reception from the present Bonn authorities.

The business federations, supported by vociferous individual business leaders, do manage to clearly get their views across to the general public. By this means they do to some extent weaken the effectiveness of the German trade unions and they are aided in their efforts by a press, which by and large is much more sympathetic to the views and aims of industry and private business than to the policies of the trade unions. It is probably incorrect to suggest that major ideological confrontations threaten to bring about the ruin of this strong industrial society. But with the mounting influence of the trade unions and clear signs of growing militancy among the unions, the business federations are correct in believing that now, more than ever before, they must seek to maintain their image of responsibility and respectability. The federations run the risk, however, of bringing about a crisis by making too many irresponsible speeches about the evil intentions of the unions and they are currently doing themselves more harm than good by continuing to criticise the Bonn Government in a negative manner and failing to try and form a healthy working relationship with the Social Democrats.

7 A General Conclusion

The international currency crisis of early 1973 resulted in a further weakening of the competitive position of German industry by producing a significant revaluation of the Deutsche Mark in terms of the currencies of Britain, the United States, Italy and a number of other countries. Decisions taken in early February 1973 by the Bonn Government, which are discussed in detail later in this chapter, added to the problems of industry by raising taxes and making it more difficult to obtain funds for investment purposes. These most recent events tend to lend weight to some of the arguments made earlier in this book that the outlook for the economy of this country is far from bright.

It would be pure folly at this moment in time to try and estimate just how great an impact the exchange rate changes since 1969, the mounting inflation, the growing militancy of the trade unions and of some of the Bonn Government's legislative plans, will have on the economy and the health of industry. This chapter will seek to draw some general conclusions and it looks at the effects that many of the matters discussed earlier in this book will have on foreign companies involved in the German market and on domestic concerns.

The many factors that have been outlined here, which suggest a somewhat pessimistic outlook for industry, will affect the subsidiaries of foreign based companies in this country to almost exactly the same extent as they will affect German owned concerns. The foreign owned subsidiaries have the advantage of being a part of organisations that can adapt to changing economic conditions in different countries and can afford to take low profits for considerable periods of time from one or other of their daughter companies. Adam Opel AG, the German-based General Motors concern, does not have the same costs as Volkswagen or BMW in terms of research and development and foreign sales. Opel is in a position to share costs to some extent with Vauxhall in Britain and to rely on its parent company in Detroit to do most basic research. Because of these factors the possible profit margins that Opel can make are greater than those of Volkswagen at a time when Germany is rapidly becoming the country with the highest level of unit production costs.

The same argument applies with equal validity to a large number of the foreign subsidiaries based here. A further important consideration is that most of these foreign owned companies in this country are not nearly as dependent on exporting from Germany as their German rivals. The need to take paper-thin profits or even losses on exports to maintain large market shares abroad is currently a major strain for many German companies. Such a strain exists for only very few of the largest foreign owned companies based here. Philips of Holland, for example, has large plants in most European countries and its German plant can to a large extent survive from turnover made in Germany alone and some of the parts the German plant needs for its products can be supplied from other Philips plants abroad, where production costs are lower. For German companies, few of which have substantial foreign subsidiaries, such opportunities as those that Deutsche Philips have, do not exist.

It seems most likely that few of the major foreign owned companies in this country will embark on major expansion of their plants in the next few years, on account primarily of the shortages of labour and the rising overhead costs here. It may also be more profitable for some companies, in view of the exchange rate changes, to increase imports to Germany from foreign based plants, rather than expand output of domestic German based plants at all. Largely the expansion of existing German based plants owned by foreign companies will be aimed at obtaining greater economies of scale. Some of the foreign owned companies may also seek to diversify in this country into sectors which suggest that high profit returns are possible. A good example of such a development can be seen in the recent move by the German subsidiary of British American Tobacco into retailing. BAT has managed to gain a cigarette market share here of around 28 per cent but, in line with other tobacco concerns, it fears that future sales expansion may be highly limited on account of the growing volume of adverse publicity to smoking. BAT in coming years will only modestly expand its tobacco operations here. However, the company has managed to obtain slightly more than a 25 per cent share in the large Horten stores group and may well expand considerably in retailing.

Fordwerke of Cologne and Opel will both continue expanding, but like other foreign companies they are going to be highly selective about where they locate plants to be built up. Ford has a plant in the Saar, which may well be considerably increased in size in coming years. As has been pointed out in an earlier chapter the Saar is an under-developed industrial region today, due mainly to the decline of such old heavy industries as steel and coal. The serious weakening competitive pressures of the German heavy industries may well make it possible for Ford to obtain labour necessary for the expansion of its Saar plant. For the same reasons, Opel may well expand its plant in Bochum in the Ruhr, for the Ruhr is increasingly becoming a depressed area as the steel and coal companies are being forced to rationalise greatly and cut their employee totals.

The location of new plants in Germany is going to be a desperately difficult matter for all companies here and it seems most likely that foreign owned concerns and their German rivals will increasingly concentrate expansion in the under-developed regions and in areas where substantial unemployment may come about. The main motive for Ford and Opel to expand in Germany, rather than open new plants in other European areas, is primarily that both companies are already so large that substantial production increases at existing plants may be possible without the need to hire a greatly increased number of workers. However, the pace of expansion of production by both these companies is unlikely to be dramatic, for both already have severe problems in filling their present labour needs and, while their present sales are at a record level, they both are far away from reaching the sort of profit levels that are likely to greatly satisfy their parent concerns.

In the electrical sector a good number of foreign companies have established major subsidiaries in West Germany. IBM Deutschland employs about 22,500 people, while Philips employs 32,000; Standard Elektrik Lorenz, which is owned by International Telephone and Telegraph, employs more than 36,600; Brown, Boveri of Mannheim, which is 56 per cent owned by the Swiss Brown, Boveri & Cie, employs more than

40,000 people. These companies are all active in business areas which look like enjoying considerable expansion in coming years. The West German Government is likely to place major orders for reactors and Brown, Boveri will almost certainly get a handsome share of the contracts, to give just one example. In the communications sphere, SEL and Siemens together dominate the market and this is likely to be a major growth sector. In computers, IBM is likely to continue enjoying significant expansion, although it seems improbable that it will be allowed to maintain its present market share of about 70 per cent in this country. The domination of the computer market by IBM and the extremely tough competitive pressures that this company produces have resulted in the last couple of years in AEG-Telefunken linking its computer operations with Nixdorf, and in Siemens reaching a broad computer co-operation agreement with Philips of Holland and CII of France. These new groups, backed to a considerable extent by public funds, are likely to produce some additional competitive pressure for IBM. Further, the general weakened competitive position of German produced goods may tempt IBM chief executives in America to slow the expansion pace of its German plants in favour of greater expansion of plants elsewhere in Europe.

All the foreign owned electrical companies in Germany are presently well managed, enjoy lengthy order books and are highly competitive on the domestic market. Their expansion is unlikely to be quite so dramatic as it has been in past years, but a gradual rate of growth for all seems fairly certain. The same, however, cannot be said with such great certainty for the foreign owned chemical companies here. The intense pressure of international competition in most chemical industry sectors places German plants with their high production costs and their highly valued Deutsche Mark at a growing disadvantage. The recognition of this has been the main spur for the German chemical industry to build up foreign subsidiaries at a swift pace in the last decade. As illustrated in an earlier chapter the German chemical companies have invested more abroad in recent years than any other industry in this country. It seems improbable that such international giants with subsidiaries here, as Imperial Chemical Industries, Monsanto, DuPont and AKZO, will strongly increase plant capacities. It may well be that some cut-backs are made, especially in the synthetic fibres sector, and Dow Chemical and AKZO have already started in a significant manner in this direction. Some petro-chemical companies, however, such as Dow, may well build new plants in the development areas in North Germany and thereby take advantage of well-placed coastal sites and substantial investment aids from public authorities.

There is little reason to expect a significant slow-down in the expansion pace of some of the food companies owned by foreign concerns in this country. The rapidly rising level of incomes here, especially the likely development of a fairer distribution of income producing greater prosperity for the lowly paid, is likely to lead to a substantial continuation of the consumer boom that is at present raging in this country. To some extent such large firms as Deutsche Nestlé with its more than 15,500 employees in Germany, and Deutsche Unilever with its more than 39,500 employees in Germany, are likely to prosper. The latter company may encounter some difficulties in the detergent sector, where the privately owned Henkel group is a most fierce competitor and one of the very few firms to have effectively forced Procter and Gamble out of a market. Other food companies, such as Cadbury-Schweppes, are also likely to continue expanding here. In many cases these companies may decide to try and buy existing medium-sized companies here to get labour and a stronger footing in certain business areas. In the food sector this is a development that many German experts expect, and a number of British companies are often mentioned as possible future purchasers of German companies. Such a development seems improbable in the brewing industry, where the shares of the largest companies tend to be highly priced and largely in the hands of major institutions. A number of foreign breweries, notably British concerns, have shown a strong interest in trying to get into the vast German market, but they are unlikely to meet with great success.*

In the oil sector the general outlook for foreign companies in Germany seems far from bright. Competition is intense and the German Government is determined to become less dependent

---

* In early summer 1973, Watney Mann of Britain managed to acquire more than 75 per cent of the medium-sized German brewery, Stern-Brauerei Carl Funke AG.

on foreign companies for its energy supplies. The Deminex concern, which is a venture owned by a consortium of German companies, which in turn are partly State controlled, gets large aid from public authorities to search for oil. Its endeavours have so far been largely unsuccessful, but as the Germans become increasingly worried about the possibility of insecure long-term energy supplies, they will increase the aid Deminex and such companies as Veba get. These aid increases may place these companies in a position to deal with Middle East oil countries directly and this aim is now being backed by substantial diplomatic pressure by the West Germans on Arab countries.*

The German authorities are somewhat resentful of the fact that, while their country is the largest consumer of oil in Western Europe, they have no direct say whatever in the negotiations that are held to set international oil prices and are utterly dependent on foreign owned oil concerns. The close Government supervision of oil price levels, the strong competition and the increased energies of the German authorities to secure their own oil supplies, make the prospect of high profits in the future here for the foreign owned oil companies far from good. The largest oil concerns in Germany are Esso, Shell, Texaco, British Petroleum and Mobil Oil. With an increasing number of international experts and politicians predicting that the next decade will see major oil shortages in the world and with the Americans becoming especially alarmed about this, it is quite possible that the foreign oil companies here will, in coming years, reduce the scale of their German operations in favour of the expansion of operations in their home countries.

Oil, chemicals, food and automobiles are the industries which concern the largest foreign owned subsidiaries in West Germany. For many of the reasons discussed earlier in this book it is likely that the pace of foreign investment in production plants in this country will slow down in coming years. A substantial increase, however, may be seen in the investment by foreign concerns in the building of sales and service organisations here. Never before in the history of the Federal Republic have foreign companies had such good opportunities as now to sell their goods in this country. The high standard of living has produced a most heavy

* Further details are given on the oil situation in the section dealing with Veba AG in Appendix 2.

level of consumer spending. The Germans buy more cars, televisions, clothes and more of most things than people of other nationalities do in Western Europe. The exchange rate changes of the last few years have greatly favoured the competitive position of most foreign producers in terms of the German market. The enlargement of the European Economic Community places Ireland, Denmark and Britain in a better position to sell to Germany than before. The conclusion of special trade agreements between the European Community and the remaining member countries of the European Free Trade Association will result in these EFTA countries having better chances to sell in Germany.

Direct American exports to Germany are likely to rise as a result of the devaluations of the dollar, the revaluations of the Deutsche Mark and the substantial advantages that have been produced in the recent past by the Americans managing to maintain an inflation rate well below the West German level. In addition, it is likely that in the course of the next few years a series of major trade agreements will be reached between the United States and the European Economic Community, which will make it easier for American concerns to export to Europe. The growing number of associate membership treaties that the European Economic Community is concluding with primarily developing countries is further opening the Community to foreign imports and Germany may well be the recipient of many of these imports.

The Japanese are in a special situation, for they have not benefitted greatly from the exchange rate changes and are unlikely to benefit substantially from multilateral trade treaties that are concluded. However, the Japanese are unlikely to voluntarily choose a course that will result in a reduction of their export volume or in a decrease in the rate of growth of their export sales. The Japanese will have a tougher time than before in penetrating the U.S. market and will in all probability pay greater attention as a result to Western Europe. The Japanese have already made substantial inroads into European markets and especially into the German market, as has been indicated in earlier chapters. Unit costs of production in Japan are still far below West German levels and it would be surprising if the volume of Japanese exports to Germany did not increase in coming years, producing a still larger trade surplus for Japan in trade with this country.

There is no single business area where increases in imports to West Germany should not be possible. The most striking rises will in all probability come in the engineering, electrical and consumer goods areas (oil imports quite naturally are also bound to rise). But while the conditions have greatly improved for foreign companies to sell in Germany and make healthy profits, it must be pointed out that only those firms which plan a long-term strategy and carefully study the market here will meet with large successes. The German market is bitterly competitive and German companies will not easily relinquish market shares to foreign products. Foreign companies seeking to gain a footing here will have to adopt similar marketing tactics to those that German companies have in the past used abroad.

The Japanese, for example, are a major headache for German car producers, for they appear to be studying market conditions here now with great care and there are fears that they will soon launch a massive offensive in this market. Surprisingly, there are few German car industry experts who fear sharp competition in this market from the British Leyland Motor Corporation, despite the fact that this company stands to benefit greatly from the sharp devaluation of the pound in terms of the German currency and from British entry into the European Economic Community. The methods that BLMC have used so far in getting into the German market are in themselves lessons on how not to try and sell in the fierce German market.

For some time BLMC appeared to content itself with simply raising its profit margins every time the pound declined in terms of the Deutsche Mark (there have been quite a few occasions of this happening since November, 1967). The result was that while BLMC increased its profits it did not increase its market share, while the French automobile makers, for example, held prices, despite French Franc devaluations, in terms of the Deutsche Mark and used this as a means to really penetrate the German market. BLMC seemed content for some time to sell just a few thousand cars a year in this market, where annually more than 2·2 million new cars are sold.

There is little doubt that the range of cars produced by

BLMC could do well in competition with the Germans in the German market. Jaguar, Rover and Triumph models could present a most serious challenge to Mercedes and BMW. Similarly, because of the price advantages produced by the currency developments, Austin and Morris models could almost certainly win a substantial share of the German market for small and medium cars. But the successful sales of these models could only result if BLMC were to establish a sales and service organisation in this country that is just as efficient as the organisations of BMW and Volkswagen. The great success that VW and BMW have enjoyed in Britain is largely due to the ability of these companies to build sales and service organisations on a par with those of British rivals. No German will opt for a British car if great difficulties exist in getting repairs done swiftly. So far BLMC has appeared unwilling to spend sufficient money on building up a strong service and dealership organisation and has done little to change its reputation in Germany of being a manufacturer of poorly finished unreliable cars.

At one point BLMC decided to leave marketing of Austin and Morris cars solely to A. Brüggemann & Co. GmbH, a Düsseldorf-based company. A wholly-owned BLMC company was established in Frankfurt to sell Jaguar, Rover and Triumph cars. This company had barely got off the ground when BLMC changed its mind and decided to take a 40 per cent stake in Brüggemann, giving Brüggemann full responsibility for selling all BLMC cars in Germany and closing the Frankfurt company. Brüggemann is a small company without the finance needed to build a strong network of sales and service companies across Germany and an efficient series of spare parts depots. Further, it would seem that this company is quite content to achieve modest sales and the total BLMC sales volume in Germany in 1972 was just 21,000 units. It may well be that BLMC will miss the present chance to get a strong footing in Germany by failing to approach the market in the thorough manner that VW has approached the British market.

Those foreign companies prepared to invest in building sales organisations here that are fully competitive with those of German rivals stand now to greatly boost sales and profits here. The growing competition from foreign companies in the German market is one of the major forces that will speed up a process of industrial concentration in this country. The only checks on this swift process of concentration will be those imposed by the new Bonn legislation on cartels and monopolies and the new rules and regulations governing monopolies that the Commission of the European Economic Community is planning. This concentration process may not be completely confined to Germany alone and may involve an increasing number of mergers between German and foreign companies. The number of such cross-border mergers, however, is likely to be relatively small. This will be on account of the immense difficulties posed for such a merger by the absence of common tax, corporation, social security and trade union laws across the European Community.

The prospect of adequate conditions being produced to make cross-border mergers no more difficult than mergers within a single country seems remote, despite all the enthusiasm and optimism on this topic continually shown by the leaders of the European Community. German companies have to some extent been adventurous in this sphere with Agfa linking with Gevaert of Belgium, Hoesch linking with Hoogovens of Holland and Vereinigte Flugtechnische Werke linking with Fokker of Holland. The difficulties of arranging cross-border mergers may well become even more difficult for German companies, as has been noted in an earlier chapter, if the German trade unions succeed with their plans for worker co-determination. But even without such a development the present problems involved in a cross-border merger are immense. The exact nature of these problems is still difficult to fully assess, for since the creation of the European Community the number of these mergers has been few and most have been too recent to allow one to make an objective judgement. Some of the problems, however, have come to the fore clearly in the case of the Agfa-Gevaert merger, which is the oldest of its kind since the establishment of the European Community.

Agfa and Gevaert merged in 1964, but the integration of the two companies is still far from complete. The great competitive pressures of the Japanese and of Eastman Kodak made the two companies conclude that only by a merger could they hope to remain competitive. Gevaert did not have the funds to buy Agfa and even if Agfa had had the necessary funds, the Belgians would never have allowed one of their top companies to fall completely into German hands. The merger was established through the creation of two main companies – Agfa-Gevaert AG in Germany and Gevaert-Agfa NV in Belgium, in which the two parent companies each had a 50 per cent stake. These two new companies had the same boards of directors. The new ten-man executive board consisted half of Belgians and half of Germans, with a Belgian and a German sharing the chairmanship and with meetings held twice a month alternately in Belgium and in Germany.

Clumsy parallel administrative organisations were established in both countries, but joint committees went ahead to devise the best ways of rationalisation and in a few years some substantial savings had been made. The merger has been most complete in third countries where the Gevaert and Agfa sales teams have been fully integrated. The fact that in Belgium and Germany two quite different types of pension schemes and social security schemes exist has made it difficult to arrange for many transfers of middle management staff among the two head offices. While the two head offices, in Leverkusen near Cologne and in Mortsel near Antwerp, are just a two-hour drive from each other, executives have sought to avoid travelling between these offices as much as possible and communication between top managers is by no means as good as would be the case if the company had a single headquarters. At first no attempts were made to arrange transfers of middle managers, for the Belgians still felt some resentment towards the Germans, due to some extent to memories from the last war, and few German employees were keen to live in Mortsel.

It took more than five years to get the new company into some sort of shape and effect fairly wide-ranging integration. In this period profits fell to levels below those that the two parent companies had prior to the merger. Positive results of the merger have been seen in the recent past and in 1972 the turnover was twice that of 1964 at around DM 2,300 million, profits were substantially ahead and the total number of employees had risen by only about 3,000 from the 30,000 at the time of the merger. A thawing in nationalistic feeling between the two partners came recently and introduced a new phase in the company's integration. In Spring 1971 Dr Gustav Schaum retired from the executive board and instead of replacing him with another German it was agreed that the two head companies should have just one chairman, the Belgian, Dr Hendrik Cappuyns. The dual nationality system in top management thus started to crumble some seven years after the merger.

The company is forced to carry a number of overhead costs that most companies do not have. It is forced to have two separate accounts departments and continually has fights with both the German and the Belgian tax authorities. The aim of maintaining an equal partnership has been difficult because the value of the Belgian part of the company's basic capital has changed considerably due to the revaluations of the Deutsche Mark and the issue of new shares is a complex procedure in view of the need to keep the 50–50 balance between the two countries. Other serious and costly problems arise from maintaining two separate head offices. While the merger has been a success in that both companies still believe that it was the only chance of remaining competitive, the attendant difficulties have been so great that the Agfa-Gevaert example is hardly an encouragement to other companies considering a cross-border merger.

While such ventures are unlikely to become numerous, it is quite possible that many more close co-operation agreements will develop in coming years between German companies and companies in other member countries of the European Community. Such joint ventures as the Siemens computer link with CII and Philips and the large number of international joint ventures involving German banks, can be seen as the start of a far greater number of similar ventures that may well cover most business sectors.

The degree of industrial concentration will most certainly vary from one business sector to another, with the key factors being the extent to which the competitiveness of German industries has been weakened by the exchange rate changes of recent years, by the rises in labour costs, by the increasing tension in the labour market and by such future developments as some of the Government's legislative plans and the militancy of the trade unions. A most substantial concentration is likely in the mechanical engineering industry, where most firms are of a relatively small size and are becoming increasingly uncompetitive in terms of foreign rivals.

From the viewpoint of the general economic development of this country the effects of the factors just mentioned are likely to be greatest in the heavy industries, such as shipbuilding, iron, steel and coal. In their present shape these industries are no longer competitive internationally and could not survive at their present scale without considerable aid from public authorities and from substantial efforts at reorganisation. The German steel industry, the largest in Western Europe, is no longer in a position to compete effectively with the heavily subsidised British Steel Corporation, with the Americans and the Japanese. The desperate aim of avoiding massive unemployment in the Ruhr is resulting in the Ruhr coal industry producing far more coal than it can sell and, to curb losses, its selling prices are far above international prevailing rates. The coal industry only manages to keep customers by strong Government restrictions on the import of coal and coking coal. The result is that in addition to the wide range of factors mentioned earlier in this book and this chapter, the iron and steel companies are forced to pay more dearly than foreign rivals for their coal and coke.

August Thyssen-Hütte is West Germany's largest steel company; it is the largest steel company in Continental Europe, but it will almost certainly be forced to make heavy redundancies if it hopes to survive in the long-term. In early 1973 the company made an agreed bid for a major rival, Rheinstahl. The acquisition can produce substantial economies of scale in the shipbuilding, sheet metals, refined metals, foundry, iron and steel divisions of the Thyssen group. A merger was probably essential for Rheinstahl, which has failed in recent years to make any profit at all on annual sales of around DM 5,700 million. About 25 per cent of Rheinstahl's turnover is due to exports and export business to some extent brought losses. The serious wages and raw materials costs explosion of recent years, coupled with the currency rate changes, have been major factors in leading to a massive drop in Thyssen's profits. In the 1970–71 financial year the company announced a net profit decline to DM 63 million from DM 219 million in the previous year, while sales deteriorated to DM 10,380 million from DM 10,881 million. For the 1971–72 year the company announced a further decline in profits and sales to DM 56 million and DM 9,835 million respectively. Most other steel companies can report even worse results for the last few years.

The declining competitiveness of the steel industry has been clearly recognised in the Ruhr and led in the last three years to a considerable shake-out. In this period Salzgitter has acquired Ilseder Peine; Salzgitter has reached a partial co-operation agreement with Thyssen in the shipbuilding sector; Krupp has heavily rationalised many of its divisions and sharply reduced the number of products it makes; Mannesmann has merged its steel pipe interests with those of the Thyssen group; Mannesmann has heavily diversified and bought a major stake in the large Demag mechanical engineering company; Hoesch of Dortmund has merged with Hoogovens of Holland and, most recently, Thyssen has acquired a major stake in Rheinstahl. Further such moves are essential if the iron and steel industry can hope to once again become strongly competitive in international markets. This shake-out in this industry will inevitably lead to some cuts in output levels and possibly sharp cuts in coming years in the number of employees in the iron and steel industry.

In the coal industry major decisions will have to be taken as the giant Ruhrkohle company produces mounting losses year after year, which its main shareholders, the steel companies, can no longer afford to cover. A substantial rationalisation scheme will be started, supported to a great extent from public funds, which in coming years will produce a substantial reduction in the output volume and number of employees of this company. The degree of unemployment in the Ruhr will probably not be severe at any single time, for the unions will ensure that this does not happen through their powerful position on the boards of the major companies. Further, substantial public authority investment grants will lead to the attraction to the Ruhr of more companies involved in modern technological business sectors. To some extent, however, the Ruhr will in the course of the next few years become a depressed industrial area and the substantial labour market tension will decline in this region.

A number of other industrial sectors will also suffer without doubt from the reduction in competitiveness of this country. To give just one example one may note the present acute difficulties of the country's largest company, Volkswagen. The latest dollar devaluation will make it almost impossible for VW in the near future to maintain sales levels of 500,000 cars a year in the United States. The company's German plants have an annual turnover of more than DM 15,000 million, two-thirds of their output is sold abroad and currently VW makes well below a one per cent net profit return on the turnover of these domestic plants. The continuing wage-cost boom here, coupled with the 1973 currency realignment, could well push VW into the red for a short period. The company desperately needs funds to finance the development of new models and it may well be forced to cut its output levels to get back to a more economic scale of operations. This could produce shock waves through a vast number of car-equipment supplying companies. A substantial concentration of industry is expected in the light electrical sector and in the tyre sector and the VW developments will be a major cause of this.

In addition to the many factors mentioned so far the difficulties of German industry have been increased recently by the fiscal decisions of the Bonn Government. With the aim of curbing inflation the Government announced in early February 1973 the abolition of a number of tax deductible allowances and the increase for twelve months of corporation taxes by 10 per cent. Further, the Government increased oil taxes, pushing the price of petrol to one of the highest levels in Europe, after having been close to the foot of the European price table just two years before. While this oil tax rise will produce substantial tax revenue, it adds to the inflation pressures and the overhead costs of a vast number of companies. These fiscal measures will make it all the harder for German companies to return to satisfactory profit levels and as a result many companies will not be able to find the funds to ensure a fast rate of growth in coming years.

Further blows were dealt by the Government to the future success of industry in early 1973, apart from the exchange rate changes; and these concerned the tightening of foreign exchange controls. The sum effect of these measures is to make it all the harder for German companies to raise capital for domestic expansion. The Bonn Government tightened the regulations on the cash deposit scheme on borrowing abroad by domestic companies, known as the 'Bardepot', by increasing the volume of foreign borrowings to be deposited by domestic companies free of interest at the Federal Bank to 100 per cent from 50 per cent and decreasing the amount that can be borrowed abroad annually for use in Germany by an individual company to just DM 50,000 from ten times this sum. This decision effectively made it impractical for German companies to seek funds for domestic investment abroad. Further, foreign companies were no longer permitted to bring capital into the country for investment purposes.

In addition to these measures, the Bonn Government decided at the same time to make all non-resident purchases of German shares subject to special approval from the Federal Bank. In summer 1972 the Government made all purchases by non-residents of fixed interest-bearing German securities subject to Federal Bank approval. These two measures together effectively closed the German stock exchanges to foreigners. In 1972 non-residents had accounted for about one-third of the total volume of business transacted on German bourses. These measures have the effect of narrowing the bourses and thereby making it all the more difficult for German companies to raise large sums of capital from the public.

German industry was further burdened in June 1973 by a Bonn mini-budget, involving further tax increases and cuts in depreciation allowances. In line with the Bonn anti-inflation policies the Federal Bank increased its credit restrictions still further in the early summer and Germany experienced its toughest credit squeeze in more than two decades. The extent of the squeeze was well illustrated by day-to-day money market rates exceeding 20 per cent at times and by yields on first class domestic bond issues rising to the record high level of 10 per cent.

The Federal Bank has in recent years become increasingly alarmed about the development of domestic inflation and tended to move strongly to the view that its present armoury of credit restrictive tools is insufficient. It has succeeded in convincing the Government of this and it is likely that new legislation will be made to increase the powers of the Federal Bank. The main new power will be the granting to the Federal Bank the right to impose minimum reserves requirements on the volume of credits granted by the commercial banks. This will amount to the imposition of credit ceilings. It will probably result in the commercial banks having to be much more selective about the clients it grants credits to, and this could result in small and medium-size companies, in particular, finding it exceptionally difficult to borrow money.

All these moves by the Government have been clearly aimed at reducing the inflation rate, but they will have the effect in due course of making it harder for industry to invest and, with profits having fallen most substantially in the last few years, the conclusion one is forced to draw is that, unless special investment aids are given, German industry will not manage to maintain anything like its former growth rates in coming years, simply because of its failure to invest sufficiently. This conclusion is supported by the striking rate of profit declines. In 1970 a vast number of companies reported profit falls of more than 25 per cent and similarly high declines were reported in the following year. Very modest increases were made in 1972 by many sectors. A few companies, notably the chemical companies, improved profits significantly in 1972, but others, such as the steel concerns, reported profit falls for the third year running. The series of Government fiscal and exchange control measures in early 1973, coupled with the substantial changes in exchange rates in this year, make it virtually certain that it will be a long time before most German companies can again report profits that come anywhere near to the record levels seen in 1969.

The degree of willingness that the Government in Bonn will show towards aiding the country's weak industries is a matter of speculation and will play an important role in determining the extent to which such areas as the Ruhr become industrially depressed. If past Bonn policies are a guide, then one must conclude that Government will be most unwilling to intervene to a substantial extent to help ailing companies. The Minister of Economics, Herr Hans Friderichs, went out of his way in the speeches he made in early 1973 to state clearly that he is a strong believer in the free market economic system. It seems likely that the Government will seek to stick rigidly to the Erhard-Schiller free market economy concepts of allowing market forces to take their course, free of intervention by public bodies. Herr Friderichs, as an ambitous member of the Free Democratic Party, will not endanger his political future by moving too far away from the free market philosophy. Further, the Finance Minister, Herr Helmut Schmidt, is unlikely to favour too much public spending on weak industries, for fear that this could produce too large a budget deficit and thereby add to the inflationary pressures.

The substantial development of large depressed areas and possibly of considerable pools of unemployment will take time. At the start of 1973 there was widespread optimism of a revival in the fortunes of the economy after two years of real economic growth rates of little more than three per cent. This optimism stemmed to some extent from the general upswing in economic activity in most Western industrial countries. Further, the pace of consumer spending was increasing rapidly. Many companies could report full order books for months ahead and the demand for labour was rising strongly. Even with all the negative factors produced by the inflation and the currency crises, there seemed at the start of 1973 few grounds for pessimism about the economy's short-term outlook. These factors suggest that if anything the volume of immigrant workers will increase substantially in the near future and that the labour market tension could become more acute.

However, these are developments of only a short-term nature; and as the full impact of inflation, the exchange rate and Government actions take effect, so the general outlook for the economy is bound to deteriorate. The German Government will almost certainly aid this deterioration by failing to cope with inflation satisfactorily; by being forced to substantially limit immigration for fears of social services being impossibly strained; by producing budget deficits through spending heavily on trying to push ahead with important social reforms; by further burdening business through higher taxes, as legislation to produce a fairer distribution of income proceeds; by weakening the position of company owners; by increasing the powers of the trade unions through new worker co-determination legislation; and by hindering the industrial concentration process through new cartel laws.

The rate of inflation in this country in coming years will determine to a large extent the degree that the competitive position of industry declines. To some extent a consolation is the fact that it is most unlikely that other West European countries will have greater success in fighting inflation than the Germans. However, a major strength for German industry in the 1950s and 1960s was that inflation rates here were substantially below those abroad. In coming years there is no reason whatever to expect that Germany will again obtain inflation rates well below those of her neighbouring countries. The high degree of trade involvement between this country and her European Community partners will make it almost impossible to ensure that inflationary pressures in one country do not spill over into other countries. Further, the growing militancy of the German trade unions is likely to ensure a relatively high level of annual wage rate rises here and a level that is certainly not below the average of other European Community countries.

A further important fact is that the system of economic management is by no means as efficient as it could be in this country. On the one hand the Federal Bank enjoys vast independent powers and the drawing up of economic policies is to some extent reliant on bargaining between the Bonn Government and the Frankfurt Federal Bank. On the other hand and more importantly, the division of responsibilities between the Economics Ministry and the Finance Ministry is somewhat absurd. Herr Helmut Schmidt became Minister of Economics and Finance in summer 1972, and had the good sense to recognise that it was an impossible task for a single man to cope efficiently with all the tasks that this vast department had to deal with. After the Federal Elections in November 1972, Herr Schmidt was one of the chief advocates of the creation of separate Economics and Finance Ministries. The resultant division was produced more on the basis of political bargaining between the two coalition parties in the Government, than on the basis of common sense.

The Free Democrats insisted that they should get some share of direct control on economics affairs and Herr Friderichs become Economics Minister as a result, leaving Herr Schmidt as Finance Minister. The Finance Ministry took full control of fiscal, money and credit policy, subject to the fact that general economic planning was left in the hands of the Economics Ministry. The Economics Ministry also was placed in charge of all industry and trade matters. The economic planning department should have been placed in the Finance Ministry, but this failure makes it essential that the two ministers continually confer and agree, for the one can in effect take few decisions without the full support of the other. A clear division should have been made with the establishment of a Treasury Ministry and a Commerce Ministry.

The split that has been agreed upon has produced some confusion among the top officials in both ministries as to their exact responsibilities. On presenting the annual economic report and the budget the two ministers were forced to give a joint press conference, where it was difficult to ascertain whether they both had a clear conception of what limits existed on their powers over all economic matters. Herr Friderichs will clearly seek to ensure that his voice becomes a powerful one, for he has ambitions of higher political offices, he represents a political party that in 1976 will seek to present an independent image of its own to the electorate and he will seek to prove some observers in Bonn wrong, who have suggested that he is in fact no more than a junior assistant to Herr Schmidt. In contrast, Herr Schmidt is a most forceful personality and the heir apparent to the leadership of the Social Democratic Party. He is not an expert economist, but he is an obstinate man, who is unlikely to change his views easily once he has committed himself in public. His ambitions also lead him to make most frequent public statements.

Thus it is difficult to imagine that a harmonious relationship will exist for long between these two ministers and this by no means bodes well for the management of the economy. The situation in this regard would not be so grave were the Federal Chancellor, Herr Willy Brandt, capable of giving firm leadership on economic affairs. Herr Brandt has been hailed abroad by politicians, newspaper editors and leading public figures, as one of the most outstanding statesmen of our time. This praise is based on his most considerable achievements in foreign policy. Herr Brandt was Foreign Minister from 1966 to 1969 and earlier he was Mayor of Berlin, which was a position that forced him to make foreign affairs, especially East–West relations, his top priority. Herr Brandt understands little about economics and has given few indications in recent years of being much interested in economic matters. As a result he is unlikely to give the sort of leadership that could produce well co-ordinated policies being swiftly reached in the Economics Ministry, in the Finance Ministry and in the Federal Bank.

A major aim of Bonn Governments in recent years has been to reduce this country's large balance of payments surpluses. The willingness to accept revaluations of the Deutsche Mark and to impose controls on the inflow of capital must be seen with this aim in mind. By early 1973 the Bonn Government had achieved its aim, but failed appallingly to convince people abroad of this. The massive inflows of foreign currency to Germany in early 1973 were due to the utter failure of people abroad to recognise the extent of the economic difficulties that industry in this country was going to face in coming years; the failure to look at the overall balance of payments position, rather than just the trade surplus; the failure to recognise that exports were producing few profits for German companies and that another revaluation of the Deutsche Mark would in time lead to a substantial decline in the rate of export growth; the failure to appreciate that Germany had an inflation rate of more than six per cent, which was the highest level it had had for over twenty years, and that the pace of the inflationary upswing was increasing. The failure by the Bonn Government was that it did not make these points perfectly clear to foreigners and this failure was largely due to the reluctance of the politicians in Bonn to admit that the general outlook for the German economy was far from bright.

The exceptionally low levels of profits of German companies in the last few years, especially of those companies deeply involved in exporting, show clearly how minimal the profit levels on exports have been. The high level of exports in 1972 was to some extent due to stagnation in the domestic economy, which allowed companies to deliver more speedily to foreign markets. The upswing in domestic demand itself forces many companies to reduce their export volumes. Further, the full impact of the 1971 currency realignment did not fully come through on to German exports in 1972 and its effects are likely to be seen more clearly at a later date. Further, despite a record trade surplus of more than DM 20,000 million, the current account balance of payments showed only a modest surplus of

DM 1,700 million. West Germany has a very sizeable deficit on the invisibles account of the payments balance, due largely to the high level of German spending abroad by businessmen and tourists, to the heavy costs of having foreign soldiers based in this country and to the transfer of a sizeable proportion of the incomes of foreign immigrant workers to their home countries. These items on the invisibles side show every sign of increasing in volume, while the trade surplus looks like declining.

Furthermore, the increase in West German company investment spending abroad, coupled with the likely decline in the volume of foreign investment in Germany, will also have an impact on the balance of payments. Finally, the tight exchange controls in this country may further add to a deterioration of the current account surplus. In total, when one looks to the medium term, it would seem most likely that this country will start to run significant current account payments deficits.

It may well be that in a few years' time many of those responsible for pouring hundreds of millions of dollars into West Germany will wonder just what motivated them to hold Deutsche Marks. There are few reasons to suggest that a major depression stares Germany in the face. However, within a few years it is likely that the structure of German industry will have changed greatly – becoming more concentrated, less export orientated and more involved in international co-operation agreements of some kind with foreign concerns. It is also likely that the shake-out in some of the weaker industries will lead to some reduction of the serious labour market tension and a stabilising of the level of foreign immigrant workers in this country. The policies of the trade unions and the development of many of the Government's legislative programmes could have a most damaging effect on the health of industry in this country. There is no reason whatever today to expect Germany to achieve in this decade the inflation and growth rates of the last two decades.

The developments within the German economy in coming years will have most serious consequences for other nations, especially the other members of the European Economic Community, the United States and Japan. For many years the Germans have been the strongest nation economically within the European Community and have in consequence been major financiers of Community developments. The growing economic problems here will make the Germans, in all probability, less willing to subsidise farmers in other European countries and may make them much harder colleagues for other Community countries to get on with. Further, the development of new tax systems, cartel laws and trade union laws, may conflict with the aims in these spheres of the European Community Commission. The economic developments and legislative plans in West Germany in coming years may only add to the integration difficulties of the Community.

For the United States and for Japan the development of the German economy is of vital importance in determining the extent to which these countries can achieve balance of payments improvements. Beyond this it is to the advantage of the Atlantic Alliance that West Germany remains economically powerful. Uncertainties within the German economy could lead to a greater degree of political instability in this country, so relatively immature in the ways of democracy. Further, the burden of supporting large battalions of North Atlantic Treaty Organisation troops in West Germany could become problematic if the German economy deteriorates too greatly and this in turn could place new strains on the general relationship between the United States and Western Europe.

This book has sought to outline many of the problems within industry in this country and give some guide to the direction in which business in West Germany is moving. The present decade is going to be one of major transition within this economy; it will be testing and difficult. It will be a period where the problems facing managers will possibly be greater than those seen in the last decade and the economic developments are bound to firmly change the opinions of those abroad, who still today remain convinced that the 'Economic Miracle' continues.

Appendix 1

THE MAJOR INDUSTRIAL SECTORS

This section provides detail on the major industrial sectors supplementary to that outlined in the main chapters of this book. Further information on general industrial matters is contained in Appendix 2, where brief descriptions of the most important manufacturing companies are given. The information contained here is based largely on data compiled by the various German industrial federations, on official reports by the Federal Statistical Office and on interviews with industrial leaders conducted by the author. The data given and general comments made are mainly based on the latest published material as of the end of 1972.

General Data

TABLE A.I.I

General Sales Statistics
1971

	Total in mln DMs	% change on 1970	Foreign sales in mln DMs	% change on 1970
All industry	563,033·1	+6·5	109,997·3	+7·8
Mining	11,959·2	+3·7	2,547·4	+7·2
Raw materials	155,780·4	+1·8	30,362·4	+3·9
Capital goods	221,513·1	+8·8	64,068·3	+9·4
Consumer goods	101,155·8	+8·5	10,928·9	+9·1

Source: Based on Federal Statistical Office Data.

TABLE A.I.2

Sales of major manufacturing industries with 10-year comparison

	Total sales in mln DMs 1971	Total sales in mln DMs 1970	Total sales in mln DMs 1962	Total foreign sales in mln DMs in 1971
Food industry	72,624·6	67,429·4	40,448·0	2,090·2
Construction	67,033·8	55,229·1	35,560·6	—
Mech. eng.	60,520·5	56,135·7	31,320·2	21,324·8
Electrical	53,920·0	49,385·9	22,286·6	11,563·6
Chemical	52,870·5	49,868·8	25,315·6	16,153·6
Automobiles	46,622·8	42,452·7	21,118·3	19,104·7
Metals	25,286·3	28,269·8	16,871·2	7,083·8
Textiles	26,069·3	24,332·5	17,660·4	3,829·8
Mining	11,959·2	11,533·9	10,902·0	2,547·4

Source: Based on Federal Statistical Office Data.

TABLE A.I.3

Company Sizes

	Companies with sales of					
	up to 5 mln DMs	from 5 mln– 10 mln	10 mln– 25 mln	25 mln– 50 mln	50 mln 100 mln	over 100 mln
Total sales 1968 (mln)	52,759	33,572	54,554	43,661	39,770	217,576
% of all Company sales	12·0	7·6	12·3	9·9	9·0	49·2
Total sales 1970	54,386	38,802	68,107	55,690	56,560	308,744
% of all Company sales	9·3	6·7	11·7	9·6	9·7	53·0
Total employed in 1,000 in 1968	1,479	759	1,144	826	715	3,226
Total employed in 1,000 in 1970	1,264	725	1,197	882	867	3,914
Total invested as % of sales						
1968	2·6	4·4	4·6	5·0	4·5	5·4
1970	3·1	5·5	6·2	6·2	6·2	7·6

Source: Deutsche Industrieinstitut (Cologne).

Company Earnings

Note: The dividends paid by public companies give a rough guide to general profit trends. It is almost impossible to make general statements on earnings on an industry-by-industry basis in view of the very great variety of types of companies to be found in any single industry. The following three tables, based on Federal Statistical Office data for 1,541 Aktiengesellschaft-type companies give, at best, a general indication of profit trends in recent years.

TABLE A.I.4

Dividend % of nominal share value	1969 No. of companies	Nominal total value of shares in mln DMs	Value of dividend payments in mln DMs
Under 6%	152	2,708·0	134·5
From 6–7%	38	584·2	40·8
7–8%	82	1,739·1	139·1
8–9%	16	247·7	22·3
9–10%	132	3,181·9	316·6
10–11%	20	1,057·6	116·3
11–12%	116	3,191·8	383·0
12–13%	20	1,552·7	197·4
13–14%	78	2,052·2	287·3
14–15%	71	1,244·7	186·0
15–16%	107	5,828·6	932·1
16–17%	25	1,729·4	291·8
17–18%	76	1,750·0	314·8
Over 18%	130	7,768·9	1,944·2
All dividend-paying companies together	1,063	34,636·8	5,306·2
Companies paying no dividend	478	5,615·4	—

TABLE A.I.5

Dividend % of nominal share value	No. of companies	1970 Nominal total value of shares in mln DMs	Value of dividend payment in mln DMs
Under 6%	154	3,272·6	128·5
From 6–7%	33	686·9	48·1
7–8%	91	1,685·2	134·7
8–9%	15	236·6	21·3
9–10%	122	1,977·0	197·6
10–11%	19	898·6	98·2
11–12%	119	3,263·0	391·5
12–13%	18	974·0	126·7
13–14%	74	5,846·2	815·8
14–15%	66	1,106·4	165·4
15–16%	83	4,816·6	770·6
16–17%	19	1,014·3	171·9
17–18%	68	2,943·4	529·8
Over 18%	151	8,120·4	1,914·8
All dividend-paying companies together	1,032	36,846·6	5,514·9
Companies paying no dividend	509	5,748·4	—

TABLE A.1.6

Dividend % of nominal share value	No. of companies	1971 Nominal total value of shares in mln DMs	Value of dividend payment in mln DMs
Under 6%	164	4,077·4	207·5
From 6–7%	28	1,775·8	124·1
7–8%	101	1,250·8	100·9
8–9%	22	1,307·9	117·7
9–10%	113	2,804·1	280·3
10–11%	12	770·0	84·7
11–12%	106	2,538·4	304·6
12–13%	19	2,900·2	377·0
13–14%	78	4,535·9	634·2
14–15%	77	4,102·6	615·4
15–16%	77	2,427·3	387·8
16–17%	22	835·6	142·0
17–18%	53	1,531·9	275·7
Over 18%	160	5,898·8	1,368·0
All dividend-paying companies together	1,032	36,756·7	5,019·0
Companies paying no dividend	509	8,435·9	—

Note: In terms of dividend payment totals a new record was set in 1970, and 1971 was the first year for over 20 years when the final total was below that of the previous year.

Food, Drinks and Tobacco Industries

The food and drinks industries are largely dominated by small and medium-sized companies. Possibly the largest food company is the Swiss owned, Deutsche Nestlé, while the DUB-Schultheiss brewery, with a market share in West Germany of approximately 14 per cent, is the only major drinks company in the country of a size that can be compared with foreign giant enterprises. In the tobacco sector three large companies dominate the market. The leader, with about 42 per cent of the cigarette market, is the private Reemtsma group, which also has significant brewing interests. The second largest company in the tobacco market in West Germany is British American Tobacco, with slightly over 28 per cent of the cigarette market.

The third large group, with about 20 per cent of the cigarette market, is Martin Brinkman, which is more than 25 per cent owned by the Ritter Family and more than 25 per cent owned by the South African Rothman's group, which in turn is owned by Mr Anton Rupert. Another major company to be mentioned is the Oetker group, which like Reemtsma is family-owned and has breweries. But this group is also highly active in a wide field of foods, including commodities of assorted types and bakery products; it also owns a large shipping fleet.

The details given here about these industries concern processed foods and exclude agriculture, for the latter topic is one about which a book alone could be written and whose general development, economic well-being and prosperity, is determined by few of the factors discussed in this book and almost totally by decisions reached by the authorities of the European Community. Under the regulations of the Common Agricultural Policy, the farmers in West Germany are assured an income, which, through subsidies from Bonn, has ensured protection from international currency developments.

In 1971 this industry employed more than 520,000 persons with total wage costs at DM 4,852·3 million and salary costs of DM 3,088·6 million. The most substantial sales rises in any of the many sectors of the food, drinks and tobacco industries has been in the manufacture of spirits, which could boast a rise in 1971 of 24·2 per cent to DM 3,753 million. In the brewing sector a certain stagnation of demand is now being noted, although the Germans can claim to drink more beer per head than people in most other countries, with an average annual per capita consumption of around 144 hecto-litres (more than 250 pints). Increased taxes are clearly affecting tobacco sales; and this, together with growing publicity about the dangers of smoking, has led some tobacco companies into other business fields in recent years. Thus, Reemtsma has entered brewing and BAT has acquired 25 per cent of the Horten stores group. Some 124,000 million cigarettes are sold annually in West Germany, with the rate of increase in 1971 some 6 per cent and about 4 per cent in 1972.

The general pace of sales increase seen in 1971 (see Table A.1.2 in this section on sales of major manufacturing industries) was maintained in 1972. Price rises have been significant, but the general rate of profitability is high, although sharp variances are to be found from sector to sector. Probably the most interesting aspect of the foods and drinks industries is the rate of industrial concentration that is now in progress. In brewing, for example, there are some 1,800 independent companies, but swiftly a few giants are being created through financial institutions organising spectacular mergers. In many food sectors similar, albeit less dramatic, developments are to be found. This is a trend that will almost certainly continue. Thus, according to Federal Cartel Office figures, there were some 16 major take-overs or mergers in the food processing sector from 1958 to the end of 1969. In 1970, however, there were alone thirteen such re-groupings, with a further nine in 1971 and fourteen in the first nine months of 1972.

The Construction Industry

Relatively mild winters in 1971 and 1972 have been a major factor in helping this industry to become possibly the most profitable industry in the Federal Republic. The visitor to West Germany cannot help but be struck by the vast amount of new construction to be seen. To some extent this is a generation question, for now many of the relatively shabby buildings that were hastily constructed after the last war are being pulled down and replaced by vast, modern edifices. The determination of public authorities to increase the number and size of schools, hospitals and roads has been a further aid. In addition, largely for prestige reasons, a large number of German cities are now intent on building their own underground railway systems.

However, the increasing inflation is producing substantial pressures on the public authorities to cut their expenditures and this could well have an impact on the construction industry. But the sharp rise in earnings, coupled with the widespread belief that an investment in property is the best protection against inflation, is resulting in the swift development of property funds and in sharply rising demand for housing. For example, according to Federal Bank figures, it took about eleven years for open-ended property funds to attract just DM 120 million, but from this level at the end of 1970, the total reached more than DM 1,000 million by November 1972.

A further great worry for the industry centres on labour

shortages. Offering some of the most unattractive type of jobs it is not surprising that this industry should employ more foreign workers than any other. The possibility that the Bonn authorities will clamp down on immigration exists, and the construction industry could find that its rate of expansion is most substantially limited by the labour shortages. Prices are rising swiftly in general in this country and the construction industry has so far comfortably managed to fully offset overhead cost rises in higher prices. The sharp anti-inflation measures of the German authorities in the first half of 1973 produced a temporary, but relatively sharp, decline in demand for private housing and this gave rise to major financial difficulties for several construction companies.

TABLE A.I.7

General Construction Industry Statistics with 10-year comparisons			
	1971	*1970*	*1962*
Private housing sales in mln DMs	23,195·8	18,232·1	12,149·2
Industrial private sales in mln DMs	16,740·0	12,716·3	6,930·6
High rise public sector sales in mln DM	6,025·8	5,380·8	3,116·6
Road construction sales in mln DMs	9,980·2	8,882·4	5,104·6
Other ground level and underground sales in mln DMs	10,403·8	9,292·8	5,310·9
Agricultural sales in mln DMs	688·1	724·7	733·9
Total employees in 1,000	1,543·7	1,528·9	1,525·5
Wage and salary costs in mln DMs	25,304·4	22,162·6	11,289·7
Industry production index 1962 = 100	142·4	138·9	100·0

Source: Hauptverband der Deutschen Bauindustrie e.V.—Frankfurt/Main.

The Mechanical Engineering Industry

A general description of this vast industry was given in Chapter 4. The downturn in economic activity in 1970 and 1971 and the slow upward trend in much of 1972 resulted in sharp profit declines in numerous sectors of this industry. Some 7 per cent of the industry's sales go to the United States and well over one-third of the industry's total output is sold abroad. The international currency developments of recent years have seriously weakened the competitiveness of this sector. This has forced major rationalisation and a considerable degree of concentration. The major steel companies have entered this sector in a big way in recent years and this is a trend that is likely to continue. This is not an industry of large companies, despite its vast size. In view of the comments made on this industry in Chapter 4, it suffices here to give the main general statistics on this sector.

TABLE A.1.8

General Mechanical Engineering Industry statistics			
	1971	*1970*	*1968*
Number of companies	5,515	5,355	5,128
Number of employees in 1,000	1,184	1,207	1,079
Wage and salary costs in mln DMs	20,802	18,831	13,821
Sales in mln DMs*	65,623	60,546	41,598
Production in 1,000 tonnes	5,827·2	5,841·2	4,608·1
Exports in mln DMs	29,061·9	26,707·3	21,365·5
Imports in mln DMs	9,420·7	8,616·8	5,084·7
Machine tools† Employees	120,000	125,000	110,000

Source: Verein Deutscher Maschinenbau-Anstalten e.V. (VDMA).

* The sales figure given here is based on returns by mechanical engineering companies rather than on a products basis, and some of the reporting companies have minor activities in non-mechanical engineering industries – hence the discrepancy in the figures in this table and those in the table at the start of this section on the sales of the major manufacturing industries.

† This figure is given, because the machine tools sector is by far the largest of all mechanical engineering branches and the employment figure gives some indication of the size of this sector, compared to the whole industry.

The Electrical Industry

The capital goods side of this industry, like the mechanical engineering industry, started to register substantial orders in the latter part of 1972, which grew in volume in the following months. Many of the capital goods sections registered most sharp profit falls in 1970 and 1971. In the consumer goods sector the competition by the Japanese, in particular, has been a major source of worry. Developments within this industry in general have varied greatly. Foreign competition has restricted a healthy development of profit margins and, for example, imports of entertainment electrical goods to West Germany from Asia rose by 40 per cent in 1972, after a rise of 37 per cent in the previous year. The variations in the trends are seen for example in the consumer goods sector, where total production rose 20 per cent in 1972, with output of colour television sets up 57 per cent (largely on account of the Munich Olympic Games), while output of black and white televisions fell 5·7 per cent.

The sharp rises in overhead costs and currency factors will in time produce major hardship for many companies and some difficulties are already being experienced (see comments on AEG-Telefunken in Appendix 2). However, at the start of 1973 the level of orders booked with the industry was so high that in the short-term a most substantial sales and profit increase is probable. The table given below for 1972 and 1971 adequately describes the scale and type of operations in this industry. The comments made in earlier chapters regarding this industry, coupled with those made in Appendix 2 concerning the three largest German electrical companies, should produce a general and rounded picture of this large industrial sector.

TABLE A.I.9

General Electrical Industry statistics

	1972	1971	% change 1971 from 1970
Sales in mln DMs*	62,998	56,963	+9·3
Production in mln DMs	55,846	50,813	+5·5
Exports in mln DMs	17,286	14,808	+9·3
Imports in mln DMs	9,056	7,918	+7·3
Total number of employees in 1000	1,069·5	1,085·0	−1·2
Wage and salary costs in mln DMs	18,827	17,113	+11·6

Source: Zentralverband der Elektrotechnischen Industrie e.V.

* This figure includes computers and office equipment, which are items not included in the table at the start of this section giving the sales of the major manufacturing industries.

The Chemical Industry

Earlier chapters have mentioned various important aspects of this industry and the brief descriptions of Farbwerke Hoechst AG, Bayer AG and Badische Anilin- und Soda-Fabrik AG given in Appendix 2 help to round out the picture. This is a modern-structured and large profit-making industry. It has invested more in building foreign production plants than any other German industry. It embraces a large number of companies of diverse sizes. The most important companies are the 'Big Three' Veba Chemie, Henkel, Degussa and Schering. Intense international competition has resulted in recent years in few price increases being possible in many sectors and profits have to a large extent been the result of substantial rationalisation. In recent years this has been one of the most swiftly expanding German industrial sectors and it is likely to maintain strong growth, although it is likely that many companies will expand their foreign subsidiaries at a swifter pace than their domestic plants. The 1973 financial year is likely to see a further major revival in profits and the general medium-term outlook for this sector is much more satisfactory than for many other sectors of industry.

TABLE A.1.10

General Chemical Industry Statistics

	1972	1971	1970
Total number of employees in 1000	577	586	590
Wages and salary costs in mln DMs	12,600	11,700	10,900
Exports in mln DMs	21,300	19,600	18,600
Imports in mln DMs	11,700	10,900	9,900
Production index 1962 = 100	262·6	246·5	230·4

Source: Verband der Chemischen Industrie e.V.

The Automobile Industry

All the industries detailed so far in this section are the largest of their kind in Western Europe and this one, as well as the iron and steel industry, is not an exception. It is an industry discussed at some length in Chapter 4. It is an industry composed of a handful of large and highly competitive companies, two of which are described in Appendix 2. As comments made elsewhere in this book have sought to show, the problems of the individual car makers vary greatly from one another. Some of the companies are certainly better managed than others and clearly Adam Opel, Fordwerke, Bayerische Motoren Werk and Daimler-Benz, must rank among the best organised and most modern of West German companies. At the moment the leading manufacturers of cars and commercial vehicles export a great percentage of their total output, yet have few foreign based subsidiaries. Major changes are likely to take place in this respect in coming years. There is still scope for some rationalisation of the commercial vehicle sector, although a considerable amount has been achieved in the last few years. The general profit outlook remains uncertain on account, primarily, of currency factors. The increases in 1973 in West German road and petrol taxes and in car insurance, are likely to have a substantial negative effect on sales.

TABLE A.I.II

General Automobile and Commercial Vehicle Industry statistics

	1972	1971	1970
Total output all vehicles	3,815,982	3,982,722	3,842,247
Total exports of vehicles	2,188,138	2,293,005	2,103,948
Total new vehicle sales in West Germany	2,291,994	2,314,472	2,271,792
Production index 1962 = 100	181·7	182·1	182·0
Number of employees	608,816	630,897	606,162
Wages and salary costs in mln DMs	12,286	11,735	10,320
Total output of passenger cars	3,521,540	3,696,779	3,527,864

Source: Verband der Automobilindustrie e.V.

The Metals Industry

A vast number of companies are involved in the production of a wide range of assorted types of metal goods in West Germany. The large iron and steel companies have increasingly diversified in recent years into mechanical engineering and into finished metal goods sectors. In addition, there are many specialist non-ferrous metal concerns. To some extent the upswing in the fortunes of the German economy in mid-1972, which gathered momentum at a considerable pace, saved many firms in this vast industry from serious financial difficulties. Many companies had recorded losses in 1970 and 1971, or had taken such devastating falls in earnings that they barely had sufficient funds to finance modest and essential investments.

The coal industry has been a key source of concern. This is an industry, included in this part of this Appendix, which is being run on uneconomic lines and which depends for its future well-being on the plans that the Bonn Government will draw up for energy as a whole. Some of the difficulties of the coal industry are given in the description of Ruhrkohle AG in Appendix 2.

The sharp competitive pressures, the rises in overhead costs, especially coal, coking coal and wages and the currency developments, have forced a substantial industrial rationalisation, which will continue. In the years since 1969 a large number of major deals have taken place, including the take-over by Salzgitter of Ilseder Peine, the acquisition by Salzgitter of the Howaldtswerke Deutsche Werft shipyard, the acquisition by August Thyssen of Rheinstahl, the merger between Thyssen's and Mannesmann's steel pipe interests, the start of serious co-operation talks in the shipbuilding sector between Thyssen's Blohm und Voss and Howaldtswerke Deutsche Werft, the acquisition by Mannesmann of more than 50 per cent of Demag, the merger of Hoesch with Hoogovens of Holland. The German shipbuilding industry is now fully controlled by the large German steel companies and major rationalisation in this area is likely. The sort of major industrial deals just described will occur increasingly frequently in coming years as the vast metal working industry, steel and iron industry and allied industries of this country are forced to come to terms with the much weaker international competitive position that has developed.

TABLE A.I.12

General Iron, Lead and Metals Processing Industry statistics

	1966	1970
Sales in mln DMs	15,607	21,038
Number of employees	414,086	418,235
Production index 1962 = 100	124·6	161·8
Exports in mln DMs	4,034	6,390
Imports in mln DMs	1,277	2,157
Wages and Salary Costs in mln DMs	3,986	5,609

Source: Wirtschaftsverband Eisen, Blech und Metall verarbeitende Industrie e.V.

Note: Compilation of figures for this industrial sector is exceptionally difficult and the general total figures at best only give an impression of general size, for the business sectors covered here range greatly from the manufacture of steel furniture, to screws and bolts and locks, to pens and non-ferrous metals.

TABLE A.I.13

General Iron and Steel Industry statistics

	1971	1970	1969
Total number of employees	354,590	374,428	371,622
Wage and salary costs in mln DMs	6,003	5,921	4,879
Total sales in mln DMs	25,286·3	28,269·8	24,507·0
Foreign sales in mln DMs	7,083·8	6,920·0	5,923·3
Crude steel output in mln tonnes	40·3	45·0	45·3
Crude iron output in mln tonnes	29·9	33·6	33·8

Source: Statistisches Bundesamt, Aussenstelle Düsseldorf.

TABLE A.I.14

General Coal Industry Statistics

	1971	1970	1969	1957
Coal production in mln tonnes	110·8	111·3	111·6	149·4
Number of employees in 1000	205·9	213·9	214·9	553·6
Output per man per year in tonnes	769	770	774	419
Weekly earnings per employee (in North Rhine–Westphalia)	318DM	314DM	273DM	149,49DM

Source: Gesamtverband des Deutschen Steinkohlenbergbaus.

TABLE A.1.15

Wages as a percentage of turnover in major manufacturing industries—1971	
	%
Coal Industry	61
Mechanical Engineering Industry	39
Electrical Industry	38
Automobile Industry	32
Textiles Industry	29
Chemicals Industry	27
Iron and Steel Industry	27
Food Industry	15
All Manufacturing Industries	30

Source: Gesamtverband des Deutschen Steinkohlenbergbaus.

The Textiles Industry

This is an industry of predominantly small companies, that is facing increasing problems as a direct result of the weakened West German industrial competitive position. One result has been a speeding up of the pace of industrial concentration. In 1972 the number of companies in this industry declined by 100 or 2·8 per cent; in the first ten months of 1972 a decline of about 3·1 per cent was seen to produce an industry of about 3,409 independent companies. Major rationalisation resulted in declines of about 4·8 per cent in the total number of industry employees in the first ten months of 1972, despite a sales gain in this period of somewhat over 2 per cent. Further cuts in labour totals are likely in the medium-term as a number of medium-size companies expand swiftly at the expense of many smaller and weaker rivals. Foreign competition will determine the medium-term developments of this industry, but in the short-term the pressing problems are to some extent outweighed by such beneficial factors as sharp upswings in consumer spending in the Federal Republic and in many developed Western economies.

The composition of the tables in this Appendix has largely been done in such a manner that the reader can see how major changes have taken place. Thus, for example, the years 1969, 1970 and 1971 are compared with each other for the steel industry or for general company earnings, for in these cases, as was the case for many industries, 1970 was a turning point and the start of a downward trend. 1972 and 1973 are likely to be temporary interruptions of the downward movement and recent important trends in the coal industry, for example, compare with the situation in the late 1950s, to show how great the transformation of this industry has been. The following table shows clearly recent developments in the textile industry.

TABLE A.I.16

General Textile Industry statistics			
	1971	*1970*	*1966*
Number of employees in 1000	853	881	945
Number of companies	3,512	3,615	4,038
Production Indes 1962 = 100 per employee	168·4	153·2	119·6
Sales in mln DMs	26,054	24,320	19,992
Wages and salary costs in mln DMs	6,094	5,702	4,430
Exports as % of total sales	14·4	13·6	9·8

Source: Arbeitgeberkreis Gesamttextil.

Appendix 2

This section provides brief descriptions of the largest, publicly quoted, manufacturing companies in the Federal Republic. At the end of this section a brief description of the leading publicly quoted retailing companies is given. The information contained here is based on interviews conducted by the author with company directors, on material published by the end of 1972 by the companies described and on studies made by several of the leading West German banks, most noteably the Commerzbank AG, the Deutsche Bank AG and the Westdeutsche Landesbank Girozentrale. Relatively detailed descriptions of those manufacturing companies with annual sales of more than DM 10,000 million are given below, followed by briefer descriptions of other important, but smaller, companies.

Volkswagenwerk AG

This is the largest company in West Germany in turnover terms. Annual sales in 1971 and 1972 were around DM 17,000 million. Heavy profit declines were registered in 1970 and 1971, to levels well below 0·5 per cent of turnover, due largely to sharp rises in wage costs, currency revaluations out-dated models and to some extent, to poor management. The poor results were a major factor in the dismissal, in late 1971, of Dr Kurt Lotz and his replacement as chief executive by Dr Rudolf Leiding. A large scale management reorganisation is now taking place. This has been partly reflected in the forced resignations in 1972 of Dr Werner Holste, the design chief and Herr Carl Hahn, the sales chief.

The VW group produces more than 2·2 million cars a year. It is the largest automobile manufacturer outside the United States. Apart from about 250,000 cars produced annually at a wholly owned Brazilian-based subsidiary, almost all of VW's output is in West Germany, although the domestic market accounts for just under one-third of total group sales. Most VW cars are produced in Wolfsburg, a town located in North-East Germany on the East German border, that is completely dominated by the vast VW plant.

The series of Deutsche Mark revaluations has hit sharply at company profits and may spur VW to build large new production plants abroad. The United States market alone accounted for sales of about 560,000 VW group cars in 1971. The Audi-NSU car company is fully owned by Volkswagenwerk. VW employs close to 200,000 people. The company had at the end of 1972 a basic capital of DM 900 million and some 900,000 shareholders. The large shareholders are the Federal State with 16 per cent, the State of Lower Saxony with 20 per cent and 4 per cent hold by the VW Foundation, which is controlled by VW employees.

Dr Leiding is confident of a strong profit upswing in the next three years. The company will invest a total of some DM 5,300 million in the four years to the end of 1975. The sales outlook is difficult to assess in view of the Deutsche Mark revaluations, which make VW cars expensive in a number of key markets. The success of the company's planned new models for the next three years will in large measure determine whether or not VW can again become a financially strong enterprise.

Siemens AG

Based in Munich this is the largest employer in the private sector in this country, with a total staff of around 300,000. The company is a highly efficient and modern manufacturer of a wide range of electrical and electro-technical equipment. Siemens is second only to Philips NV of the Netherlands as the largest electrical manufacturer in Western Europe. It has a large number of foreign production subsidiaries and currently devotes about 20 per cent of its annual investment spending (which is around DM 1,000 million) on plants located abroad.

The executive board chief, Dr Bernhard Plettner, was appointed to the top job in late 1971 on the retirement of Dr Gerd Tacke, who is widely seen in this country as having been one of the ablest and most imaginative managers in German industry. The top management works closely as a team and its ability is best reflected in the profit results, which are among the best consistently in German industry. In the year to the end of

September 1972 Siemens increased its net profit by DM 173 million to DM 411 million on total sales that rose DM 1,512 million to DM 15,147 million. Foreign sales account for slightly more than 40 per cent of total sales.

At the end of the 1971–72 financial year Siemens had a basic capital of DM 1,193,410,250. The company has about 340,000 shareholders with some 60,000 of these being company employees. The von Siemens family has a minor holding, but otherwise there are no large shareholders. The company's prospects are excellent and it will in all probability grow into a major multinational giant at a swift pace, although its management notes that company profit as a percentage of turnover is still considerably below that of its chief foreign rivals, but well ahead of domestic competitors.

August Thyssen-Hüette AG

The acquisition of 60·5 per cent of the shares of Rheinstahl AG strengthened the Thyssen group's position as the largest steel manufacturing concern in continental Europe. Including Rheinstahl, the group has annual sales of about DM 15,900 million. Thyssen intends to fully integrate Rheinstahl, which it took over in March 1973, and plans to become a modern and highly diversified steel, iron, shipbuilding and machinery producing group. The acquisition of Rheinstahl should in time produce substantial rationalisation in the sheet metals, refined steel and shipbuilding sectors. The task of rationalisation is an immense one, but essential, for Thyssen has been losing money heavily in many of its key sectors, due largely to the toughness of foreign competition and the sharp rise in domestic German wage costs.

At the Thyssen annual meeting in April 1973, the man who chiefly rebuilt and restructured Thyssen in the last twenty years, Dr Hans-Günther Sohl, retired as chief of the executive board and handed over to the man whom Sohl had groomed for the top job for many years, Dr Dieter Speethmann. The latter months of 1972 and early months of 1973 showed a substantial rise in Thyssen order book levels and indicated that the worst days of Thyssen's recession were over. In the year to 30 September 1972 Thyssen's net profit fell to DM 53 million, from DM 63 million in the previous year and DM 219 million in 1969–70.

Group sales in the 1971–72 year totalled DM 9,835 million, which was a decline of DM 500 million on the previous year and DM 1,000 million on 1969–70. Thyssen's total steel output is now around an annual 12 million tonnes.

Rheinstahl produces about 1·5 million tonnes of steel a year, it has wide-ranging interests in numerous engineering sectors, it owns a large shipbuilding company, as does Thyssen and owns large blast furnace capacity in the Ruhr. Rheinstahl has not made a profit for some years, but has spent heavily on rationalisation and modernisation. Rheinstahl's annual sales are around DM 5,700 million and the Thyssen-Rheinstahl group has a labour force of some 150,000. At the end of 1972 Thyssen had a basic capital of just over DM 1,010 million. Somewhat more than 25 per cent of the company's capital is held by the Thyssen Vermögensverwaltung GmbH, which is largely owned by the Anita Thyssen Foundation and by Gräfin Anita Amelia Thyssen de Zichy. The Fritz Thyssen Foundation holds a further 11 per cent and the remaining shares are widely distributed.

Farbwerke Hoechst AG

In terms of turnover this Frankfurt-based company is of a very similar size to its chief German rivals, Bayer AG and Badische Anilin- und-Soda Fabrik AG. These three companies follow Imperial Chemical Industries Ltd of Britain as the largest chemical companies in Europe. Hoechst's total sales in 1972 totalled DM 13,500 million, with DM 7,850 million accounted for in foreign markets. It has vast foreign holdings, notably in the United States, various parts of Europe and can claim to be the heaviest German investor in Great Britain.

The Hoechst group employs some 145,000 people and invests around DM 1,700 million a year. It is active in a vast range of chemical sectors. Its output of fibres alone in 1972 produced sales of DM 1,800 million and other particularly strong fields are organic and inorganic chemicals, paints and dyes and pharmaceuticals. The company, like its other key domestic rivals, is a descendant of the vast pre-war I.G. Farben empire and was largely rebuilt and reorganised in the last 20 years by Dr Karl Winnacker. In mid-1969, Dr Rolf Sammet became chairman of the company's executive board.

Company profits are moving ahead slowly and in 1972 they were modestly ahead of the 1971 total of DM 320 million. The company is well managed, with the top board working well as a team and maintaining a generally low public profile. Hoechst is likely to continue its foreign expansion at a brisk pace in coming years and sees its foreign plants as the major source of company growth in the medium-term future. It has a basic capital of just over DM 1,500 million and some 370,000 shareholders. There are no major shareholders in the company, but like the other two leading chemical concerns in West Germany, bankers believe that up to 20 per cent of the Hoechst shares are now owned by non-Germans.

Bayer AG

Based in Leverkusen, which lies between Cologne and Düsseldorf, the vast and sprawling Bayer plants represent one of the largest chemical industry industrial complexes in Europe. The company has total annual sales of DM 12,930 million (1972) and a profit level somewhat higher than that of Hoechst. The Bayer group has large foreign operations and like Hoechst it produces a wide range of chemical products. The company's investment volume is of similar dimensions to that of Hoechst but, rather than concentrate most of its major future development abroad, the company plans a massive new chemical industry complex on the German north coast, which in time may develop into a centre of similar proportions to the Leverkusen operation. Up to the end of 1969 Bayer had some 92 foreign companies which involved a total acquisition cost of 102 million dollars. The company is run in somewhat of a dictatorial manner by Dr Kurt Hansen, who has successfully established Bayer as a modern and streamlined organisation. The company is the largest single shareholder in Agfa-Gevaert, the largest photographic materials company in Western Europe. Further, Bayer has strong and diverse interests in the rubber industry. It owns the Metzler tyre company, it owns Hüls, the largest synthetic rubber company in Europe and it is likely to have a major stake in the tyre giant that may be formed through the merger of this country's two largest tyre producers, Continental Gummi and Phoenix Gummi.

The general outlook for Bayer is good, with order book levels

in early 1973 likely to produce serious shortages of capacity.
The continual revaluations of the Deutsche Mark, however,
will force Bayer to supply its foreign markets more greatly from
foreign based plants and currently more than 50 per cent of the
company's sales are accounted for abroad. Bayer had a basic
capital at the end of 1972 of DM 1,865 million with no major
shareholders, but some 450,000 small shareholders.

BASF

Badische Anilin- und Soda-Fabrik AG is based at Ludwigshafen
near Mannheim and differs in many respects from Hoechst and
Bayer. For many years it was much smaller than its two rivals,
but in the late 1960s, under the leadership of its aggressive
executive board chief, Professor Bernhard Timm, it went on a
massive acquisition and expansion drive. The result was
spectacular. Company sales advanced from DM 5,580 million
in 1968 to DM 8,892 million in 1969, to DM 10,520 million in
1970, to DM 12,139 million in 1971 and then up 12·5 per cent to
DM 13,661 million in 1972. But only in 1972 was a relatively
good profit seen, with an increase of over 30 per cent on the
previous year. Many of the purchases had initially produced
heavy losses and in 1971 the group net profit of DM 288 million
was even below that of 1968.

Slowly, but surely, BASF now appears to be fully coming to
terms with its new size. The company is more diversified than
its rivals, making almost every type of chemical product
between fertilisers and tape recorder tapes and cosmetics. It
employs slightly fewer persons than does Bayer at 104,000 and,
like its chief rivals, more than 50 per cent of its sales are outside
West Germany. The company has built up strong foreign subsidiaries in recent years, most notably in Antwerp, Belgium and
in the United States. It has achieved a certain name for itself
in the United States as an aggressive and highly competitive
concern, through its purchase of the large Wyandotte Chemicals Corporation in 1969. For the moment BASF's chief
priority is rationalisation and it has ended its expansion drive
through acquisition for the time being at least, and in consequence its 1973 investment spending volume is likely to be
around DM 1,000 million, compared with considerably higher
levels in previous years.

BASF had a basic capital at the end of 1972 of DM 1,513 million and does not have any major shareholders. However, like Siemens, it makes share distributions to its employees and the BASF employees account for a small proportion of the capital. Altogether BASF has about 330,000 shareholders. Between them, BASF, Bayer and Hoechst own a very sizeable proportion of the German chemical industry and have large numbers of important domestically based subsidiaries. While outwardly bitter rivals, the three concerns are partners to some extent in a number of subsidiary chemical companies.

Daimler-Benz AG

The company's sales development has consistently been impressive and, like Siemens, it boasts a reputation of modern and highly efficient management. Total turnover rose 12·8 per cent in 1972 to DM 13,800 million, which compares with a total turnover volume of just DM 5,900 million in 1967. Based in Stuttgart it, like Volkswagen, has a foreign subsidiary of considerable size in South America, but is otherwise more or less totally dependent on domestic German output. The company accounts for over 38 per cent of its turnover from foreign sales. The company is one of the most important manufacturers of luxury class saloon and sports cars in the world and the leading heavy commercial vehicle manufacturer in Western Europe.

Daimler-Benz daily car output is around 1,300 units, with annual car production totalling 323,878 in 1972, with exports accounting for 140,045 units. Total commercial vehicle output, including production by Hanomag-Henschel, which is a Daimler subsidiary, amounted to 168,482 units in 1972, with exports in the first eleven months of the year totalling 77,641 units. The company plans a gradual expansion of capacity and is currently investing about DM 600 million a year. In the West German market Daimler-Benz holds about 63 per cent of the market for cars priced above DM 15,000. While continuing to produce some of the best designed cars on today's roads, the company faces increased foreign competition, largely due to currency considerations and this is likely to result in a much slower rate of profit growth than is desirable. The main problems here will be in the commercial vehicle sector, where Daimler-Benz is now spending heavily on the full integration of Hanomag into the Daimler group. The company is strongly led by Dr Joachim Zahn, a former lawyer and recognised internationally as a brilliant motor industry expert.

Net profit rose to DM 275 million in 1972 after DM 207 million in 1971 and DM 246 million in 1970. As a percentage of turnover the net figure in 1972 was below that of 1970 at 2·51 per cent against 2·73 per cent. An improvement in profits is most likely for 1973, with order book levels for many products ensuring that plant capacity is fully utilised for many months ahead. The autonomy that Dr Zahn has is curbed by the existence of powerful shareholders in the company. Some 40 per cent of the capital is held by the Flick group, about 27 per cent is held by the Deutsche Bank and about 14 per cent is held by the Quandt group. The company had a basic capital at the end of 1972 of DM 951 million.

Veba AG

Sooner or later the style of management, ownership and business in general of this company will change radically. Currently the Federal State is the only large shareholder, having 40 per cent of the basic DM 1,031 million capital. The Bonn Government is anxious to see Veba become a major oil company and to ensure this the company will need vast additional capital, which may have to be supplied in part by the State and which could result in the State's stake rising. Veba is currently something of a conglomerate, with particulary strong interests in coal (it owns 14·1 per cent of Ruhrkohle AG and is the biggest shareholder in this company), in chemicals (it fully owns the large Veba Chemie AG, as well as having 25 per cent of Chemische Werke Hüls and 36 per cent of Chemie-Verwaltung), it has significant holdings in transport and trading companies and large and diverse interests in the energy sector, which are about to be greatly expanded.

In July 1973 Veba started negotiations with Rheinische-Westfälisches Elektrizitätswerk AG to take over a number of this latter company's oil interests, including its 48·5 per cent stake in Gelsenberg AG. These negotiations are strongly supported by the Bonn Government, and the eventual hope of the authorities in Bonn and of the Veba directors is that most of the German-owned companies active in the oil business will be merged into the Veba organisation. This will include not only such large refining companies as Gelsenberg, but also the Aral AG petrol station company.

If the complicated negotiations reach a satisfactory solution, which seems most probable, then Veba AG would control about 25 per cent of the petrol stations in the country and have a refining capacity by 1980 of some 40 million tonnes, which is about equal to 25 per cent of the total refining capacity of all oil companies in this country. Veba would have a turnover of similar dimensions to that of Volkswagenwerk AG.

Turnover for the Veba AG group in 1972 rose from DM 9,405 million to DM 10,332 million, with the net profit up at DM 293 million from DM 191 million in the previous year. The structure of the company may be further changed when the government finally decides the future of Ruhrkohle AG. Veba is based in Düsseldorf, it has a total of more than one million shareholders, which is a larger number than any other continental European company, and it employs over 58,000 persons. This giant concern is managed by an able, if somewhat colourless team, led by Herr Rudolf von Bennigsen-Foerder.

AEG-Telefunken AG

Few companies have been so deeply hit by the strong rise of Japanese competition in international markets as this one. The company's management has been slow to recognise that in many sectors it is impossible to compete with German made goods against the Japanese. The Frankfurt-based company, led by Dr Hans Groebe, has a sorry record to boast of in terms of profits and comes off most shabbily by comparison with Siemens. Profits in 1972 were modestly above the 1971 level of DM 61 million (this figure is only for the parent company, representing about 60 per cent of sales, with total group figure not available). Total sales in 1972, including value added tax, for the AEG group rose 7 per cent to DM 10,700 million, with foreign sales accounting for DM 3,400 million of the total.

The company makes a large and varied range of electrical and electro-technical equipment. It suffers extreme competition from the Far East in the entertainment electrical sector and in the office equipment sector (AEG owns Olympia, which makes typewriters and desk calculators). It is conceivable that the company will in time run down many of its consumer goods sectors and concentrate more fully on the manufacture of capital goods. It has an excellent research department, which can claim among its successes the PAL television system, which is used in most West European countries. The company has a staff total of 166,000. It is likely to do well in the near-term having booked a vast volume of advance orders by early 1973, which its directors see as signifying the long-awaited turn-around in company fortunes. Plant closures and heavy rationalisation have been made in the past few years to make AEG more internationally competitive.

The company has also saved on investment spending with a cut in 1972 of 25 per cent to DM 355 million. The company already is reliant for two-thirds of its sales on capital goods and in the consumer goods sector it has increasingly sought cheaper production locations than Germany. Thus, for example, it is a major shareholder in Zanussi, the Italian domestic appliances manufacturer. Sales by foreign subsidiaries have increased ten times in the last decade and close to 40 per cent of all AEG foreign sales are accounted for by foreign subsidiaries. New AEG plants are currently being developed in Brazil, South Africa and Greece. The basic capital stood at DM 704 million at the end of 1972 and it is not generally known that the only large shareholder, with a stake of more than 10 per cent, is the General Electric Capital Corporation, Shenectady, New York.

The following pages give somewhat briefer descriptions of those German owned manufacturing companies with annual sales of more than DM 3,500 million.

Ruhrkohle AG

Created in late 1968 through the concentration of most of the coal mines in the Ruhr area. It has its head offices in Essen and its future depends entirely on Bonn Government energy policy decisions. It is making heavy losses, largely because it owns numerous small and out-dated pits and has suffered from sharp wage-cost rises, which do not make it possible for the company to offer coal and allied products at internationally prevailing levels. It desperately needs vast public subsidies if it is ever to get on to a financially sound footing. The losses made by this company have to be borne to some extent by the shareholders, which adds substantially to steel company financial problems. Ruhrkohle sales have to some extent been assured by Government restrictions on coal and coking coal imports.

In 1971 the company produced 84·7 million tonnes of coal and 24·7 million tonnes of coking coal. It employed 179,000 people and had coal and coking coal stocks of 2·9 million tonnes and 5 million tonnes respectively. By the end of 1972 the company employed just 160,700 people, its output of coal was down to 77·5 million tonnes and its output of coking coal was down to 21·8 million tonnes. Substantial economies were achieved during the year. However, coal and coking coal stocks at the end of 1972 had risen to record levels of 5·6 million tonnes and 8·3 million tonnes respectively. Some pit closures have been made, attempts at other forms of rationalisation have met with some success, but demand fell so greatly that vast stocks have been the result, adding to the company's financial burden.

In coming years it is virtually certain that the scale of operations of the company will be greatly reduced and heavy rationalisation will be made. The company lost more than DM 380 million in 1971 and an even greater sum in 1972. Its annual turnover is around DM 7,500 million. The company's management face the extremely great difficulty of trying to run a concern well that has massive debts and insufficient financial aid from the Government. The company has a basic capital of DM 534·5 million, with the main shareholders being Veba AG with 13·3 per cent, Gelsenberg AG with 11·8 per cent, Mannesmann AG with 7·7 per cent, Hoesch AG with 6·4 per cent, Ewald AG with 6 per cent, Fried. Krupp Hüttenwerke AG with 5·8 per cent, Rheinstahl Energie GmbH with 5·4 per cent, Hüttenwerk Oberhausen AG with 5·2 per cent, Harpener AG with 4·8 per cent, Klöckner Industriewerte AG with 4·7 per cent and sixteen other companies, each of which has less than a 4 per cent holding.

Mannesmann AG

This Düsseldorf-based concern is rapidly moving into a highly diversified giant group from a company that largely concentrated on steel products. Under the guidance of Dr Egon Overbeck, Mannesmann has grown substantially in recent years and proved to be more profitable than many of its Ruhr rivals. It has won in recent years some of the largest orders ever concluded between a Western company and the Soviet Union, and the Russians appear to be keen to do still more business with this company. Mannesmann is the largest steel pipe manufacturer in Western Europe. The company acquired a 51 per cent stake in the large Demag AG engineering company in summer 1973, to aid its diversification programme. Machinery and plant construction business produced sales of DM 1,248 million in 1972. The Mannesmann group employs around 84,500 persons and its group sales in 1972 were DM 7,155 million after DM 7,178 million in the previous year. The company produced 2·97 million tonnes of steel pipe and 3·9 million tonnes of crude steel in 1972 and foreign sales account for 40 per cent of total company business. The company is expanding at a fast rate, especially abroad and into various sectors of the machinery and engineering industry. Mannesmann had a basic capital at the end of 1972 of DM 656·8 million, with no large shareholders and shares distributed among some 120,000 persons and organisations. Net profit in both 1971 and 1972 stood at DM 66 million and a considerable improvement is expected for 1973.

Gutehoffnungshütte AG

Based in Oberhausen, this is one of the largest engineering companies in Western Europe. In many respects it is a large holding company, owning large shares in such large companies as Maschinenfabrik Augsburg-Nürnberg AG, Büssing Automobilwerke AG, Schloemann AG, Ferrostahl AG, Kabel- und Metallwerke GHH AG. Among other things, through some of these subsidiaries, GHH is one of the largest commercial vehicle manufacturers in Europe.

GHH's sales in the year ending 30 June 1972 totalled DM 7,618 million (including value added tax), composed of DM 4,181 million in the machinery and plant, building and transport equipment sectors, then DM 2,363 million in the engineering, trading and metalworking sectors, and DM 1,074 million in the cable-making and non-ferrous metal working sectors. Foreign sales account for about 30 per cent of total sales. The company is in the midst of large-scale rationalisation and reorganisation, which has involved, among other things, its selling its shipbuilding interests and substantially linking together its various commercial vehicle interests. Net profit in 1972 fell to DM 49 million from DM 60·5 million, but the strong upswing in demand for capital goods in late 1972 and in 1973 should assure a substantial short-term profit improvement, at least. The chief of the executive board is Dr Dietrich Wilhelm von Menges. The company has a basic capital of DM 225 million and substantial shareholders are the Jacobi, Haniel and Huyssen families as well as the Allianz insurance group.

Fried. Krupp GmbH

While not a public company, this giant concern and the two others mentioned below hold a special place of importance in German industry. Saved from bankruptcy in 1967, the Krupp company moved out of family hands into the hands of a special foundation, which holds all the shares, but which after 1977 can issue shares to the general public. The parent company on the operating side of Krupp's diverse businesses is Fried. Krupp GmbH, based in Essen. The company has had serious management problems, due largely to the Supervisory Board chairman, Herr Berthold Beitz, being determined to be master of the House of Krupp. The man who did most to ensure the recovery of Krupp after 1967, Herr Gunther Vogelsang, left Krupp in October 1972. His successor, Dr Jurgen Krackow, lasted just eleven weeks and was then replaced by Herr Ernst Mommsen.

The total Krupp concern is divided into seven main business sectors, which cover such diverse activities as running a bakery and a modern shipbuilding company. The following were the sales of the major sections in 1972: steel with DM 2,146 million, industrial plant construction with DM 1,237 million, trading with DM 2,250 million, mechanical engineering with DM 848 million, shipbuilding with DM 583 million, metal-working with DM 441 million and services with DM 173 million. Total group sales in 1972 were DM 7,678 million, after DM 7,437 million in 1971. The group employs a total of close to 75,000 people. Total group profit in 1972 was DM 13·4 million, after DM 16 million in 1971 and DM 109·6 million in 1970. Most old debts have been fully repaid. Vogelsang pushed through a major management reorganisation and it is only the continual changes in the top management positions that hold one back from stating that Krupp is once more a financially sound and well organised enterprise. Apart from some naval contracts, the company no longer is in any respect involved in the manufacture of arms.

Friedrich Flick KG

This is possibly the largest privately owned family company in Europe. It is a vast and secretive conglomerate, created by Friedrich Flick, who died at the age of 89 in the summer of 1972. The company is owned by Friedrich Flick's heirs in the following way: 12·12 per cent is held by old Flick's youngest son, Dr Friedrich Karl Flick (the eldest son died in the war and the second eldest left the company after major arguments with his father); 12·12 per cent is held by the eldest son of old Flick's second eldest son, Dr Gert-Rudolf Flick; 12·12 per cent is held by the latter's brother, Dr Friedrich Christian Flick and 6·06 per cent is held by the sister of these brothers, Dagmar Flick. Further, 42·43 per cent is held in the Friedrich Karl Flick Foundation, 12·12 per cent is held in the Friedrich and Marie Flick Foundation and 3·03 per cent is held in the Dr Friedrich Flick Foundation, and all these foundations are controlled by Dr Friedrich Karl Flick.

The Flick KG holding company fully owns the Feldmühle AG paper company, which has annual sales of DM 1,126 million. It fully owns the Maxhütte steel company with sales of DM 1,122 million a year. It owns 84 per cent of the dynamite company, Dynamit Nobel, which has annual sales of DM 1,380 million. It owns 95 per cent of the Buderus Group iron concern, which has annual sales of DM 2,823 million. Further, it holds majority stakes in over 200 companies, which between them have total annual sales of well over a couple of billion marks. In addition, the Flick family owns 40 per cent of Daimler-Benz.

Robert Bosch GmbH

This Stuttgart-based concern is 13·67 per cent owned by the Bosch family, with the remaining shares owned by the family controlled Robert Bosch Foundation. It is a large manufacturer of assorted electrical consumer goods and is the largest producer of automobile industry electrical accessories in Western Europe. The company is heavily involved in foreign business, it has a multitude of joint ventures with such diverse companies as Siemens of Munich and Joseph Lucas of Great Britain. It has annual sales now of close to DM 6,000 million, it is highly profitable and ably managed by a team led by Herr Hans L. Merkle. The total number of employees is over 110,000.

Rheinisch-Westfälisches Elektrizitätswerk AG

Based in Essen, this company is the largest company of its kind in this country. It is deeply involved in the energy business, with its future largely dependent on the energy policies determined in Bonn. The rise in overhead costs, primarily caused by the soaring cost of coal, has resulted in the company experiencing some financial difficulties. The company has its own plans for the substantial development of nuclear reactors in coming years. Its ambitious plans demand vast investment spending, and outlays have amounted to DM 1,862 million in 1970–71 and DM 2,575 million in 1971–72. The total turnover volume of the concern was DM 6,800 million in the year to 30 June 1972 with the sharp rise of close to 12 per cent largely due to price increases. In 1970–71 the company had a net profit of close to DM 300 million. It employs around 56,000 persons. It had a basic capital of DM 1,500 million. The shares are most widely distributed among some 180,000 persons, but special voting shares, plus a large portion of ordinary shares, are held by the Federal State and public authorities. The executive board chairman is Dr Alfred Einnatz.

Hoesch AG

This Dortmund company merged with Hoogovens of Holland to form 'Estel' in mid-1972. The merger was on an even partnership basis, but Hoogovens already held 14·5 per cent of the Hoesch capital of DM 569 million and was in fact the only large shareholder in the company. The merger will take time to complete and it is likely that eventually the Dortmund plants will decline in importance as new plants, possibly on the Dutch coast, are established. The executive board chairman of Hoesch is Dr Friedrich Harders. In the year to the end of September 1971 (the last full year prior to the merger) Hoesch had sales of DM 5,439 million, it employed 52,452 persons, it produced 6·3 million tonnes of steel and 4·2 million tonnes of iron, and had a net profit of DM 56·1 million, after DM 224 million in the previous year.

Salzgitter AG

This is a large conglomerate that is wholly owned by the Federal State. It is a major steel manufacturer, it has substantial engineering interests and is the chief shareholder in the country's leading shipbuilding company, Howaldtswerke Deutsche Werft AG. In the year to 30 September 1972 the company boosted sales by 3·4 per cent to DM 6,100 million. Total number of employees was 59,372 at the end of the 1971–72 year, with steel output at 4·1 million tonnes and iron output at 3·4 million tonnes. The company is increasingly moving towards a greater concentration on the production of finished and semi-finished steel goods. It is based in Salzgitter, a small town close to Wolfsburg. The executive board chairman is Herr Hans Birnbaum. The company claimed in late 1972 that it was still making a small profit, but in line with other German steel companies, the profit level has fallen sharply in recent years.

Metallgesellschaft AG

This is one of the largest metal working companies in West Germany and is based in Frankfurt. The management, headed by Dr Helmut Ley, is unimpressive and has largely been paying dividends out of reserves in the last couple of years. Earnings have been minimal and to some extent net profit has been the product of real estate sales. Group sales in the year to the end of September 1972 fell back to DM 4,309 million, from DM 4,459 million in 1970–71 and DM 5,098 million in the 1969–70 financial year. In recent years developments on international metal markets have clearly had an adverse effect on the company's results. It employs about 29,000 people. It had a basic capital at the end of 1972 of DM 206·75 million with the chief shareholders being the Dresdner Bank with more than 25 per cent, the Schweizerische Gesellschaft für Metallwerte with 16·85 per cent and the Allgemeine Verwaltungsgesellschaft für Industriebeteiligungen with more than 25 per cent (this latter concern is jointly and equally owned by the Allianz insurance group, the Deutsche Bank and Siemens).

Gelsenberg AG

One of the most important German-owned oil concerns, this Essen-based company faces most considerable difficulties. The strong foreign competition on the petroleum markets in West Germany has resulted in the company making next to no profit, after a profit of DM 38·2 million on sales of DM 4,121 million in 1971. The future of this company will be determined to a very large extent by Government policies. It is managed by a team headed by Dr Walter Cipa, it employs about 14,500 persons and has a considerable number of important holdings in assorted types of companies, such as Ruhrgas AG, Aral AG, DEMINEX (the State-run oil exploration concern, in which the chief German oil companies all have an interest). Gelsenberg had a basic capital at the end of 1972 of DM 485 million with the largest shareholder being Rheinisch-Westfälisches Elektrizitätswerk AG, with 48·5 per cent. As stated in the section on Veba AG the control of Gelsenberg is likely to change and Veba is likely, in time, to obtain a majority share-holding in Gelsenberg, which, in the medium-term, is likely to see Gelsenberg fully absorbed into the huge Veba organisation.

Klöckner-Humboldt-Deutz AG

Based in Cologne this is a sizeable commercial vehicles and engineering company. It faces immense competition and has sought to strengthen its position by entering into a number of international joint ventures. The executive board chairman is Dr Karl-Heinz Sonne. It is a modern and well managed company, with total group sales in 1971 of DM 3,477 million, with a net profit of DM 21·8 million and with a staff total of around 28,000. Its future development will largely depend on how it manages to maintain an internationally competitive position, on the success of present rationalisation moves and on the development in the commercial vehicle sector of its joint venture with Volvo of Sweden, Saviem of France and Daf of the Netherlands. The company had a basic capital at the end of 1972 of DM 180 million with the main shareholder, having a holding of between 25 per cent and 50 per cent, being Klöckner

& Co, which in turn is owned by Dr Günter Henle and by the
Peter Klöckner Family Foundation.

Klöckner-Werke AG

This Duisburg steel company faces a difficult future in that it is
in many respects too small to remain highly competitive with
the giant international steel combines in Britain, the United
States, Japan and to some extent in continental Europe.
However, under the management of Herr Hans-Jörg Sendler,
the company is increasingly carving a niche for itself as a

TABLE A.2.I

The Largest Retailing Organisations

Company	Description	1971 sales in mln DMs	Chief owners
Karstadt AG	Multiple stores	4,800	Commerzbank AG and Deutsche Bank AG with each having more than 25 per cent
Hertie Waren- und Kaufhaus GmbH	Multiple stores	4,700	98 per cent owned by the Karg family trust, 2 per cent owned by Herr Georg Karg
Kaufhof AG	Multiple stores	4,200	Commerzbank AG and Dresdner Bank AG with each having more than 25 per cent
Quelle	Mail Order and photo shops	4,200	Schickedanz family
Horten AG	Multiple stores	2,400	British American Tobacco and Deutsche Gesellschaft für Anlageverwaltung GmbH with each having 25 per cent and with the latter company in turn jointly owned by the Deutsche Bank AG and Commerzbank AG
Neckermann	Stores, Mail Order, Travel Agencies	2,200	Mainly Josef Neckermann family

specialised enterprise, producing a range of semi-finished and finished steel products and having a most active trading division. Company sales in the year to the end of September 1972 totalled DM 2,165 million, after DM 2,339 million in the previous year. Iron output in 1971–72 fell to 2·05 million tonnes from 2·15 million tonnes in 1970–71, while steel output fell to 2·95 million tonnes from 3·11 million tonnes. The total number of employees is just over 24,000. The company's net profit rose slightly in 1971–72 to DM 20·3 million from DM 20 million. In the steel production sector the company may well ask to strengthen its position by building its own 'mini-mills' and has formed a joint venture with the European 'mini-mill' patent-holder, Herr Willy Korf. The company has a basic capital of DM 339 million and its main shareholder, with more than 25 per cent, is the Dutch concern, Internationale Industriele Belegging Maatschappij 'Amsterdam' NV.

Appendix 3

STATISTICS

This section aims to give a general picture of the size of the German economy and of West Germany's industry in statistical form. The rapid development of the economy produces important changes in the key statistics, yet the tables given here do provide a general picture of the developments in recent years and serve to make most recent figures more intelligible, while also serving to support many of the general comments made in the chapters of this book.

TABLE A.3.1

Key Domestic West German Economic data						
			1963	1968	1971	1972
Gross National Product at current prices	1000 mln DMs	384·0	540·0	758·8	830·8
Gross National Product at 1962 prices	1000 mln DMs	372·6	462·3	544·4	561·5
Use of National Product at current prices	1000 mln DMs				
Private consumption		218·2	301·8	411·0	448·0
Government consumption		59·6	84·3	130·6	147·5
Fixed capital investment		100·1	124·8	202·8	215·2

Source: Federal Statistical Office.

Notes: Figures for 1968 and 1971 are provisional.
       Figures for 1972 are partially based on Federal Bank estimates.

The tables reproduced here regarding domestic German economic data are based on the reports of the West German Federal Bank (Statistische Beihefte zu den Monatsberichten der Deutschen Bundesbank, February 1973). Some of these are in turn based on statistics from the Federal Statistical Office and are therefore so ascribed.

TABLE A.3.2

Index of Industrial Net Production

(1962 = 100.   Figures adjusted for working day variations, with averages given for the years quoted)

	All industries		Capital goods industries		Consumer goods industries	
Year	Index	% Change	Index	% Change	Index	% Change
1960	90·2	+ 11·4	90·1	+ 15·8	89·6	+ 9·8
1962	100·0	+ 4·3	100·0	+ 2·6	100·0	+ 5·6
1963	103·4	+ 3·4	102·5	+ 2·5	101·9	+ 1·9
1964	112·3	+ 8·6	110·2	+ 7·5	108·6	+ 6·6
1965	118·2	+ 5·3	117·8	+ 6·9	115·6	+ 6·4
1966	120·3	+ 1·8	117·3	− 0·4	118·4	+ 2·4
1967	117·4	− 2·4	109·1	− 7·0	113·2	− 4·4
1968	131·2	+ 11·8	122·7	+ 12·5	129·5	+ 14·4
1969	148·2	+ 13·0	146·5	+ 19·4	144·2	+ 11·4
1970	157·2	+ 6·1	160·1	+ 9·3	147·7	+ 2·4
1971	160·1	+ 1·8	158·8	− 0·8	153·7	+ 4·1
1972	166·0	+ 3·7	160·9	+ 1·3	162·7	+ 5·9

Source: Federal Statistical Office.

Notes: Figures for Consumer Goods Industries do not include food, drink and tobacco industries.
The 1972 figures given are provisional.

TABLE A.3.3

The Labour Market

Year	Total number of persons employed	Year	Total number of unemployed
1960	20,331,000	1960	271,000
1964	21,547,000	1964	169,000
1968	21,330,000	1968	323,000
1971	22,583,000	1971	185,000
1972	22,500,000	1972	246,000

Source: Federal Statistical Office.

Notes: Figures for 1971 and 1972 are provisional.

TABLE A.3.4

Prices and the Cost of Living
(All index figures have 1962 = 100)

Average for Year	Index of producer prices of industrial products in home market sales		Cost-of-living index for all households	
	Index	% change on previous year	Index	% change on previous year
1960	97·6	+1·1		
1961	98·9	+1·3		
1962	100·0	+1·1	100·0	
1963	100·5	+0·5	102·9	+2·9
1964	101·6	+1·1	105·4	+2·4
1965	104·0	+2·4	108·7	+3·1
1966	105·8	+1·7	112·7	+3·7
1967	104·9	−0·9	114·7	+1·7
1968	99·3	—	116·4	+1·6
1969	101·5	+2·2	119·5	+2·7
1970	107·5	+5·9	124·0	+3·8
1971	112·5	+4·7	130·4	+5·2
1972	116·1	+3·2	137·9	+5·8

Source: Federal Statistical Office.

Notes: For the producer prices table the figures from 1968 exclude value-added tax. Value-added tax is included in the figures from 1968 in the figures for the cost of living.

TABLE A.3.5

Level of wages and salaries in the economy based on hourly rates
(All index figures have 1962 = 100)

Year	Index	% change on previous year	Year	Index	% change on previous year
1960	84·5	+7·5	1967	135·0	+ 4·0
1961	91·9	+8·7	1968	140·4	+ 4·0
1962	100·0	+8·8	1969	150·2	+ 7·0
1963	105·8	+5·8	1970	169·6	+12·9
1964	112·5	+6·4	1971	193·7	+14·2
1965	121·2	+7·8	1972	211·7	+ 9·3
1966	129·8	+7·1			

Source: West German Federal Bank.

Notes – Figures for 1971 and 1972 are provisional.

TABLE A.3.6

Monetary reserves of the West German Federal Bank
(Figures in mln DMs)

Year	Net total	of which gold	U.S. dollar investment portion of reserves
1960	32,767	12,479	14,982
1964	32,754	15,374	11,669
1968	40,292	18,156	8,561
1969	26,371	14,931	2,239
1970	49,018	14,566	28,576
1971	59,345	14,688	37,413
1972	74,433	13,971	51,965

Source: West German Federal Bank.

Notes: The value of the totals given has changed greatly in terms of the
U.S. dollar in view of the revaluations of the Deutsche Mark in 1961,
1969, 1971. Further changes resulted from the monetary crises of
1973.

TABLE A.3.7

Major items of the Balance of Payments
(the Current Account)
(Figures in mln DMs)

Year	Current account total	Balance of Trade	Balance of Services	Balance of Transfer payments
1950	− 407	− 3,012	+ 540	+ 2,065
1955	+ 2,205	+ 1,245	+ 1,794	− 834
1960	+ 4,493	+ 5,223	+ 2,758	− 3,488
1965	− 6,723	+ 1,203	− 1,549	− 6,377
1966	+ 68	+ 7,598	− 1,595	− 6,295
1967	+ 9,436	+ 16,862	− 1,004	− 6,422
1968	+ 10,906	+ 18,372	− 154	− 7,312
1969	+ 6,226	+ 15,584	− 908	− 8,450
1970	+ 2,673	+ 15,670	− 3,938	− 9,059
1971	+ 584	+ 15,892	− 4,765	− 10,543
1972	+ 1,714	+ 20,251	− 6,148	− 12,389

Source: West German Federal Bank.

Notes: 1972 figures are provisional.

Re Balance of Trade figures – special trade according to the official foreign trade statistics: imports c.i.f., exports f.o.b.; re Balance of Services figures – excluding expenditure on freight and insurance costs contained in the c.i.f. import value, but including balance of merchanting trade and supplementary trade items. West Germany does not consider East Germany as a separate and independent country, hence payments transactions between the two German countries are not included in the West German balance-of-payments figures.

TABLE A.3.8

Major items of the Balance of Payments
(the Capital Account and Basic Balance)
(Figures in mln DMs)

Year	Over-all balance of capital transactions	Balance of recorded transactions	Balance of unclassifiable transactions	Balance of all transactions
1950	+ 207	− 200	− 364	− 564
1955	− 450	+ 1,755	+ 96	+ 1,851
1960	+ 1,782	+ 6,275	+1,744	+ 8,019
1965	+ 2,362	− 4,361	+3,078	− 1,283
1966	+ 881	+ 949	+1,003	+ 1,952
1967	− 9,998	− 562	+ 422	− 140
1968	− 7,235	+ 3,671	+3,338	+ 7,009
1969	−19,008	−12,782	+2,520	−10,262
1970	+11,005	+13,678	+8,234	+21,912
1971	+ 7,163	+ 7,747	+8,611	+16,358
1972	+ 7,355	+ 9,069	+6,621	+15,690

Source: The West German Federal Bank.

Notes: 1972 figures are provisional.

Re balance of unclassifiable transactions – net errors and omissions in current and capital accounts (=balancing item); short-term fluctuations mainly due to seasonal factors and to changes in the terms of payment; re Balance of all transactions – overall balance on capital and current accounts including the balancing item.

TABLE A.3.9

International comparison: Balance of Payments current account

Country	1966–70 average % of G.N.P.	Official reserves end-1970: % of imports of goods in 1970	Change from Nov 1971 to Nov 1972 in $ million
West Germany	1·0	45·6	6,200
United Kingdom	0·2	13·0	324
United States	0·1	36·3	1,176
France	−0·4	26·0	2,525
Japan	0·9	25·6	3,576

The Source for all the international comparative tables in this section is the Organisation for Economic Co-operation and Development.

TABLE A.3.10

International comparison: Foreign Trade

| | Imports 1970 | | Exports 1970 | |
| | in $ | as % | in $ | as % |
Country	million	of GNP	million	of GNP
West Germany	40,270	21·5	43,270	23·1
United Kingdom	28,250	23·3	30,520	25·2
United States	59,310	6·0	62,900	6·4
France	24,580	16·6	25,140	17·0
Japan	20,920	10·6	23,110	11·7

Notes: Imports and exports cover goods and services, including factor income. Dollar values given at current prices and exchange rates.

TABLE A.3.11

International comparison: Production, Investment, Saving

			Gross fixed investment	
	GNP	GNP annual	total	Gross saving
	per head	volume growth	1966–70	1966–70
	1970	1965–70	as % of	as % of
Country	in $	in %	GNP	GNP
West Germany	3,040	4·6	25·4	26·9
United Kingdom	2,170	2·4	18·6	18·5
United States	4,870	3·2	16·6	17·9
France	2,920	5·8	25·8	26·5
Japan	1,910	12·1	36·6	38·7

Notes: Dollar values given at current prices and exchange rates. GNP annual volume growth and gross fixed investment total given at constant (1963) prices with U.K.s GNP annual volume growth figure based on GDP in purchasers values, with U.S.'s gross fixed investment figure measured noting that government and government enterprise expenditure on machinery and equipment is included in government current expenditure.

TABLE A.3.12

International comparison: Standard of Living					
Indicator	W. Germany	U.K.	U.S.	France	Japan
Private consumption per head in 1970 in U.S. $	1,650	1,340	3,010	1,720	840
Education expenditure in 1969 as % of GNP	3·08	4·97	5·41	4·75	3·93
Total number of dwellings completed per 1,000 inhabitants in 1970	8·1	6·5	7·0	9·1	14·4
Passenger cars in 1969 per 1,000 inhabitants	237	213	432	245	85
Television sets in 1969 per 1,000 inhabitants	262	284	399	201	214
Telephones in 1969 per 1,000 inhabitants	212	253	567	161	194
Doctors in 1969 per 1,000 inhabitants	1·54	1·18	1·65	1·23	1·12

Notes: The figure given for doctors is for 1967 in the case of the United Kingdom. The private consumption per head figure given for Japan is for 1969, while also in the case of Japan the expenditure on education figure is for 1968.

For statistics on German industry see Appendix 1.

Index

Abs, Hermann J., 42, 50, 97
Adam Opel AG, 53, 114, 225; marketing strategy, 120–2; foreign investment, 147; profit margins, 191–2; expansion, 193
Adenauer, Dr Konrad, 6, 7
AEG-Telefunken, 130, 154, 164, 194, 223, 238–9
Africa, trade with, 110, 126, 128, 151–2
Africa, North, workers from, 101
AG Weser, 96, 106
Agfa-Gevaert AG, 36, 115, 234; cross-border merger, 200–2
Aktiengesellschaft (share company), 66, 162; organisation and control, 34–43; general meeting of shareholders, 34, 53–64; Vorstand, 34–43; Aufsichtsrat, 34–43; balance of power, 35, 36–39, 41, 66; personalities, 41–3; total number, 69–70; share capital volume, 165
AKZO, 159, 194, 195
Allgemeine Verwaltungsgesellschaft für Industriebeteiligungen, 245
Allianz insurance group, 242, 246
America, South: trade with, 110, 126, 151–2; production subsidiaries in, 126, 128, 230, 236, 239
America, United States of, see United States
Amerongen, Otto Wolff von, 76n., 174, 179
Aral AG, 238, 246
Arbeitsgemeinschaft der Deutschen Wertpapierbörsen, 182
Asia, trade with, 126, 223
associations: business, 81, 172–82; special interest, 182–3
Atlantis AG, 55
Audi NSU auto Union AG, 36, 57–64, 231
Aufsichtsrat (supervisory board of directors), 34–43; balance of power, 35, 36–9, 41, 66; power to dismiss Vorstand members, 36–8; size and

responsibility, 40–1; and general meeting, 54–5; dismissal of, 54–5; trade unions and, 76–7, 78, 81
Austria, trade with, 15, 16
Auto Union (Audi), 114; and merger with NSU, 57–64
automobile industry, 22, 23, 134, 143, 225; exports, 110, 225; concentration of, 114, 120; marketing methods, 120–9; sales figures, 126, 215, 225; investments abroad, 148, 151; foreign competition, 198–9; statistics, 225, 228

Babcock & Wilcox AG, 117
Baden-Württemberg: population, 2; strikes in, 86, 89; foreign workers, 102; investment in, 157
Badische Anilin- und Soda-Fabrik AG (BASF), 3, 165, 170, 233, 235–6; foreign bourse listings, 164
balance of payments, 14, 211–13, 152–153
Banco di Roma, 166
Bank für Gemeinwirtschaft, 52
banks: shareholdings by, 44–8; influence on mergers and takeovers, 45–7; promotion system, 92–5; and investment finance, 160–2, 167–70; foreign, 167–9; small companies' increasing dependence on, 169–70; national federation, 180–1
'bardepot' (cash deposit system), 27, 206
Bavaria: foreign workers, 102; investment in, 157
Bayer AG, 3, 114, 151, 159, 234–5, 236; structure and control, 36, 234–5; wage costs, 100, 129; marketing problems, 129–30; foreign investment, 148, 164, 165, 234
Bayerische Hypotheken und Wechsel-Bank AG, 114; shareholders in, 42–3; holdings in other companies, 47
Bedford vehicles, 121
'Beetle' car, 112, 122, 127, 128